MW01590711

Relations and Networks in South African Indian Writing

Cross/Cultures

READINGS IN POST/COLONIAL
LITERATURES AND CULTURES IN ENGLISH

Edited by

Gordon Collier
Geoffrey Davis
Bénédicte Ledent

Co-founding editor

†Hena Maes-Jelinek

VOLUME 203

The titles published in this series are listed at *brill.com/cc*

Relations and Networks in South African Indian Writing

Edited by

Felicity Hand
Esther Pujolràs-Noguer

BRILL

RODOPI

LEIDEN | BOSTON

Cover illustration: Grupo Actialia (15 January 2015)

Library of Congress Cataloging-in-Publication Data

Names: Hand, Felicity, editor. | Pujolras-Noguer, Esther, editor.
Title: Relations and networks in South African Indian writing / edited by
   Felicity Hand, Esther Pujolras-Noguer.
Description: Leiden ; Boston : Brill Rodopi, 2018. | Series: Cross/cultures ;
   203 | Includes bibliographical references and index.
Identifiers: LCCN 2018008091 (print) | LCCN 2018019901 (ebook) | ISBN
   9789004365032 (E-Book) | ISBN 9789004364967 (hardback : alk. paper)
Subjects: LCSH: South African literature (English)--East Indian
   authors--History and criticism. | Identity (Psychology) in literature |
   East Indians in literature. | Ethnic relations in literature. | South
   Africa--In literature.
Classification: LCC PR9358.2.E24 (ebook) | LCC PR9358.2.E24 R45 2018 (print) | DDC
   820.9/891411068--dc23
LC record available at https://lccn.loc.gov/2018008091

Typeface for the Latin, Greek, and Cyrillic scripts: "Brill". See and download: brill.com/brill-typeface.

ISSN 0924-1426
ISBN 978-90-04-36496-7 (hardback)
ISBN 978-90-04-36503-2 (e-book)

Printed by Printforce, the Netherlands

Contents

Acknowledgements

The Spanish Ministry of Economy and Competitiveness funded the research that has contributed to this volume (project references FFI2012-37626 & FFI2015-63739-P), and the Ministry of Education and Culture awarded a mobility grant to Felicity Hand (reference PRX15/00102) which enabled her to conduct research at the Centre for Indian Studies in Africa, University of the Witwatersrand, Johannesburg.

The editors would also like to thank most warmly Dr. Sandra Saayman of the Université de La Réunion for her kindness, friendship, and timely scholarly advice.

The conference held at the Universitat Autònoma de Barcelona in November 2015 *Relations and Networks in Indian Ocean Writing* was an exciting forum of debate, as we were able to discuss our work with other colleagues in Indian Ocean studies. The two panels on South African Indian writers were extremely stimulating. We are sorry that some of the participants were unable to contribute their revised papers to this volume.

Notes on Contributors

Isabel Alonso-Breto
is a lecturer in Postcolonial Literatures and Cultures at the Architectural Projections of a 'New Order' in Interwar Dictatorships. She has done work on different areas of postcolonial literatures in English, and has published on authors of Caribbean, South Asian, African, and Canadian origin. Her articles mostly focus on issues of cultural identity, migration, and displacement, and on the various forms in which fiction and poetry negotiate and transgress boundaries of different types. At present, she is Vicedirector of the Centre for Australian Studies at the University of Barcelona (http://www.ub.edu/dpfilsa/welcome.html) as well as a member of RATNAKARA (http://grupsderecerca.uab.cat/ratnakara/).

M.J. Daymond
is Professor Emerita in English Studies and a Fellow of the University of KwaZulu–Natal. Her published articles are mostly on writing by women in Africa, and her most recent books are *Women Writing Africa: The Southern Volume* (2003), *Africa South: Viewpoints 1956–1962* (2011), and *Everyday Matters: Selected Letters of Dora Taylor, Bessie Head and Lilian Ngoyi* (2015). She was a founder editor of the journal *Current Writing*. Besides fiction, her research interests include autobiography, letters, and travel writing.

Salvador Faura
studied English Literature at the University of Edinburgh and at the Universitat Autònoma de Barcelona, where he now lectures. His areas of interest range from postcolonial studies to contemporary poetry. Salvador Faura has also translated several English-speaking authors into Catalan and Spanish (Tahir Shah's *In Arabian Nights*), has published some poetry ("Caixa d'Olivera"), and has been granted several prestigious awards for his creative work.

Felicity Hand
is a Senior Lecturer in the English Department of the Universitat Autònoma de Barcelona. She has published articles on various Indian and East African writers, including M.G. Vassanji and Abdulrazak Gurnah, and a book-length study of the Mauritian author Lindsey Collen. She is the head of the research group RATNAKARA (http://grupsderecerca.uab.cat/ratnakara) which explores the literatures and cultures of the south-west Indian Ocean. Felicity is also the editor of the electronic journal *Indi@logs (Spanish Journal of India Studies)*.

Farhad Khoyratty
is Senior Lecturer at the University of Mauritius. His publications are mostly in film and cultural studies. A member of the RATNAKARA Research Group in Barcelona, and of South African PEN, he has been made Honorary Fellow, University of Iowa, Fellow of the Cambridge Commonwealth Society, the English-Speaking Union, twice the British Chevening, and Hughes Hall, Cambridge. He has delivered keynotes at three international conferences.

Esther Pujolràs-Noguer
is a lecturer in American and postcolonial literature at the Universitat Autònoma de Barcelona. She specializes in African literatures and cultures, and has published articles on the convergence of race, ethnicity, and constructions of whiteness in Indian Ocean writing ("The Scramble for Home: World War I in the East African Imagination"; "Between Memory and Desire: The Historical Novel as a Shadow-Genre in Abdulrazak Gurnah's *Desertion*"). Her current research focusses on postcolonial life writing and, more specifically, on how a creative writing methodology can contribute to overcome the trauma of gender violence. The project she is presently involved in, the Nalubaale Creative Writing Workshop 'Healing, Loving Writing' (http://blogs.uab.cat/nalubaale/), aims at constructing a body of life writing texts from victims of gender violence.

J. Coplen Rose
currently works as a contract lecturer in the Department of English at Lakehead University, Canada. He recently completed his PhD in English and Film Studies at Wilfrid Laurier University. Coplen's dissertation, "National Crises and Moments of Laughter in 'Second Interregnum' South African Drama, 2001–2014," analyzes political criticism and humor in eight plays produced after Nelson Mandela's retirement. This project was completed through international fieldwork in 2012 and 2013. His other research interests include postcolonial studies, geography and digital mapping, trauma studies, and memory. In addition to his degree from Wilfrid Laurier University, Coplen holds an MA from Lakehead University and a BA from Bishop's University.

Modhumita Roy
teaches in the English Department at Tufts University, Boston. Most recently she has co-edited, with Elizabeth Ammons, *Sharing the Earth. An International Environmental Justice Reader* (2015). Her publications include essays on South African literature, feminism, black British fiction, and cultures of the British Empire.

Lindy Stiebel

is Professor Emerita of English Studies at the University of KwaZulu–Natal. Her research interests have in common a profound interest in the relationship between writers and place: these include the South African colonial and post-colonial novel; Indian Ocean studies, particularly literary interconnections between South Africa, India, and Mauritius; and literary tourism. Her latest book, published in 2016, is *Writing Home: Lewis Nkosi on South African Literature* (with Michael Chapman). Accepted for publication in 2017 is *A Literary Companion to KwaZulu–Natal* (with Niall McNulty), a book which collects over fifteen years of the KZN Literary Tourism project, which she leads.

Juan Miguel Zarandona

obtained his doctorate from the University of Zaragoza, Spain, in English Studies. He is a senior lecturer in the Department of Translation Studies, University of Valladolid at Soria, Spain. He has teaching experience in English studies and general and specialized translation. Among his general research interests are literary translation, history and translation, and cultural studies and translation. His specific research interests include Arthurian, African, and utopian studies. He is the editor of *Hermēneus: Journal on Translation Studies* (www.uva .es/hermeneus) and is the promoter of two research groups (Afriqana www .afriqana.org and Clytiar www.clytiar.org).

CHAPTER 1

From Cane Cutters and Traders to Citizens and Writers

Felicity Hand and Esther Pujolràs-Noguer

This introductory chapter provides a brief history of the South African Indian community and their struggle to be acknowledged as citizens of the nation. Likewise, it outlines the pitfalls and obstacles that South African Indian writers have had to overcome in order to be considered fully-fledged South African writers.

Delineating a South African Indian Cartography

It is true that the first Indians had been brought as slaves to the Cape Colony in the seventeenth century. These people were mixed with other captives from Sri Lanka, South East Asia, and Macao, among other diverse places, and their common religion, Islam, would later lead to their being classified as 'Cape Malays.'[1] However, historians tend to date the origins of a recognizable Indian community to the arrival in Durban in 1860 of the ship SS *Truro*, which carried the first indentured laborers who would work on the canefields of Natal province. As far as large-scale immigration is concerned, for over fifty years from 1860 onwards, over 150,000 people were recruited, often by devious means, to toil for meagre wages in semi-slavery. Ten years after the docking of SS *Truro*, a new kind of immigrant from the Indian subcontinent began arriving. These were the so-called 'passenger Indians,' mostly traders from Gujarat, who paid their own fare. The two groups had little in common, but the white population lumped them all together as 'coolies,' despite the fact that the passenger Indians rapidly set up retail shops and prospered. Soon more professional people arrived, including teachers, lawyers, and accountants, but this only led to jealousy and outright hostility towards the Indian community. The colonial administration enacted

---

1 Nigel Worden, "Indian Ocean Slavery and Its Demise in the Cape Colony," in *Abolition and Its Aftermath in Indian Ocean Africa and Asia*, ed. Gwyn Campbell (London: Routledge, 2005): 30–31; Uma Dhupelia–Mesthrie, *From Canefields to Freedom: A Chronicle of Indian South African Life* (Cape Town: Kwela, 2000): 10.

© KONINKLIJKE BRILL NV, LEIDEN, 2018 | DOI 10.1163/9789004365032_002

a series of discriminatory laws against them, including the 1895 law of the
Orange Free State which excluded them completely from the province. In fact,
Indians remained fairly restricted to—and thus concentrated in—southern
Natal because of government restrictions on inter-provincial movement after
1910.[2]

Apart from the initial recruitment to work in the plantations, Indians were
employed in various sectors, such as the railways, the dockyards, coal mines,
municipal services, and domestic service. After indenture was officially ter-
minated, the former laborers often turned to hawking and to a large extent
took over the small garden produce of the coastal areas of Natal. The passenger Indians who were involved in the retail trade gradually began to compete
with the more expensive stores run by whites. In addition to shopkeepers, this
group of Indians consisted of professional people such as teachers, accountants, and lawyers, and their success did little to ingratiate them with the white
settlers, who sought to curb their activities. The colonial administration soon
enacted a series of discriminatory laws against the Indians, the obligation to
carry a pass becoming one of the most notorious and provoking the public
burning of passes, led by Gandhi. On 16 August 1908, 3,000 Indians of diverse
religions and geographical origins gathered outside the Hamidia Mosque in
Jennings Street, Johannesburg and burned their passes. The huge bonfire, lit in
a cauldron, marked the first burning of passes in South Africa and the beginning of Gandhi's satyagraha, or passive resistance, campaign.[3]

No history—however brief—of the establishment of an Indian community
in South Africa would be complete without mention of the twenty years that
Mohandas Karamchand Gandhi spent in South Africa as the *Mahatma* provided the community with the inspiration and leadership required to resist
the racist policies of the white colonists. It is true that some scholars question the importance attached to the role played by Gandhi in the sense that
he worked primarily for the rights of the merchant class rather than for the
Indian proletariat.[4] Although his sojourn in South Africa may have been mythologized, as the Indian working class was in fact already politically aware
and passive resistance would turn out to be ineffectual in the violent South
African context, Gandhi is still regarded as a model to follow and an icon in

---

2   Anthony Lemon, "The Political Position of Indians in South Africa," in *South Asians Overseas.
    Migration and Ethnicity*, ed. Colin Clarke, Ceri Peach & Steven Vertovec (Cambridge: Cam-
    bridge UP, 2009): 132.

3   *Sunday Times Heritage Project* http://sthp.saha.org.za/memorial/mohandas_gandhi.htm (ac-
    cessed 3 December 2015).

4   Maureen Swan, *Gandhi: The South African Experience* (Johannesburg: Ravan, 1984).

the struggle for equal social and political rights. Certainly with regard to the forging of a sense of Indian unity, Kaarsholm celebrates Gandhi's Phoenix Settlement as "the centre for a new Indian public culture of schools and media within it, which brought Hindus and Muslims together in terms of a common Indian identity."[5] Until the violent years of 1985–86, when the settlement was burned down, it was a beacon of peaceful cohabitation among Indians and Africans alike.

In 1894, the Natal Indian Congress was founded; by the time the *Mahatma* had left South Africa, a certain number of concessions had been obtained from the government and, perhaps more importantly, cautious collaboration between Indians and the black majority was starting to take shape. This was clearly difficult, as both ethnic groups were inherently unequal, economically and socially, at this point in history, which would prevent an easy transition towards anti-apartheid solidarity in later years. Kaarsholm highlights the difficulties that Gandhi and his followers encountered in establishing an ideal common cause against racism between Indians and Africans during the early twentieth century.[6]

The Natal and the Transvaal Indian Congresses gradually drifted towards a multi-racial struggle of all oppressed peoples in South Africa, and charismatic figures such as Monty Naicker and Yusuf Dadoo emerged from within their ranks. The apartheid years witnessed courageous attempts by many South African Indians to assert their rights and lead dignified lives. The double discrimination suffered by South African Indian women needs to be highlighted; it should be remembered that not all Indians were willing to embrace the kind of gender equality promulgated and fought for in the West and to throw in their lot with the blacks. In this respect Dr. Goonam—the 'coolie doctor'—stands out for challenging conservative Indians in Durban both by her social behaviour and by her political activism.

In 1942, the Restriction of Trading and Occupation of Land Act was promulgated.[7] The government passed this so-called Pegging Act following complaints from white traders who insisted that they were being forced to

---

5 Preben Kaarsholm, "Transnational Spaces, Islam and the Interaction of Indian and African Identity Strategies in South Africa During and After Apartheid," in *Eyes Across the Water: Navigating the Indian Ocean*, ed. Pamila Gupta, Isabel Hofmeyr & Michael Pearson (Pretoria: U of South Africa P, 2010): 229.

6 Kaarsholm, "Transnational Spaces, Islam and the Interaction of Indian and African Identity Strategies in South Africa During and After Apartheid," 223.

7 Bill Freund, *Insiders and Outsiders: the Indian Working Class of Durban 1910–1990* (Petermaritzburg: U of Natal P, 1995): 58.

compete with their Indian counterparts or business opponents. The whites wanted Indians to be banned from residing in white areas. This Act meant that Indians could not acquire or own property in the area reserved for whites for a period of three years. Further racist legislation was passed in the form of the Asiatic Land Tenure and Indian Representation, also known as the 'Ghetto Act,' which was designed to curtail Indian property ownership in white areas in Natal. The controlled areas in Natal would be white areas in which Indians could no longer purchase land, whereas the uncontrolled areas were open to both whites and Indians. In controlled areas, Indians could continue to own land purchased before 21 January 1944 (the date when the Bill was announced) but could no longer purchase new properties. They had to lease land from whites on condition it was used for trading purposes. The Ghetto Act included some 'political representation' to Indians, "possibly to soften the blow of the restrictions."[8] This in fact meant that three whites would take seats in the Assembly and two in the Senate, together with two provincial councillors who could be Indian. Despite the apparent political rights granted to the Indian community in the Ghetto Act, the Act was ineffectual, as Indians could not elect their own people. The Natal Indian Congress rejected the Act and took the lack of citizenship of the Indian community to both the Indian government and the United Nations in 1946. This brought international attention to South Africa's racial policies, possibly for the first time.[9]

When the South African government ignored both the international community and its own citizens, the Natal Indian Congress embarked on a campaign of passive resistance. This campaign saw African, Indian, and Coloured people united in South Africa. A 'Joint Declaration of Cooperation' was signed in 1947 between the African National Congress, the Transvaal Indian Congress, and the Natal Indian Congress, with a view to working together for an end to the denial of rights by the apartheid state. Despite this somewhat idyllic scenario, from the early 1950s onwards two distinct ideological grounds of protest and compromise become manifest. The more radical South African Indian Congress sought mass support and identification with Africans and thus promoted interracial political action. Indians were becoming increasingly identified with the oppressed black majority.[10] On the other hand, the South African Indian Organisation, who defended the interests of traders and merchants, feared

---

8   South African History Online. *Towards a People's History* (nd), http://www.sahistory.org
      .za/topic/segregationist-legislation-timeline-1940-1949 (accessed 15 September 2015).

9   Lemon, "The Political Position of Indians in South Africa," 132.

10   Rehana Ebr.-Vally, *Kala Pani: Caste and Colour in South Africa* (Cape Town: Kwela, 2001):
      95.

African nationalism, as they believed it would seriously challenge their hard-won position. However, Lemon argues that it was their weak position rather than their accommodation with whites that forced them into accepting the status quo.[11]

In her analysis of the representation of the South African 'Indian,' Rehana Ebr.-Vally reminds us that historians have tended to focus their narratives on the political processes affecting the community from the perspective of the elites, as if the masses deferred to the dominant social group and had no political perception of their own.[12] She argues that the Indian struggle was far more complex and was not just based on the tensions between Indian and white power. From the 1970s onwards, coinciding with the intensification of the anti-apartheid struggle,

> 'Indian' intellectuals as well as some sections of the 'Indian' population identified themselves as 'Black,' that is to say as non-White South African victims of the same segregation as the rest of the non-White population of the country.[13]

Indians ceased to be so isolated and the sufferings of the Indian working class were gradually revealed. Internal differences, nevertheless, would be blurred if a common South African identity was the objective. As Sara Upstone argues,

> the nation is founded on subsuming cultural difference to a communal image: a population of a nation may not naturally be homogeneous, but they are encouraged to see themselves as such, with cultural difference discouraged. This unity is obviously central to the importance of the nation for anticolonial resistance.[14]

Conversely, when the National Party set up a tri-cameral Parliament in 1984, the inclusion of Indian representation was only possible if the Indians were classified as a homogeneous group. This naturally suited their segregationalist policies, whether it involved excluding them from power or ensuring their cooperation.

---

11   Lemon, "The Political Position of Indians in South Africa," 137.

12   Rehana Ebr.-Vally, *Kala Pani*, 92. The author uses the term 'Indian' in inverted commas in order to query the validity of the label to describe a highly heterogeneous community.

13   Ebr.-Vally, *Kala Pani*, 94.

14   Sara Upstone, *Spatial Politics in the Postcolonial Novel* (Farnham & Burlington VT: Ashgate, 2009): 27.

To create a sense of belonging this 'fictitious' Indian identity was passed down from generation to generation, perpetuated by the apartheid state and accepted by those who were categorised as such.[15]

From the passing of the Group Areas Act in 1950 until 1991, working-class Indians—who made up the largest number of Indians in South Africa—were removed from white-designated areas and rehoused in the new townships created for this purpose. Chatsworth was built in southwest Durban in the 1960s and Phoenix in northwest Durban in the 1970s. Middle-class Indians went to live in more upmarket areas such as Reservoir Hills, Isipingo Beach, and Effingham Heights. The passenger Indians, mainly of Gujarati origin and concentrated mainly in trade and commerce, formed what Kalpana Hiralal calls "middlemen minorities" by maintaining intra-ethnic solidarity through the establishment of family-orientated businesses which relied on fellow Gujaratis for capital and labour.[16] When, in 1961, Indians became South Africans at the height of apartheid, they were a permanent population and the high degree of urbanization among Indians, which is even higher than among whites (91% in 1980), made Indian inclusion in any new political structures inevitable.[17]

In the final years of the apartheid regime and despite Indian participation in the struggle for freedom, the relative prosperity of the Indian community singled them out as objects of envy and resentment, feelings that have not totally dissipated in the post-apartheid era. While it is true that Nelson Mandela appointed various Indians to ministerial positions, his successor, Thabo Mbeki, retained only Kader Asmal and Vali Moosa in his new 1999 government. The belief in flagrant economic disparity separating the Indians from the blacks focusses only on the wealthy members of this community, whereas poverty and unemployment are also rampant among many South African citizens, including the Indians. An example of this in contemporary post-apartheid South Africa can be found among the student population, who appear to be visibly divided along lines of social class.

The 'upper' class 'Indian' students have a greater purchasing power so they naturally locate themselves in spaces that provide expensive offerings,

---

15   Kathryn Pillay, "The Minority Report: Undressing 'Indians' in Durban," in *Undressing Durban*, ed. Rob Pattman & Sultan Khan (Durban: Madiba, 2007): 328.

16   Kalpana Hiralal, "The Gujarati Trading Class Within the Indian Community—Shaped and Styled by Historical Contradictions," in *Undressing Durban*, ed. Rob Pattman & Sultan Khan (Durban: Madiba, 2007): 309.

17   Lemon, "The Political Position," 138.

whereas the 'lower' class 'Indian' students can be found in places where they are charged at student rates. But these divergent spaces also become cultural signifiers of class difference.[18]

If we assess South Africa's credentials in Indian Ocean membership, it seems that "Indian Ocean interactions only came to the fore with the arrival of indentured Indian labourers and 'passenger' Indian tradespeople from the 1860s."[19] In this respect, it is worth remembering that Gandhi's Phoenix Settlement has been rehoused in a buffer zone between Bhambayi and Phoenix and, thanks to subsidies from the Indian Government, the buildings and printing press have been restored.[20] Thus, the Indianness of the South African Indians has, somewhat ironically, been reinforced in the post-apartheid era, which is when they wish to emphasize more than ever their loyalty to a South African identity.

South African Indian Writing and the New South Africa

Writers of Indian origin have largely been omitted from studies of South African literature and, curiously enough, their work rarely finds its way into studies of the cultural productions of the South Asian diaspora. The shady area they occupy in terms of national belonging links them to East African writers of South Asian origin, whose African credentials have frequently been questioned. Arlene A. Elder (1992) provides a careful reading of the short stories of Ahmed Essop, together with a discussion of the novels of the Ugandan Asian authors Bahadur Tejani and Peter Nazareth. In his mammoth study *The Literature of the Indian Diaspora: Theorizing the Diasporic Imaginary* (2007), Vijay Mishra claims that in South Africa "the multiracial disappeared under the politics of apartheid, [so] the writing of the Indian diaspora remained muted, and politically less agonistic."[21] Mishra devotes a page to the work of Ahmed Essop, who, he claims, offers a critique of South African supremacist ideology; but, like Elder, Mishra fails to mention any other South African Indian writer in his study. Naturally, this shows that in the late twentieth century few South African writers of Indian origin had been able to publish their work, a reminder

---

18   Kathryn Pillay, "The Minority Report: Undressing 'Indians' in Durban," 324.
19   Kaarsholm, "Transnational Spaces," 233.
20   "Transnational Spaces," 230.
21   Vijay Mishra, *The Literature of the Indian Diaspora: Theorizing the Diasporic Imaginary* (London: Routledge, 2007): 59.

of the political restraints on production and publication during the apartheid era.

More recent studies engage with what Mariam Pirbhai calls a "broadening of [post-apartheid South Africa's] literary frontiers." She classifies the writing into two waves as well as two generations of diasporic writing in South Africa: the writing that responded to apartheid and that of the post-apartheid years, after the demise of the regime in 1990.[22] She claims: "It is in the later fiction that ethnic self-assertion is approached more forcefully."[23] Pallavi Rastogi agrees that "there is a direct and determinate relationship between politics and identity in South African Indian writing" but argues that a South African identity is the primary affiliation, even though Indian idiosyncrasies are not wholly erased.[24] Ronit Frenkel similarly tackles the thorny category of 'race,' which, she claims, still lies at the root of contemporary sociocultural divisions in post-apartheid South Africa. Her study "destabilise[s] such taxonomies by exploring what they mean and how they continue to inform culture."[25] Finally, we can mention Sissy Helff (2013), who discusses Farida Karodia's novel *Other Secrets* as a fictional autobiography which both traces the collective experiences of violence during apartheid and makes a plea for reconciliation.

Therefore, while critics are beginning to examine the recent writing of South African Indians, with the notable exception of Govinden's sensitive study of South African Indian women writers, no study has, to date, provided a comprehensive analysis of the patterns of connectedness that are being forged between diverse communities in South Africa;[26] indeed, South African Indian writers are often still ignored in mainstream publications.[27] While it is clear that racial and class categories cannot be ignored in a country with a recent history of brutal exploitation and statutory oppression, many studies explore what we are calling 'relations and networks' in the post-apartheid era, hence

---

22   Mariam Pirbhai, *Mythologies of Migration, Vocabularies of Indenture. Novels of the South Asian Diaspora in Africa, the Caribbean, and Asia-Pacific* (Toronto: U of Toronto P, 2009): 70.

23   Mariam Pirbhai, *Mythologies of Migration*, 71.

24   Pallavi Rastogi, *Afrindian Fictions: Diaspora, Race, and National Desire in South Africa* (Columbus: Ohio State UP, 2008): 9.

25   Ronit Frenkel, *Reconsiderations: South African Indian Fiction and the Making of Race in Postcolonial Culture* (Pretoria: U of South Africa P, 2010): 6.

26   See Devarakshanam Govinden, *Sister Outsiders: The Representation of Identity and Difference in Selected Writings by South African Indian Women* (Pretoria: U of South Africa P, 2008).

27   See, for example, *Modern Fiction Studies* 46.1 (Spring 2000), a special issue on South African writing after apartheid.

delineating a social geography in which subjectivities are being constructed beyond—and despite—constraining racial and ethnic parameters. Although scholars such as Gaurav Desai, Pallavi Rastogi, and Ronit Frenkel have engaged in an exploration of relational subjectivities in their work, thus already adhering to a 'relations and networks' paradigm, they have never formally conceptualized the term. Our 'relations and networks' framework should therefore be acknowledged as an attempt to foreground a methodology whereby ethnicity, class, and gender inextricably coalesce to map out the national space of post-apartheid South Africa. Through the analysis of a selection of writers, many of whom are emerging as leading voices in the 'new' South Africa, we aim to bring to the fore the sociality and patterns of connectedness that are being forged between South Africa's hitherto divided communities. Our starting point is that literature inflects productions and performances of identities in relation to the long history of trade and encounter that has been conceptualized largely from the perspectives of economic history and geographical studies.

Stemming from a Foucauldian perspective on subjectivity which measures the subject as an active participant in a strategic interplay of power relations, in this volume we aim at fostering consideration of South–South subjectivities by *strategically* locating South African Indian literature within the relations and networks paradigm that shapes the Indian Ocean world and its cosmopolitanisms. These South–South subjectives, which speak of relations and networks across the Indian Ocean, will be seen to coexist with and also to pre-date colonialism. Henceforth, we claim that the experience of history as embedded in literary texts evinces an unceasing transformation of self. The literary texts under examination display a varied range of mechanisms whereby institutional bodies, desires, and discourses are deconstructed in order to lay out the script for an aesthetics of resistance. To understand and thus situate the South African Indian experience as a constitutive component of Indian Ocean thassalogy requires a more nuanced investigation of the relationship between self and other than that elicited so far. We contend that the South African Asian community, despite having followed a different settlement pattern from Mauritius or Kenya, must take its place as part of the Indian Ocean experience. Moreover, we consider that a thorough study of South–South subjectivities can throw light on alternative ways of being in the world and can thus contribute to the creation of fairer, more humane societies. The various chapters that configure this volume are *connected* and *related* by this aesthetics of South–South subjectivities.

The contributors deal with notions of in-betweenness (Alonso, Daymond, Pujolràs, Roy); crossing boundaries (Alonso, Hand, Pujolràs); disappointment in post-apartheid South Africa (Daymond, Zarandona, Rose); ambiguity (Hand,

Daymond, Khoyratty); and remembering the past (Faura, Hand, Stiebel, Roy, Pujolràs, Khoyratty). Lindy Stiebel's chapter aims at giving visibility to works by South Africans of Indian descent set on the sugarcane plantations. In 2010, the one hundred and fiftieth anniversary of the arrival of the first indentured laborers in South Africa brought forth a considerable number of literary texts that sought to commemorate this event. The survival and upward mobility of successive generations of indentured laborers (and the descendants of passenger Indians) in South Africa now affords the possibility to travel to other places and other countries, the freedom in fiction and reality to imagine an 'elsewhere,' the ability to branch out, leaving only nostalgia for the South African landscape. Stiebel contends that the movement in the writing of this latest generation of South Africans of Indian descent is transnational, outward, not necessarily inward and nostalgic. At the turn of the millennium, many people of Indian descent in South Africa rediscovered the 'Indian' part of their identity, which was reinforced, emphasized, and cherished even though, as Stiebel points out, the tendency in literature written by South African Indians is to reach out and assume a more cosmopolitan identity.

Felicity Hand's chapter focusses on the debut novel by Aziz Hassim, *The Lotus People*, which traces the evolution of two families of Indian origin through four generations from close-knit ethnicity toward complete identification with South Africanness. Hand explores the relationship of the South African Indian community with the other South Africans, their fit into white-dominated society, and their evolution as politicized actors both before and during the apartheid era. Hassim carefully plots his novel with references to the sociohistorical context for the events; thus, *The Lotus People* deserves to be heralded as the first attempt to chronicle the history of South Africa's Indians in a literary text. Juan Zarandona directs his attention to the translated corpus of contemporary postcolonial South African literature in Spain. In his chapter, he discusses the extent to which the race factor is still significant when it comes to translating certain South African works into Spanish, as white authors tend to be favored over black, Indian, or Coloured writers. He argues that writers such as Ahmed Essop should be translated, as their work throws light on the complex racial make-up of contemporary South Africa.

Salvador Faura has unearthed links between Achmat Dangor's novel *Kafka's Curse* and a fifteenth-century Persian poet. His article suggests that Dangor responds to the work of the poet Fuzuli in the same way that Fuzuli himself reinterpreted the work of a fellow Persian, Nizami of Ganja, the twelfth-century romantic epic poet. Faura argues that Dangor's novel can only be understood through an analysis of Fuzili's characters Leyla and Mejnun, who, he contends, resurface in twentieth-century South Africa. Accordingly, Faura traces the patterns of connectedness forged between the present-day Indian community and their forebears in relation to the long history of trade and encounter in the Indian Ocean. Isabel Alonso-Breto essay on Farida Karodia's novel *Boundaries* searches for the transnational connections that, she claims, are manifest in the literature of the post-transitional phase. Her focus on the entry of the New South Africa into the ranks of globalization highlights the need to acknowledge that this ideal shifting of and release from constrictive boundaries is far from being a reality, and that social and economic inequalities have actually been exacerbated by the advent of transnational practices and globalization.

Esther Pujolràs-Noguer discusses Shamim Sarif's novel *The World Unseen* as an example of how the national space that was imagined under apartheid laws was a 'border space' as a consequence of internal colonialism. She argues that South Africa's Others—the non-whites—inhabited this 'border space' but were in fact essential components of the nation. The article thus highlights the arbitrariness of boundaries which were a consequence of the institutionalization of apartheid in 1948 and the Population Registration Act of 1950. The South African national space became a network of racial boundaries where whites, blacks, Coloureds, and Indians had, paradoxically, to cohabit separately. Sarif's 'world unseen' is introduced as a counter-hegemonic national space where 'home' can be a site of ultimate estrangement but also—and simultaneously—a ground where belonging can be explored. The nation-space that is being imagined steps beyond the confines of India and South Africa and lays out a script for the configuration of a 'home' in which 'gender'—unlike 'roots'—is allotted a prominent role. Modhumita Roy focusses on the work of the playwright and short-story writer Ronnie Govender. She looks closely at his collection of stories *At the Edge* and his family saga *Black Chin White Chin*, which chronicles five generations of South African Indians in order to analyze how history and cultural identity are reconstructed.

M.J. Daymond highlights South Africa as a land of division, collision, and ambiguity, problems the Indians had to face because of the conditions imposed on immigrants by legislation that was passed in South Africa before and during the apartheid era. The Indians were a highly heterogeneous people who did not think of themselves in collective terms and did not at first experience anything like group coherence or a shared sense of identity. Daymond discusses two of Imraan Coovadia's Durban novels, *The Wedding* and *High Low In-between*, which, despite being set a century apart, invite a historical comparison of the fortunes of members of the non-heterogeneous community which they depict. Composed of the descendants of indentured laborers and of traders, the Indian community in Durban has suffered internal fissures but it has invariably been compelled to occupy a marginalized position. Individual

members have been materially and professionally successful but the community as a whole has had to endure the indignities of political oppression and
cultural disparagement. J. Coplen Rose analyzes one of Ashwin Singh's plays,
To House, which highlights how stereotypes based on ethnic, cultural, and economic differences fragment the community on both the public and the private level. Ashwin Singh portrays the heterogeneity and cultural complexity of
South African Indians through his range of characters, who would have been
lumped together simply as 'Indians' during the apartheid era. Rose argues that
even after the demise of apartheid race still wields immense power in South
Africa as a social construct. Like many of the authors in this volume, Rose in-
sists on the heterogeneity of both immigrant groups—the indentured laborers
and the passenger Indians—who, despite originating in the subcontinent, did
not share a common religion or language and in fact came from different regions and classes. Rose highlights the improbability of successful integration
in the short term. He suggests that this is further complicated in urban centers
such as Durban where the same economic and geographical resources have to
be shared among multiple ethnic identities. The final chapter in this volume
pays homage to two fearless freedom fighters, Dr. Goonam and Fatima Meer,
through an analysis of the narratives they wrote about their experiences of
apartheid prisons. Farhad Khoyratty analyzes their work from a philosophical perspective, drawing on Heidegger's ideas of temporality. He claims that
the public space provided by the autobiography moves centrifugally from the
private identity constructed in the home both as women and as members of
'Indian' identities, which are also carceral.

The chapters in this volume deal with different genres—novel, play, short
story, poetry, historical memoir—illustrating the diversity of the community,
the object of this study. Older, more established writers are juxtaposed with
younger, lesser-known writers, male and female, Hindu and Muslim, forging
links between present-day communities and those of the past. South African
Indians are seen to be caught between the poles of the black–white binary,
but the texts analyzed in the following pages demonstrate how racial-ethnic
connections are substantially more complex than the white–black polarity
discourse that sustained the apartheid regime. Ultimately, what South African
Indian writing stands for is but another instantiation of the unfeasibility of
racial classifications. In short, the relations and networks that structure this
book contribute decisively to the dismantling of boundaries—racial, social,
cultural, geographical, and so forth—in an attempt to imagine a space more
substantial than the one delimited by the nation-state.

Relations and Networks in South African Indian Writing urges readers to
acknowledge how a specific and yet permanently fluid South African Indian

identity is reinforced through literature. The volume demands that 'Indian-ness' be re-conceptualized alongside the South African national identity struggle while maintaining a stronghold in an imaginative and ever-elusive Indian Ocean subjectivity.

Works Cited

Dhupelia–Mesthrie, Uma. *From Canefields to Freedom—A Chronicle of Indian South African Life* (Cape Town: Kwela, 2000).

Ebr.-Vally, Rehana. *Kala Pani: Caste and Colour in South Africa* (Cape Town: Kwela, 2001).

Elder, Arlene A. "Indian Writing in East and South Africa: Multiple Approaches to Colonialism and Apartheid," in *Reworlding: The Literature of the Indian Diaspora*, ed. Emmanuel S. Nelson (Westport CT: Greenwood, 1992): 115–139.

Frenkel, Ronit. *Reconsiderations: South African Indian Fiction and the Making of Race in Postcolonial Culture* (Pretoria: U of South Africa P, 2010).

Freund, Bill. *Insiders and Outsiders: The Indian Working Class of Durban 1910–1990* (Scotsville: U of Natal P, 1995).

Goonam, Dr. (Kesaveloo Goonam). *Coolie Doctor: An Autobiography by Dr. Goonam* (Durban: Madiba, 1991).

Govinden, Devarakshanam Betty. *Sister Outsiders: The Representation of Identity and Difference in Selected Writings by South African Indian Women* (Pretoria: U of South Africa P, 2008).

Helff, Sissy. *Unreliable Truths: Transcultural Homeworlds in Indian Women's Fiction of the Diaspora* (Cross/Cultures 155; Amsterdam & New York: Rodopi, 2013).

Hiralal, Kalpana. "The Gujarati Trading Class Within the Indian Community—Shaped and Styled by Historical Contradictions," in *Undressing Durban*, ed. Rob Pattman & Sultan Khan (Durban: Madiba, 2007): 309–315.

Kaarsholm, Preben. "Transnational Spaces, Islam and the Interaction of Indian and African Identity Strategies in South Africa During and After Apartheid," in *Eyes Across the Water: Navigating the Indian Ocean*, ed. Pamila Gupta, Isabel Hofmeyr & Michael Pearson (Pretoria: U of South Africa P, 2010): 220–237.

Lemon, Anthony. "The Political Position of Indians in South Africa," in *South Asians Overseas: Migration and Ethnicity*, ed. Colin Clarke, Ceri Peach & Steven Vertovec (1990: Cambridge: Cambridge UP, 2009): 131–148.

Mishra, Vijay. *The Literature of the Indian Diaspora: Theorizing the Diasporic Imaginary* (London: Routledge, 2007).

Pillay, Kathryn. "The Minority Report: Undressing 'Indians' in Durban," in *Undressing Durban*, ed. Rob Pattman & Sultan Khan (Durban: Madiba, 2007): 319–329.

Pirbhai, Mariam. *Mythologies of Migration, Vocabularies of Indenture: Novels of the South Asian Diaspora in Africa, the Caribbean, and Asia-Pacific* (Toronto: U of Toronto P, 2009).

Rastogi, Pallavi. *Afrindian Fictions. Diaspora, Race, and National Desire in South Africa* (Columbus: Ohio State UP, 2008).

South African History Online. *Towards a People's History* (nd), http://www.sahistory .org.za/topic/segregationist-legislation-timeline-1940-1949 (accessed 15 September 2015).

Sunday Times Heritage Project (nd). http://sthp.saha.org.za/memorial/mohan das_gandhi.htm (accessed 3 December 2015).

Swan, Maureen. *Gandhi: The South African Experience* (Johannesburg: Ravan, 1984).

Upstone, Sara. *Spatial Politics in the Postcolonial Novel* (Farnham & Burlington VT: Ashgate, 2009).

Worden, Nigel. "Indian Ocean Slavery and Its Demise in the Cape Colony," in *Abolition and Its Aftermath in Indian Ocean Africa and Asia*, ed. Gwyn Campbell (London: Routledge, 2005): 29–49.

CHAPTER 2

Planted Firmly in South African Soil

Literary Recollections of Indenture

Lindy Stiebel

The extraordinary volume of writing which has emerged over the past few years on the subject of indenture has proved that the broad field of study surrounding South African Indians is rapidly attracting attention from many quarters but particularly from South Africans of Indian descent themselves. In recent years many people from all walks of life seem to have expressed a desire to record their history; not only are academics writing extensively on their community but medical doctors, journalists, lawyers, accountants, and teachers have also put pen to paper.

The most popular expression of this drive to record the past—whether in fiction, history, memoir, short story, article, play or poetry—was the various 'memory' projects launched by Durban-based newspapers in 2010 which urged people of Indian origin to send in their story to mark a momentous event: the 150th anniversary of the arrival of the first indentured Indian laborers in 1860. The so-called '1860 Project' in the *Sunday Tribune* sought to encourage South Africans of Indian descent to rediscover their ancestral culture—and, by extension, themselves—as it may be in danger of becoming lost to memory.[1] However, the idea of celebrating such an event was queried by Aziz Hassim, author of *The Lotus People* (2002) and *Revenge of Kali* (2009), who insisted that there was little to be proud of when it came to remembering the exploitation of human beings. "Celebrate? Really! Can you celebrate slavery? Can we get it right, just this once? We can commemorate that despicable event in our history, not glorify it with false attributes."[2] Hassim's counterpointing of 'commemoration' and 'celebration' was at the heart of the 150th anniversary: it points directly to the bitter-sweet nature of such an occasion. The contemporary

---

1 For further information on Indian indenture in South Africa, see the website of the Christian Revival Centre, "The 1860 Project," http://www.crconline.co.za/the-1860-project/.

2 Aziz Hassim, "Celebrating Slavery? Commemorate, but do not glorify," *The Post* (1 September 2010), https://www.pressreader.com/south-africa/the-post7573/20100901/282226597041379 (accessed 25 January 2017).

© KONINKLIJKE BRILL NV, LEIDEN, 2018 | DOI 10.1163/9789004365032_003

gains and successes have come on the back, as it were, of a very harsh start.[3]

Another newspaper in the same Independent Newspapers stable, the *Daily News,* ran a similar project called the '1860 Settler Project.' The rubric of this project was, however, significantly more upbeat:

> The *Daily News* will celebrate the contribution these brave pioneers have made by telling the stories of the treacherous journey and their new life here, as handed down to the generations who followed.

One such story carried within the pages of the newspaper was an extract drawn from Jay Naidoo's memoir, *Fighting for Justice,* in which he records his great-grandmother's shipping number (28330), and ironically observes that, as an organizer in the Sweet, Food and Allied Workers' Union, he had "to engage with the very sector that had treated my ancestors as nothing more than hard-working serfs in a feudal colony."[4] An even more ironic twist is contained in the article "White Gold" carried in the *Sunday Times* (6 June 2010), which describes activities surrounding a locally made film of the same name,[5] filmed in Tamil, Hindi, and English, released on circuit in November, and thus timed to coincide with the 150th anniversary. The film tells the story of four friends who leave India as indentured laborers for South Africa and follows them and their descendants over three generations. According to the scriptwriter, Jayan Moodley, the response to the call for extras was overwhelming—it seems the people who arrived—over two hundred—were attracted by much more than the pay.

Running parallel to the stories sent in to the press and the articles reprising the history of indentured labor in this country were the many newspaper letters, poems, and columns written in 2010 on the question of South African Indian identity. The combination of sixteen years since the first democratic elections in 1994, and 150 years since indenture, provoked intense debate on this issue. The following poem captures the question of identity clearly:

---

3   See Lindy Stiebel, "Crossing the *kala pani*: cause for 'celebration' or 'commemoration' 150 years on? Portrayals of indenture in recent South African Indian writing," *Journal of Literary Studies* 27.2 (2011): 77–90, for a fuller discussion of this issue.

4   Jay Naidoo, *Fighting for Justice: A Lifetime of Political and Social Activism* (Johannesburg: Picador Africa, 2010): 17.

5   Paul Railton & Jayan Moodley, dir. *White Gold,* screenplay by Jayan Moodley (Serendipity Productions / African Lotus Production Studios, South Africa 2010; 113 min.).

"Who Am I?"

1860 I arrived. Classed Indian Coolie, I was called!
Sugarcane farms
Bitter conflict
Divided by race—African, Indian, Coloured, White
From humanity I was deprived
1946,'52,'60,'76,'85 the struggle continued
1990 the land filled with joyous cheers
So much friendship
Viva Mandela Viva!
A nation appears.
No more black, white, or brown or blue?
But...
Who am I?
I am Indian by creed, by race I am African
I am Indian by religion, by race I am African
I am Indian by tradition, by race I am African
I am an African Indian in Africa
I am.[6]

Needless to say, there is nothing really new about these questions. The late Fatima Meer, in her early pioneering work *Portrait of Indian South Africans* (1969), summarized the historical context of the arrival of indentured labor to South Africa, and in so doing made a clear statement about nationality and identity in the last sentence to be quoted below. The passage outlines the historical context in which Indian immigration to South Africa from 1860 to 1911 (when Indian legislation halted sending indentured laborers to Natal), and 1913 (when South African legislation prohibited immigration for all Indians) can be understood:

> The majority of Indian South Africans are the descendants of indentured workers brought to Natal between 1860 and 1911 to develop the country's sugar belt. White colonists despaired of exploiting the country's agricultural resources, due to the scarcity of labour. Slavery had been abolished and the Zulu, relatively secure in the tribal economy, refused to market their labour.

---

6   Tshque Harcharan, "Searching for my identity," *Sunday Tribune* (3 June 2010): 6.

India, convulsed by the British occupation, offered a solution. Peasants and craftsmen, often deluded by unscrupulous recruiting agents, bound themselves for five years and more to unknown masters, under little known conditions, to fill the vacancies created by the emancipated slaves on the world's tropical plantations [...] Free, or passenger Indians as they came to be called, followed in the wake of the indentured to Natal, but White colonists became alarmed by the competition offered by these merchants and by those whose labour contracts had expired. By 1913 Indian immigration was generally prohibited by law.

The result is today, with few exceptions, Indian South Africans, are South African citizens by birth.[7]

Just over twenty years later, Dr. Goonam started her autobiography *Coolie Doctor* (1991) with the problem of identity:

I was born in May Street, in Durban, in 1906 on the southern part of the East African coast. That made me African, but not quite, for my father had immigrated from South Asia and my mother from Mauritius. I would be identified as a South African Indian or Indian South African.[8]

In contrast, Ela Gandhi, great-granddaughter of the Mahatma, is quoted in Uma Dhupelia–Mesthrie's book *From Cane Fields to Freedom* as resisting the coupling of 'South African' and 'Indian' in defining her identity:

I'm a South African. A very proud South African [...] The Indianness comes in at the level of culture, the way we eat, the kind of things we eat, the kind of things we [...] appreciate like music, drama, the language we speak [...] We only enrich our country by having all these different tastes and habits. What I'm basically saying is that is where the Indianness stops.[9]

Given the large number of Indians who arrived in South Africa during the years of indenture—Diesel estimates "altogether, just over 150,000 individual Indians were brought to Natal in the fifty year period between 1860 and

---

7   Fatima Meer, *Portrait of Indian South Africans* (Durban: Avon House, 1969): 7.

8   Dr. Goonam, *Coolie Doctor* (Durban: Madiba, 1991): 41.

9   In Dhupelia–Mesthrie, *From Cane Fields to Freedom: A Chronicle of Indian South African Life* (Cape Town: Kwela, 2000): 9.

1911"[10]—together with passenger Indians, and their combined descendants, who, like their forefathers represent a number of trades, professions, income levels, languages etc., any uniformity on the question of identity would be unusual. Dhupelia–Mesthrie observes:

> Unlike the rest of Africa, where Indians were primarily a trader class, the majority of South Africa's Indians have never constituted a homogenous group and their attitudes to significant issues such as identity and political affiliation will vary.[11]

In a similar vein, Ronit Frenkel suggests that the very ambiguity of South African Indian identity can become "central to understanding the ideological underpinnings of South African culture broadly, as it destabilizes unintegrated conceptions of cultural forms."[12]

But it seems that, as the millennium turned, for many people of Indian descent in South Africa the 'Indian' part of their identity came to be reinforced, emphasized, and cherished. Among South African historians and writers, this intense interest in the past is clearly evident in the last decade and more, and intensified in the five years building up to the 150th anniversary. Whether the writers are literary critics, historians, creative writers or 'ordinary' people writing their stories and sending them to the papers, there is general recognition that an important process of reclamation is underway. Chetty, in the Introduction to the first South African work to look specifically at South African Indian writers, stresses the importance of reclamation, of memory:

> This 'audit' of a marginalized sub-genre would hopefully result in a more inclusive South African literary history, an affirmation of South African Indian writers' distinctiveness and a celebration of differences [...] Writers like Farida Karodia, Ahmed Essop, Ronnie Govender, Indres Naidoo and Kesavaloo Goonam relocate the South African Indian as an integral part of the African landscape.[13]

---

10   Alleyn Diesel, "Hinduism in KwaZulu-Natal, South Africa," in *Culture and Economy in the Indian Diaspora*, ed. Bhikhu Parekh, Gurharpal Singh & Steven Vertovec (London: Routledge, 2003): 34.

11   Dhupelia–Mesthrie, *From Cane Fields to Freedom*, 28.

12   Ronit Frenkel, "Reconsidering South African Indian Fiction Postapartheid," *Research in African Literatures* 42.3 (2011): 1.

13   Rajendra Chetty, "Introduction" to *South African Indian Writings in English*, ed. Chetty (Durban: Madiba, 2002): 9, 21.

Desai and Vahed, in their acclaimed text *Inside Indenture* (2007), reissued in 2010 as *Inside Indian Indenture* to mark the 150th anniversary, explain their goal of reclamation in writing their book:

> At its core, this book seeks to recover the biographies of those whom history has tried to ignore and to give 'voice' to those hitherto silenced [...] If the indentured system tried to turn people into numbers, then this book seeks to turn numbers into people, empirical detail into a foundation for a deeper understanding of the life of indenture, and of 'our' past into a basis for reflection on the challenges of the present. You *see*, journeys like Shiva's dance, are unending.[14]

As the literary critic Devarakshanam Betty Govinden presciently noted, "South Africa at the present moment is living through a time of memory. It is a time when we are considering the past histories of individuals, families, institutions, events and periods."[15] Indenture on the sugarcane plantations of KwaZulu–Natal, as shown through a quick look at the newspaper projects mentioned earlier, is providing writers with one such powerful event or sequence of events. South African Indian writers of the past decade who, by and large, have been engaged in 'memory' projects of one sort or another, often with indenture at the core, prove the point about the substantial rise in number and variety of recent published texts on this theme, certainly leading up to the 150th anniversary. Past that anniversary, too, research continues into the 'plantation system.' Desai and Vahed write, in a recent collection of essays, the following:

> While the contract provided guarantees on paper, in practice indenture was a period of brutality, poverty and moral disintegration for many as employers failed to fulfil their end of the bargain. Appalling servitude defined the indentured system, with many narratives of brutality on the plantations. Take the story of Mungi, for example. She had arrived with her husband Halhori from Shahabad in July 1881. She was in an advanced stage of pregnancy and, according to Dr. Lindsay Bonnar, gave birth to a stillborn child in Durban on 12 August. The following day, still weak, she was forced to go by rail to Isipingo with a group of Indian migrants and

---

14   Ashwin Desai & Goolam Vahed, *Inside Indenture: a South African story, 1860–1914* (Durban: Madiba, 2007). Re-released as *Inside Indian Indenture: A South African Story, 1860–1914* (Cape Town: HSRC Press, 2010): 26, 27.

15   Devarakshanam Betty Govinden, *A Time of Memory: Reflections on Recent South African Writings* (Durban: Solo Collective, 2008): 9.

from there, made to walk 40 miles to Umzinto on a 'cold and rainy day' because 'there was no wagon or means of shelter, the want of which was doubtless the cause of the poor young woman's untimely death.'[16]

The number of titles, and the amount of research these texts involve, speaks for an exceptionally busy 'time of memory,' especially considering that many of these are first time writers. This is true of Tholsi Mudly's memoir *A Tribute to Our Forefathers*, which is a well-researched and lavishly illustrated account of one family's experience of indenture placed in its historical context. It is, in essence, a memory project inspired by the 150th anniversary. Written simply by a retired teacher, herself descended from indentured laborers, this account is told as one of survival and triumph over adversity:

> Our forefathers worked their fingers to the bone to ensure that we, their descendants, live a far better life than theirs. They persevered against all the odds stacked against them. They scrimped and they saved, and they put up with the worst indignities with us in mind. Their commitment, their resoluteness and their pride in everything they did should serve as a reminder to all of us to strive for success in all aspects of our lives.[17]

Mudly's efforts were rewarded by having the long-lost family gravesites, on the property of the sugar giant Tongaat Hulett, restored and declared a Memorial Garden in 2010 in a ceremony attended by sugarcane plantation owners and growers, together with those whose ancestors' remains lay beneath the vegetation. *A Tribute to Our Forefathers* is one example of 'plantation literature' in South African Indian writing. Sugarcane plantations, defined as single units of agricultural production that raise crops for local consumption and export, were largely situated on the KwaZulu–Natal coastal belt. Chetty notes that a "host of writers have written about Grey Street,"[18] an urban space synonymous with Durban Indian settlement, but less attention has been devoted to those works by South Africans of Indian descent which have the sugarcane plantation as their spatial focus.

---

16   Aswin Desai & Goolam Vahed, "Indenture and Indianness in South Africa, 1860–1913," in *Contemporary India and South Africa: Legacies, Identities and Dilemmas*, ed. Sujata Patel & Tina Uys (London: Routledge, 2012): 24–25.

17   Tholsi Mudly, *A Tribute to Our Forefathers* (Wandsbeck: Reach, 2011): 172.

18   Rajendra Chetty, *The Vintage Book of South African Indian Writing* (Johannesburg: STE, 2010): v.

Plantations are more commonly associated with the Americas, but they formed a vital part of South Africa's economy in the nineteenth century. These sugar farm communities were characterized by the existence of two clearly differentiated ranks: a wealthy elite of plantation owners and a large population of poor laborers. In the South African context, the descendants of these Indian indentured workers are engaging with the history of their forebears, which is, of course, their own. The literature that has emerged from these experiences, what I am calling 'plantation literature,' deals with issues of memory, belonging, suffering, and gender.

As applied to the American South, plantation literature is a nostalgic genre that had its origins in the first attempts by Southern writers to counter the growing abolitionist sentiment of the 1830s to 1850s. The plantation system, such texts convey, was like a family, with deep bonds of loyalty uniting white and African American members under the white patriarchal master. Nostalgia is linked to the landscape of the plantation literature of the South: the hills and fields, the columned mansion, the courtly master and his family taking their ease on the veranda, their contented black retainers filling the evening air with song.[19] Plantation literature linked to sugar farms in South Africa rarely carries the same uncomplicated nostalgia even when written by descendants of white sugar farm owners who were privileged in their ownership—see, for example, *Ratoons* (1953) by Daphne Rooke, set on a south coast sugarcane farm; or *The Arrowing of the Cane* (1986) by John Conyngham, set on the north coast of KwaZulu–Natal). The exception to this is perhaps possible when nostalgia is attached to the natural beauty of the countryside only, separated from the racial tensions that play upon its surface. The following passage from Conyngham's *The Arrowing of the Cane* captures a love of place which is, however, made uneasy by the political context. The natural beauty of the sugar plantations doesn't quite escape the political context in which it is written, as its hierarchical spatial demarcations parallel a hierarchy of power relations:

> The road from Nonoti into the hills rises slowly out of the mugginess of the town, switchbacking its way past deep old houses seething with wispish Indian children, mango trees with their glossy leaves, car and bus carcasses, and fluttering flags on tall bamboo poles. Slowly, reluctantly, the sprawling suburb succumbs to the ubiquitous cane. Labouring under its load, the Land Rover edges into the sighing greenness, rising and falling with its ebb and flow.

---

19   See Richard Gray & Owen Robinson, *A Companion to the Literature and Culture of the American South* (London: Blackwell, 2004).

Clusters of palms indicate farmhouses hugged to their outbuildings by high hedges. Signs on the verge announce the company's sections— Carrickfergus, Quantock, Umsundu and Kerry Dale—each with its own manager, overseers, sirdars, indunas and army of labourers. Next the polo club, its team once provincial champions, holders of the Waterford Cup, but now fighting relegation to the third division. Then the company hospital with its two white doctors and shuttered wards, and the little St John's Church with its cemetery. Planter families lie neatly in rows while the Indians' crosses wander from the bottom fence into a grove of gums.

Gradually the air becomes more rarified. Coolness jets through the vents. Far below to the left the Umvoti River coils through another finger of KwaZulu which was a hotspot during the Bambata Rebellion. Now overpopulated, overgrazed and rutted, the valley looks idyllic to strangers crossing this neck miles above it. There is a lay-by from which tourists can take photographs of the picturesque hutted kraals. As with anything gross, distance placates the onlooker.[20]

Similarly, if there is any nostalgia expressed by anyone in the texts written by the descendants of the Indian indentured laborers who toiled in the fields, and who are the focus of this chapter, it is for the natural beauty of the surroundings. Even such nostalgia is, however, expressed ironically, as in the following passage found in a recently published novel, *What About Meera* (2015), by Z.P. Dala. The novel moves between the sugarcane town of Tongaat on the KwaZulu–Natal North Coast and Dublin, Ireland. The following passage comes from a chapter entitled "What Happened in Tongaat":

Surrounding the buildings, none of them over one storey in height, were fields and fields of sugar cane, and flourishes of bougainvillea. Tongaat was famous for its sugar. The oldest sugar barons from the British Empire and the Dutch East India Company had settled there, in grand manor houses that stood hawkishly looking over the town like distant relatives. Manor gardens on large estates with large bay windows that looked out onto the spreading sugary invitation and where men in too-tight khaki shorts with whiskies in the hands kept beady eyes on their Indian labourers, who were housed in barracks and occasionally thanked the Sugarman for the roof over their heads.

---

20   John Conyngham, *The Arrowing of the Cane* (Craighall: Ad. Donker, 1986): 5.

When Indians were freed from their indenture, after Mahatma Gandhi had starved and fought like a nappy-wearing bulldog for their freedom, the Indians remained in their barracks, grateful still for the roof over their heads. They kowtowed still to the Barons and their Baroness wives, and their children who had fully grown horses for pets, and happy golden retrievers.[21]

In common with plantation literature of the American South, it is evident that the plantation literature which emanates from the sugar farms of the coastal regions of KwaZulu–Natal also carries a heavy ideological burden. Plantation literature is, as Grammer maintains, "a version of the literary pastoral, a mode, as Raymond Williams and others have shown, which can seldom avoid saying something about politics."[22] What the following selected texts will illustrate most definitely is the truth in this statement: the 150th anniversary (2010) of the arrival of the first indentured Indian laborers in South Africa saw a sudden increase in the number of works written by South African Indian writers, with what I have called 'sugar texts' prominent among them.[23] Tholsi Mudly (*A Tribute to Our Forefathers*, 2011), Neelan Govender (*Girrmit Tales*, 2008), Rubendra Govender (*Sugar Cane Boy*, 2008), and Aziz Hassim (*Revenge of Kali*, 2009) are all examples of 'plantation literature' by South African Indian writers. All four texts—two historical memoirs and two novels respectively—draw on the history of indentured labor in South Africa, particularly as experienced on the north coast of KwaZulu–Natal, the locus for all four texts. What emerges, I will argue, is a repeated pattern of oppression, resistance, and survival as depicted by the descendants of early sugar plantation workers, the authors of these texts. The ending of all four narratives draws attention to the importance of memory, of remembering, of bearing witness to the past and—most important—of belonging to the South African soil.

At the heart of these examples of 'plantation literature' is an assertion by the writers of their identity as South Africans of Indian origin. This assertion is made through a revisiting of history, in this case, the history of their forefathers who arrived in this country as manual laborers with very few rights

---

21   Z.P. Dala, *What About Meera* (Cape Town: Umuzi, 2015): 47.

22   John M. Grammer, "Plantation Fiction," in *A Companion to the Literature and Culture of the American South*, ed. Richard Gray & Owen Robinson (London: Blackwell, 2004): http://www.blackwellreference.com/public/tocnode?id=g9780631224044_chunk_g9780631224045 (accessed 25 January 2017).

23   See Lindy Stiebel, "Sugar-Coated Stories? Plantation Literature by Selected South African Indian Writers," *English Academy Review* 33.1 (2016): 7–23.

but whose descendants nonetheless rose to positions of respectability, their voices powerful enough to articulate their experience and that of those who came before them. The starting point for the texts is clearly identifiable: on 16 November 1860, the arrival in Durban on the ss *Truro* of the first shipment of Indian workers destined to serve a five-year period of indenture in the sugarcane fields of Natal. The harsh beginnings of what has been likened to slave labor for *girmityas*—"from English, agreement, referred to indentured workers, those who had signed an agreement"[24]—defined the 150th anniversary in 2010 as a profoundly ambivalent one. From the various commemorative projects launched in the course of that year, the overriding tone was one of pride at the achievements of the descendants despite their very tough start on African soil; plus celebration of their resilience, not only then but throughout their sojourn and settlement in South Africa.

For many writers, including Neelan Govender, the centrality of the voyage over the sea, crossing the *kala pani*, is evident.[25] Govender re-creates the apprehension and hardship of the ocean crossing in one of his *girrmit* tales, "The Dowry":

> There was talk of people leaving for Fiji, Penang and Natal to work in the sugarcane fields. They considered India a cursed country for the wretched and the poor. [... My] mother fell in with the grandparents of Young Archie's bride Ramanna Naidoo and his wife Jutchmee, who were also out to seek their fortune beyond the oceans. Many people advised against this madness as it was preached by the *brahmins* that once one ventured across the oceans, one lost one's caste status. Tell this to the wretched, the hungry, and the homeless. What lesser misfortune can they fall into? Where has caste ever protected and nurtured them?[26]

The position of the widow or unaccompanied woman on the crossing was precarious, but Govender depicts opportunities, too, for the brave. In his short

---

24   Uma Dhupelia–Mesthrie, *From Cane Fields to Freedom*, 14.

25   This is true, too, of the literary movement described as 'coolitude' which can be defined as "an intellectual interpretation, a poetic and artistic immersion into the world of the vanished coolie"; Marina Carter & Khal Torabully, *Coolitude: An Anthology of the Indian Labour Diaspora* (London: Anthem, 2002): back cover. Torabully wrote in 1996: "It is impossible to understand the essence of coolitude without charting the coolies' voyage across the seas. That decisive experience, that coolie odyssey, left an indelible stamp on the imaginary landscape of coolitude" (Carter & Torabully, *Coolitude*, 11).

26   Neelan Govender, *Girrmit Tales*, preface by Phyllis Naidoo, foreword by Pat Poovalingam (Durban: Rebel Rabble, 2008): 169.

story "Where the River Flows," he shows the young widow Aoujiamma and her small children desperately weeping when the voyage starts. However,

> by the time they reached the Port of Durban, her despair gave way to hope; her anxiety to expectation. Perhaps, all the evil that had befallen her and her children would now be a thing of the past. Perhaps there was, after all, a brighter destiny for her and all on board. A kinship closer than a blood bond had arisen amongst those on board. Already some relationships such as *Akka* (elder sister), *Anna* (elder brother), *Mamman* (maternal uncle) and *Muchan* (wife's brother) were being invoked. Some of these were to become very strong bonds. There would be relationships and even marriages, as they took root in their country of adoption.[27]

Girrmit Tales, in summary, consists of fourteen stories told to the writer, a medical doctor, over a forty-year period during his medical rounds and retold to us, the readers. Neelan Govender, "himself a descendant of Natal *girrmityas*" as the back cover of the book states, intends this book to be a project of memory, reclamation, and, indeed, commemoration. It begins with a facsimile of an indenture agreement (reconstructed for a modern reader); a time line of Indian indenture 1834–1920 worldwide, not just in South Africa; a preface by Phyllis Naidoo and a foreword by Pat Poovalingam, both activists and writers, both of whom refer to indenture as a kind of slavery in their respective pieces. The stories cover accounts of indenture experience from varying individual angles, from families with rivalries carried over the water from India to Natal, from the hopeless who then hope for a better life in Natal: "In the market place he had learnt that there was a place across the ocean called Natal, where the land was so rich with gold that the chilli plants bore chillies that turned green to yellow first before turning red."[28] The position of the *sirdar* is given voice in one of Govender's *girrmit* tales, "Land of Last Content." In this tale, an old man, Thatha, tells his tale of promotion to *sirdar* by the white boss and how this was resented by his fellow workers, who then tried to poison him:

> You know, *nayna*, the Head Sirdar's job was not easy. I had to take care of everything in the settlement. I was the Mayor, Magistrate and Councillor. I was like a father to all the people. I had to settle all disputes, worry about the families, the neighbours and their relatives. I had to be at every wedding and every funeral. I was also in charge of two temples. I had to

---

27   Govender *Girrmit Tales*, 87–88.
28   *Girrmit Tales*, 64.

encourage people to work in their own gardens, as we were given land to do our own planting.[29]

This is a far more genial image of *sirdar* control than Aziz Hassim presents in his novel, discussed below—perhaps understandable, given the partial narrative position of the *sirdar* himself in the above quotation. Govender's stories are of extreme misery on the part of those tricked into service by unscrupulous recruiters; of prosperity; of families of convenience formed to gain access to the boats; and finally of African Zanzibaris, whose lot was thrown in with Indians in Durban. The stories respond to Vijay Mishra's urgent call for "a massive archeology of the 'Girmit' phenomenon"[30] before memories fade, or die out, and the details become harder to recover.

Of all the writers and their works selected, Aziz Hassim's *Revenge of Kali* is the most accomplished. This is not surprising, as Hassim is an established writer, having won the Sanlam award in 2001 for his debut novel *The Lotus People*, whereas the other three are first-time published writers. Hassim's searing fictionalized account of the lives of indentured laborers located on the Natal sugarcane farms begins the book. It is the story of Ellapen, who was forcibly put aboard the *ss Truro* in 1860 to work in the sugarcane plantations of Natal, his wife Angamma, and their son Kolapen. Thiru, Kolapen's son and the narrator, is called to tell this story by the spirits of his ancestors. By Thiru's telling their story, their ghosts are released:

> When Ellapen joined his palms together and raised his hands to his lips, then nodded down at me, I understood, absolutely, the message: the anguish of their bondage had finally been told. Their nightmare had ended, they had been released: their incubus at last interred in the very fields from which it had haunted them.[31]

As Hassim was also the author of the letter advising a lasting commemoration of the 150th anniversary rather than an 'ephemeral' celebration, it is also not surprising that his is a powerful story which roundly condemns indenture as slavery by another name:

---

29   *Girmit Tales*, 24–25.

30   Vijay Mishra, "The Girmit Ideology Revisited: Fiji Indian Literature," in *Reworlding: The Literature of the Indian Diaspora*, ed. Emmanuel S. Nelson (Westport CT: Greenwood, 1992): 1.

31   Aziz Hassim, *Revenge of Kali* (Johannesburg: STE, 2009): 75. Further page references are in the main text.

> It was a brilliant contrivance, brilliantly executed. By a stroke of the pen
> India replaced Africa as the source of slave labour [...] It was a confidence
> trick of unequalled scale.
>
> *Revenge of Kali*, 78

However, the different twist to this novel is that it shows how oppression was
not all one-way traffic: this is also a story about, again in Hassim's own words,
"what Indians did to each other."[32] Thus, the role of the hated Indian *sirdars* in
maintaining discipline and the pace of daily cane cutting quotas on the farms
are not overlooked—although it must be said that not all *sirdars* were ruthless
sadists, as Govender's tale mentioned above illustrates.

Indian complicity in their own exploitation is not skirted in the book's pro-
gression through four generations of the descendants of Ellapen. Whether the
setting moves in Parts Two and Three to the Duchene or Grey Street areas of
Durban respectively, oppression is shown as being complex and multiple—
of one caste towards another, of one belief system set up against another, of
rich landlords evicting poorer tenants, of the strong against the weak, of men
against women resulting in domestic violence. Hence the title's reference to
Kali: in this book, she is the avenging goddess "ensuring justice for the power-
less" (54). It is a justice promised by the book's rain-soaked ending: rain that
washes away, rain that causes the cane to grow, a torrent of water that allows
the logjam to break through.

Despite *Revenge of Kali*'s dark and weighty themes, this is an eminently
readable novel with plenty of pace and, above all, a wonderfully authentic
evocation of place. Divided into three sections: The Canefields, The Duchene,
The Casbah, *Revenge of Kali* is a deeply Durban book as this example of a de
Certeau-like urban stroll illustrates:

> Careful now—take a left into Ajax Lane and you will be lost in a maze of
> alleys and dead-ends; unless you happen to bump into the cantankerous
> Mister Akoon who, depending on his mood, will take you by the hand and
> lead you out of the labyrinth and deposit you safely back onto Old Dutch
> Road—a hundred feet from the ill-famed Etna Lane, the home-base of
> the notorious Duchene Gang.
>
> *Revenge of Kali*, 85

---

32   Aziz Hassim, "By a stroke of the pen, India became a source of 'slaves'," *Sunday Independent*
     (4 October 2009), https://www.pressreader.com/south-africa/the-sunday-independent/
     20091004/281921654098906 (accessed 25 January 2017).

It is the street world of Benjamin's *flâneur*, Dickensian in its twists and turns, its low life. In this respect, *Revenge of Kali* follows on from Hassim's first, award-winning novel, *The Lotus People* (2002), which also had as its locus 'Indian' Durban, particularly Grey Street, where Hassim spent years as a *laaitie* (young boy) himself.[33] The Canefields section, in contrast to those sections based in the city, is rendered in less detail—it is the characters and their suffering that Hassim evokes here, rather than a sense of place. There is heat, fields, sugarcane, floggings, and back-breaking labor. This is what Hassim imagines and records; despite being a descendant of rural indentured laborers, he was a city man and his description of the city spaces is much more detailed and engaged from a place-specific point of view.

Hassim's prose is peppered with words from the street and everyday speech—Thiru, the central character and descendant of grandfather Ellapen, is variously referred to as a *bro, boet, scoten, laaitie, charou* who eats the *vadeh* and *murku* made by his Tamil-speaking grandmother or *parti*. The glossary, with its mix of Afrikaans, Hindi, Tamil, Gujarati, and Zulu words, thoughtfully provided at the end, bears witness to the melting-pot that was the 'old' Grey Street of years gone by and, indeed, of the world of indenture which had to adapt so rapidly to a South Africa of competing cultures. This, then, is *Revenge of Kali*'s strength—it contains an authoritative central voice set in a densely visualized place telling a South African story of survival in hard times, generation after generation. That the past needs to find expression in tales such as these is made evident in the evocative chiding of Thiru by the spirits of his forefathers whom he seeks out: "Come *kanna*. What took you so long!"(14).

Rubendra Govender's *Sugar Cane Boy* draws its setting from an Inanda sugarcane farm owned by the Murugappa family, themselves descendants of indentured laborers who improved their lot dramatically over time. The Indian ownership of the sugar farm sets it apart from the other three texts which describe indentured life on white-owned sugar plantations. It is important to note that although many indentured laborers were destroyed by the system in which they found themselves in Natal, this was not the only outcome (as, indeed, the tales selected all record survival and even eventual success, combined with tragedy, along the way). As Desai and Vahed point out,

> Indenture was not slavery. It was for a limited time and was not passed on to one's descendants, the system underwent changes over time, the plantation was not a 'total' system of control and migration was a

---

33   See Felicity Hand's chapter on *The Lotus People* in this volume.

liberating experience for some who may have sought an escape from India.[34]

They go on to quote the example of Boodha Dulel Sing, who, after serving his indenture on the north coast, bought a few acres of land in Nonoti and planted sugarcane, tobacco, and vegetables. By the time of his death in 1919, "his farm 'Hyde Park' measured almost 5,000 acres, and employed over 100 Indian workers."[35] As Frenkel points out, there is a danger of stereotyping 'Indians' in South Africa into one homogeneous group, including seeing all indentured Indians as one homogeneous grouping as well. This, she and others have said, is partly explained by the ignorance of the authorities who received the migrants and saw one 'different' people who could be described as 'Indian' for ease of administration; and then the later "apartheid taxonomies [which] reified Indianness into a distinct racial category, setting one population group against another in its enforcement of imposed difference."[36] This was not a homogeneity imposed from the outside only, but was also occasioned from within in the face of anti-Indian sentiment. In the same way as anti-Indian sentiment, where it occurred, did not differentiate between caste or language groupings among Indians, a pan-Indian identity emerged in groupings such as the Natal Indian Congress to present a united front against discrimination.[37]

The other difference to be noted in *Sugar Cane Boy* is that it highlights the relationship between an Indian boy on the sugarcane farm and his best friend, a Zulu boy, Boniwe Mkhize. As Desai and Vahed point out, it was African (cheaper) labor that white farmers were keen to employ rather than the more expensive Indians:

> Slowly at first, and then with greater intensity after the defeat of the Bambatha Rebellion of 1906, the African dispossessed were turned into cheap labour that began to replace Indians in the colonial workforce. The availability of African labour rendered Indians superfluous in the farming, mining and the public sectors. As the 'cheap bodies' of indenture left the plantation, so the 'cheapened bodies' of the Zulus took their place in most economic sectors.[38]

---

34   Desai & Vahed, "Indenture and Indianness in South Africa, 1860–1913," 32.

35   "Indenture and Indianness in South Africa, 1860–1913," 32.

36   Ronit Frenkel, *Reconsiderations: South African Indian Fiction and the Making of Race in Postcolonial Literature* (Pretoria: Unisa Press, 2010): 13.

37   Frenkel, *Reconsiderations*, 12.

38   "Indenture and Indianness in South Africa, 1860–1913," 31–32.

Boniwe's existence on the Indian-owned farm indicates the changing face of the workforce and is intended as a hopeful signifier of potential harmonious interrelationships between Indian and African which can defy the stereotype of animosity between these two groupings, as expressed in, for example, the Cato Manor riots of 1949 and 1959.[39]

Thus, in summary, the novel, set in the 1970s, is a story of friendship between Soya Sivaraman whose family works on the farm, and Boniwe Mkhize, a fellow farm 'boy.' Soya's father, Deena, works on the Groenberg farm as assistant farm manager-cum-truck driver as his father had done before him. The Sivaraman family also works in the farm's five-acre market garden, the produce of which is sold in the town markets. The narrative takes the reader through Soya's teenage years on the farm: working in the garden, fighting with other boys, participating in festivals, and helping in the cane fields at harvest time. Though marked by hard work, these times are described with nostalgia:

> A few hours after the cane floor had completely cooled down, the cane cutters took their assigned portions of the field and got to work armed with cane knives. Soya stayed behind to watch them cutting the fields so effortlessly. Their task seemed to have been made easier by the beautiful Zulu songs they sang in unison. Soya walked up to one of the cane cutters, Sipho, and asked if he could help.
>
> "Yebo, but be careful," said Sipho.
>
> Soya took to cutting like a duck to water. Even though he had not had an opportunity to do this before, he was able to cut the cane quickly and skillfully.
>
> "I'm a Sugar Cane Boy, just like my forefathers," he boastfully said to Sipho, referring to those who had come to South Africa as indentured labourers.[40]

Tough times include his father's injury on the farm, battles over possession of the farm within the Murugappa family, experience of apartheid in the cruel shooting by a white policeman of a black boy stealing bread and parting with his friend Boniwe, who leaves for northern Zululand with his family. It takes us through Soya's teenage years on to student times at the University of Durban–Westville, where he attains political maturity. This is definitely a novel of the

---

39   For further details on the riots, see Bill Freund, *Insiders and Outsiders*: *The Indian Working Class of Durban 1910–1990* (Scotsville: U of Natal P, 1995): 57–58.

40   Rubendra Govender, *Sugar Cane Boy* (Reservoir Hills: Bambata, 2008): 51. Further page references are in the main text.

celebratory type—the author himself being a success story as a descendant of a pioneering Indian sugar-farming family risen from indenture status, a university graduate, and a science teacher. From the opening pages: "Despite the harsh life, a unique spirit, culture and zest for life permeated the community" (2); to the middle: "'I'm a Sugar Cane Boy, just like my forefathers'" (previously quoted, 51); to the end, when the hero gets his girl, the mood is one of triumph over adversity, with relatively few complications. It is simply written and has for some years now been set as an English textbook in a few predominantly Indian schools.

Despite being published several years before the 2010 commemoration, Praba Moodley's debut novel, *The Heart Knows No Colour* (2003) captures the bewilderment of the new arrivals in 1879 and traces the evolution of the Suklal family and the harshness of work on the Natal sugarcane plantations with skill and compassion. Moodley's novel is woven around a forbidden relationship between Sita, the daughter of an indentured Indian worker, and Albert, the brother-in-law of the white estate owner. Sita's rebellious nature and apparent refusal to conform to tradition and an arranged marriage leads her into an unexpected and impossible relationship with Albert. Discovering herself to be pregnant, she is forced to marry to save her family's honor. When Albert returns to Natal with his new wife and child after several years in England, their passion is rekindled, giving the author the opportunity to contrast colonial attitudes towards the Indian workers.

It may be worth mentioning one last text, as it, too, is set on the sugarcane plantations, but this time those of the south coast of Natal, unlike the others set on the north coast. Life on the sugar plantations on both coasts would nevertheless have been similar. *Reeds of Wrath* (2008) by Fiona Khan is, similar to Moodley's novel, a 'Barbara Cartland'-style historical romance which shows that, like all significant world movements, indenture can be tackled from a variety of angles, in a number of genres, both serious and popular. The story is a family drama extending from India to Natal focussing on the trials and tribulations of Cassiopeia Pennywhistle's daughter, Jahan (an Anglo-Indian), who is tricked into working on a sugarcane farm in the 1880s, but who triumphs over adversity to marry her true love, Patrick Buchanan, a white sugar farm manager in Natal. The passionate narrative is, however, punctuated sporadically by lengthy descriptions of the terrible conditions suffered by indentured laborers, passages which sit uneasily in this frothy frolic:

> Harvesting proved to be backbreaking work, as with blistered hands the labourers proceeded to gather the crop, duly delivered by wagons to the mill [...] The influx of labour increased the production of sugar in a

limited time, during which many were flogged to ensure the expansion of production or else wages were withheld, moreover the rations were halved.

Coolie labour atrocities had become widespread encouraging agitation in groups resulting in fire to barns and fields especially after news had spread of a ten-year old shepherd thrashed with a riding crop and his parents beaten on suspicion of taking food to him at night. In the north an entire field of cane had been burnt and Indians protested by abstaining from work. Labourers served imprisonment terms petitioning the governor to transfer them to a new employer, only to be disillusioned. While one stood condoned and another punished, there was nothing more painful and mortifying than being ordered to continue work for the same employer pardoned with so much as a rebuke. Their revenge was ever so sweet as they increased the workload and cut back on rations.[41]

Poorly edited in parts, this narrative nonetheless offers further evidence of the number of texts focussing on sugarcane plantations, and indenture generally, which the 150th anniversary occasioned in its descendants.

As Govinden pointed out in a talk given at the 'Words on Water' India–South Africa writers festival in Durban in 2009,

> Since the first democratic elections we see a further flourishing of the theme of indenture in literary writings by South African Indians. The presence of 'girmitya' or 'coolie' texts points to the way the history of indenture continues to shape the psyche of Indians in South Africa.[42]

Uneven in quality though some of the offerings may be, their very number indicates interest in the past—both that of indenture 150 years ago and, more recently, of apartheid. In this regard, the actor and playwright Rajesh Gopie's *The Coolie Odyssey* deserves a brief note. The play, which was first performed in 2002 but reworked to commemorate the 150th anniversary, focusses on the Indian workers on the sugar plantations in Natal between 1860 to 1911. A compassionate and humorous play, it reveals the significant role that South African Indians have played in the building of a new South Africa.

---

41   Fiona Khan, *Reeds of Wrath* (Durban: Washesha, 2009): 170.

42   Devrakshanam Betty Govinden, "The Cane Is Singing: South African Indian Literature on Indenture," paper given at India-South Africa Shared Histories Words on Water Conference (September 14–15 Durban, 2009): 8–9.

Z.P. Dala's novel *What About Meera*, mentioned earlier in this chapter, perhaps heralds a new way of writing about plantation life as experienced in Natal in the late-nineteenth century: the narrative progresses from the protagonist's childhood in sugarcane country, specifically the town of Tongaat on the north coast, to adulthood as an emigrant to Dublin in the far country of Ireland. The trajectory is up and away. Similarly, Imraan Coovadia's novel *The Wedding* (2001), set in Durban, in its closing pages takes the grandson of a passenger Indian couple—therefore not indentured—to New York.[43] The movement in the writing of this latest generation of South Africans of Indian descent is transnational, outward, not necessarily inward and nostalgic as Govinden's pronouncement quoted above suggested it might be. This is a tendency worth watching—what Frenkel calls "an ascendant cosmopolitanism":[44] which suggests that the survival and upward mobility of successive generations of indentured laborers' descendants (and those of passenger Indians) in South Africa now affords the possibility of travel to other places and other countries, the freedom in fiction and reality to imagine an 'elsewhere,' despite having their feet firmly planted in South African soil.

Works Cited

Carter, Marina, & Khal Torabully. *Coolitude: An Anthology of the Indian Labour Diaspora* (London: Anthem, 2002).

Chetty, Rajendra, ed. *South African Indian Writings in English* (Durban: Madiba, 2002).

Chetty, Rajendra, ed. *The Vintage Book of South African Indian Writing* (Johannesburg: STE, 2010).

Chetty, Rajendra, & Pier Paolo Piciucco. *Indias Abroad: The Diaspora Writes Back* (Johannesburg: STE, 2004).

Christian Revival Centre. "The 1860 Project," http://www.crconline.co.za/the-1860 -project/.

Conyngham, John. *The Arrowing of the Cane* (Craighall: Ad. Donker, 1986).

Coovadia, Imraan. *The Wedding* (New York: Picador, 2001).

Dala, Z.P. *What About Meera* (Cape Town: Umuzi, 2015).

Desai, Ashwin, & Goolam Vahed. "Indenture and Indianness in South Africa, 1860–1913," in *Contemporary India and South Africa: Legacies, Identities and Dilemmas*, ed. Sujata Patel & Tina Uys (London: Routledge, 2012): 21–34.

---

43   See M.J. Daymond's chapter on *The Wedding* in this volume.

44   Frenkel, "Reconsidering South African Indian Fiction Postapartheid," 15.

Desai, Ashwin, & Goolam Vahed. *Inside Indenture: A South African Story, 1860–1914* (Durban: Madiba, 2007). Repr. as *Inside Indian Indenture: A South African Story, 1860–1914* (Cape Town: HSRC Press, 2010).

Dhupelia–Mesthrie, Uma. *From Cane Fields to Freedom: A Chronicle of Indian South African Life* (Cape Town: Kwela, 2000).

Diesel, Alleyn. "Hinduism in KwaZulu-Natal, South Africa," in *Culture and Economy in the Indian Diaspora,* ed. Bhikhu Parekh, Gurharpal Singh & Steven Vertovec (London: Routledge, 2003): 169–184.

Frenkel, Ronit. *Reconsiderations: South African Indian Fiction and the Making of Race in Postcolonial Literature* (Pretoria: Unisa Press, 2010).

Frenkel, Ronit. "Reconsidering South African Indian Fiction Postapartheid," *Research in African Literatures* 42.3 (2011): 1–16.

Freund, Bill, *Insiders and Outsiders: The Indian Working Class of Durban 1910–1990* (Scotsville: U of Natal P, 1995).

Goonam, Dr. (Kesaveloo Goonam). *Coolie Doctor: An Autobiography by Dr. Goonam* (Durban: Madiba, 1991).

Gopie, Rajesh. *The Coolie Odyssey* (unpublished play, first performed 2002).

Govender, Neelan. *Girrmit Tales,* preface by Phyllis Naidoo, foreword by Pat Poovalingam (Durban: Rebel Rabble, 2008a).

Govender, Rubendra. *Sugar Cane Boy* (Reservoir Hills: Bambata, 2008b).

Govinden, Devarakshanam Betty. "The Cane Is Singing: South African Indian Literature on Indenture," paper given at India-South Africa Shared Histories Words on Water Conference, 14–15 September, Durban, 2009.

Govinden, Devarakshanam Betty. *A Time of Memory: Reflections on Recent South African Writings* (Durban: Solo Collective, 2008).

Grammer, John M. "Plantation Fiction," in *A Companion to the Literature and Culture of the American South.* ed. Richard Gray & Owen Robinson (London: Blackwell, 2004), http://www.blackwellreference.com/public/tocnode?id=g9780631224044_chunk _g97806312240445 (accessed 25 January 2017).

Gupta, Pamila, Isabel Hofmeyr & Michael Pearson, ed. *Eyes Across the Water: Navigating the Indian Ocean* (Pretoria: Unisa Press, 2010).

Harcharan, Tshque. "Searching for my identity," *Sunday Tribune* (3 June 2010): 6.

Hassim, Aziz. *Revenge of Kali* (Johannesburg: STE, 2009a).

Hassim, Aziz. "By a stroke of the pen, India became a source of 'slaves,'" *Sunday Independent* (4 October 2009b), https://www.pressreader.com/south-africa/the-sunday -independent/20091004/281921654098906 (accessed 25 January 2017).

Hassim, Aziz. "Celebrating Slavery? Commemorate, but do not glorify," *The Post* (1 September 2010), https://www.pressreader.com/south-africa/the-post7573/20100901/ 282226597041379 (accessed 25 January 2017).

Khan, Fiona. *Reeds of Wrath* (Durban: Washesha, 2009).

Meer, Fatima. *Portrait of Indian South Africans* (Durban: Avon House, 1969).

Mishra, Vijay. "The Girmit Ideology Revisited: Fiji Indian Literature," in *Reworlding: The Literature of the Indian Diaspora*, ed. Emmanuel S. Nelson (Westport CT: Greenwood, 1992): 1–12.

Moodley, Praba, *The Heart Knows No Colour* (Cape Town: Kwela, 2003).

Mudly, Tholsi. *A Tribute to our Forefathers* (Wandsbeck: Reach, 2011).

Naidoo, Jay. *Fighting for Justice: A Lifetime of Political and Social Activism* (Johannesburg: Picador Africa, 2010).

Nelson, Emmanuel S. *Reworlding: The Literature of the Indian Diaspora* (Westport CT: Greenwood, 1992).

Railton, Paul, & Jayan Moodley, dir. *White Gold*, screenplay by Jayan Moodley (Serendipity Productions / African Lotus Production Studios, South Africa 2010; 113 min.).

Rooke, Daphne. *Ratoons* (London: Victor Gollancz, 1953).

Stiebel, Lindy. "Crossing the *kala pani*: cause for 'celebration' or 'commemoration' 150 years on? Portrayals of indenture in recent South African Indian writing," *Journal of Literary Studies* 27.2 (2011): 77–90.

Stiebel, Lindy. "Sugar-Coated Stories? Plantation Literature by Selected South African Indian Writers," *English Academy Review* 33.1 (2016): 7–23.

CHAPTER 3

Daku or *Dukan*?

Surviving within and without the Indian Community of Durban

Felicity Hand

Aziz Hassim's *The Lotus People* has been read as a saga of a family of passenger Indians who settled in the Durban area in the late-nineteenth century,[1] which in turn plays an important role in inscribing Durban—and, by extension, the whole of South Africa—in a wider Indian Ocean context.[2] It spans four generations, starting with the first patriarch, the Muslim Pathan Yahya Ali Suleiman, and his unexpected friendship with the Gujarati Hindu Pravin Naran. The two men remain close for the rest of their lives and pass on their values to their children. One of the recurrent motifs of the novel is the insistence of retaining the essence of Indianness despite the changing sociopolitical context of the Indians' adopted country. These values are constantly put to the test through the responses to the contingencies of apartheid South Africa and in fact are seriously questioned by the third generation. "Duty, tradition and obedience, Sam thought, it holds us together and tears us apart."[3] For Yahya Ali Suleiman's grandsons, Sam and Jake, there are two kinds of Indians, those who play the white man's game and those who fight. Nithin, one of their friends and a street thug like Jake, goes into more detail and classifies Indians in the following way:

> There are three types of Indians: there are those that openly defy the system, to the point of losing everything they possess. They deserve our admiration. There is a second group that is so completely intimidated into

---

1 Devarakshanam Betty Govinden, *A Time of Memory: Reflections on Recent South African Writings* (Durban: Solo Collective, 2008): 9; Govinden, "Healing the Wounds of History," in *SA Lit: Beyond 2000*, ed. Michael Chapman & Margaret Lenta (Scotsville: U of KwaZulu–Natal P, 2011): 287–289; Lindy Stiebel, "'Last Stop Little Gujerat': Tracking South African Indian Writers on the Grey Street Writers' Trail," *Current Writing* 22.1 (2010): 1–20.

2 See, for example, Isabel Hofmeyr, "The Black Atlantic Meets the Indian Ocean: Forging New Paradigms of Transnationalism for the Global South—Literary and Cultural Perspectives," *Social Dynamics* 33.2 (2007): 3–32; Meg Samuelson, "Making Home on the Indian Ocean Rim: Relocations in South African Literatures," in *Indian Ocean Studies: Cultural, Social, and Political Perspectives*, ed. Shanti Moorthy & Ashraf Jamal (London: Routledge, 2010): 298–317.

3 Aziz Hassim, *The Lotus People* (Johannesburg: STE, 2002): 216. Further page references are in the main text. I have respected Hassim's use of italics in all the quotations.

> servitude that all they have left to fall back on is their dignity. [... They de-
> serve] our sympathy. Then there is the third kind, the despicable wretch
> who energetically reduces himself to the level where he resembles a
> clone that not only imitates his oppressors but actually outclasses them
> in his effort to emulate their behaviour. [...] He should be completely os-
> tracised from our ranks.
>
> *The Lotus People*, 356

For the great-grandchildren, however, the rift will become even wider. Despite
Nithin's tripartite ethnoclassification, the novel is in fact focussed on the convergence of the *daku* and the *dukan*, represented by Jake (Yacoob) and Sam
(Salim) respectively. With the notorious Group Areas Act in the background,
Dara, of the second generation and now in his sixties, decides it is time for his
second son to take a momentous decision. Either he joins his father in the family business and becomes a full-fledged retailer or else he turns his back on his
family and joins his brother, Jake, in his gangster-style street life.

> "It is a question of my *izzat*," Dara explained, "my respect, without which
> I am nothing. And I must make this clear, if you choose the path of the
> thuggie, follow in the footsteps of your brother, then my door is closed to
> you for good. You must leave us, never to return. Speak now, Salim. *Daku*
> or *Dukan*! One or the other, for now and forever."
>
> *The Lotus People*, 217–218

Sam agrees to follow his father, and his words "spoken like a Pathan" (218)
endear him to his parents but, ironically, also seal his fate as a bystander to
South Africa's fight for democracy. *The Lotus People* traces the fortunes of both
brothers, third-generation South African Indians, who diverge in their understanding of politics and justice but whose children will show that the only
route left to non-whites is armed resistance.

The novel moves backward and forward in time from 1882 to 1986, the last
five chapters being entirely centered on the dying throes of apartheid. Chapter
3, which contains almost a hundred pages, spans over sixty years from 1882 to
1948, ending with the Ghetto Act, which was "aimed specifically at the Indian
and it's [sic] prime purpose is to ruin him economically" (117).[4] The emphasis
is on continuity, with Chapter 3 functioning almost like a complete novel within the whole saga. The assymetrical organization of the novel and the great

---

4   The Ghetto Act refers to the Asiatic Land Tenure Act passed in 1946 which curtailed Indian
    property ownership in white areas. See Chapter 1 for further details.

weight attached to the third chapter underline Hassim's aim to chronicle the
life stories of a selected number of Indians who fought for their community
and its survival in the racist colonial society of South Africa throughout most
of the twentieth century. Hassim has described his first novel as a kind of "personal Truth and Reconciliation Commission," as he believes that the history
of South African Indians has lain hidden and "a truth that remains untold is
the beginning of a lie."[5] In this chapter, I aim to explore the relationship of the
South African Indian community with the other South Africans, their fit into
the white-dominated society, and their evolution as politicized actors both before and during the apartheid era. As apartheid was based on the physical segregation of racialized population groups, my analysis of the novel will focus on
spatial demarcations and the violent tensions that the National Party imposed
on the people. Subversions of the racist frontiers are highlighted in *The Lotus
People* and signpost the growth of a politically active community that fought
for its rights.

The First Generation and the Old Values

The early struggles of first-generation patriarch Yahya to eke out a living as
a street vendor come abruptly to a halt when the anti-Indian sentiments
"verged on hysteria and [the whites] were determined to put even the lowli-
est of traders out of business" (55). He manages to make ends meet as a tinker
but the oppressive colonial laws strike another blow when he is caught on the
streets during the curfew, which only applied to Indians, and is thrown unceremoniously into jail when he is on his way to fetch the midwife for his wife
Nadia's second delivery. The baby dies, another voiceless victim of a heartless
colonial structure. The early hardships suffered by Yahya and Nadia are narrated from his viewpoint only, with his wife's daily trials firmly relegated to the
background. *The Lotus People* lacks a more nuanced gendered narrative; the
experiences of the early migrants from the Indian subcontinent are focalized
through the men. I will return to Hassim's treatment of gender issues in the
third part of this chapter.

   The early part of the novel is concerned with the trials and tribulations of
Yahya Ali Suleiman and, by extension, with those of many of his compatriots
who migrated to South Africa in the second half of the nineteenth century to
improve their lot. Curiously, we are not told his actual reasons for migrating, so

5 Pallavi Rastogi, *Afrindian Fictions: Diaspora, Race, and National Desire in South Africa*
   (Columbus: Ohio State UP, 2008): 212–213.

one is led to take his case as being representative of the majority. The opening pages of Hassim's saga dramatizes the forging of a lifelong friendship between two diametrically opposite characters. On one hand, Yahya is introduced as "a descendant of that fierce tribe of India, a man who asked for no quarter and gave none" (11). On the other, Pravin Naran is a Hindu, "the offspring of gentle, cultured people […] steeped in the concept of *Ahimsa*" (11–12). From the very first pages of his novel, Hassim locates his characters within a wider world that reaches back to the time of Alexander the Great, who was stopped from expanding into India by the warrior Pathans. Thus, the novel not only speaks to and of a South African Indian diaspora but also anchors the narrative of this community within a larger Indian Ocean history.[6] The Indian Ocean experience forms the backbone of *The Lotus People* from the very beginning by reinserting South Africa into the Indo-Oceanic historical narrative from which the years preceding and following apartheid had inadvertently isolated it. The two patriarchs come to an agreement over a botched business deal that the inexperienced Yahya has fallen foul of. Naran shows his solidarity and perspicacity by helping the other man, unversed in business matters. Curiously, this opening chapter sets the scene for what I see as the embedded critique of the novel: what choices are left to South African Indians? Naran, a clever *bunya*, follows a strict code of honor when it comes to negotiations. Yahya is cheated by *dakus*, in Naran's words, "the parasites of the business community" (14) and is warned to commit all deals to writing and, above all, to be aware of the rules of the game. His traditional methods of achieving satisfaction are useless in a country like South Africa. Yahya follows the Pathan code of honor, which, ironically, could be construed as being that of acting like a *daku*, as far as exacting revenge is concerned, whereas Naran is a courteous man of the business world to whom physical violence is anathema but who is capable of using his talents to ruin anyone who crosses him. In the years that follow their encounter, Yahya becomes a true *dukan*, although he refuses to forget his Pathan heritage. This early encounter heralds the budding friendship and mutual respect that will develop and become cemented between the two men's opposing worldviews and which epitomizes the dilemma that the novel hinges upon: *daku* or *dukan*? The fine balance between the honor of the *dukan* and the expediency of the *daku* is finally resolved by the fourth generation of South African Indians, but only after much bloodshed and countless humiliations.

The first generation, typified by the figure of Yahya, live in their own community with little or no connection with other South African groups. Blacks

---

6   Hofmeyr, "The Black Atlantic Meets the Indian Ocean," 19; Samuelson, "Making Home on the Indian Ocean Rim," 306–307.

and Coloureds form no part of their social landscape and whites merely lurk menacingly in the background as the makers of the oppressive laws that seek to reduce the Indian community to penury. Like so many first-generation migrants, Yahya never reveals the real circumstance of his life in the new land to his family back in India.

> He stubbornly ignored the limitations placed on his race by the rulers of the land in which he had settled. He wrote copious letters to his family in India without once mentioning the hardships of his existence. He stoically accepted every indignity heaped on his once proud bearing and made a covenant with himself that he would, ultimately, overcome the vicissitudes of his capricious fortunes.
>
> *The Lotus People*, 52

Hassim provides the sociohistorical context for the events in his novel. Anti-Indian sentiment was gradually growing and preventing people like Yahya from earning a decent living, let alone prospering.

> All hawkers' licences were withdrawn at the whim of the Licencing Officer. The right to appeal to any court of justice was expressly forbidden. [...] Virtually overnight, the Indians were in danger of being reduced to near poverty.
>
> *The Lotus People*, 55

The arrival of passenger Indians was a grueling experience and one that would condition the new arrivals. Yahya denies being arrogant; pride is what keeps him going. He recalls his initial disappointment on arriving in Durban:

> Look, when I first came here I truly believed that I was coming as a free man. A pioneer. On the first day that we docked in Durban they held all the Indians on board our ship as virtual prisoners, on the pretext that the ship was in quarantine. the European passengers who had traveled so closely with us had been happily welcomed and allowed to desembark.
>
> *The Lotus People*, 61

However, life on the cane fields was even harsher than the urban existence of the passenger Indians:[7]

---

7   Hassim's second novel, *Revenge of Kali* (Johannesburg: STE, 2009), discussed in Lindy Stiebel's chapter, uncovers the history of the sugar plantation workers and reveals the internal

> the white sugar barons help themselves to our women and make them
> into concubines while their husbands are out in the fields. They insist on
> the right to sleep with every new bride that enters their domain, on her
> very first wedding night.
>
> *The Lotus People*, 63

The young Dara, Yahya's son, is soon introduced to Gandhian philosophy, which
will help him in his own personal struggle. A young man called Jammu relates
his awakening to a group of Indians. The day his master abused him unfairly
was a turning point in his life when he realized that "their strength is derived
from our weakness. Refuse to cooperate with them and they are helpless" (65).
Jammu soon stands aside and Dara, six years old at the time, comes face to face
with Mohandas Karamchand Gandhi, whose speech electrifies the child and
will influence his own view of the South African situation. Gandhi reminds the
men present that "you cannot obtain liberty by violent rebellion—the one ne-
gates the other—you cannot destroy civilization in order to save it" (67). These
words will become etched on Dara's consciousness and prevent him from
seeing a third way. As Meg Samuelson notes, there is "a sense of ontological
insecurity in the second generation; Yahya's son, Dara, sees the Indian caught
between two groups: unyielding whites and militant blacks."[8]

Hassim's hagiographical portrait of Gandhi ignores the fact that the latter
worked primarily for the rights of the merchant class rather than for the Indian
proletariat as the novel seems to suggest. Gandhi's sojourn in South Africa has
been mythologized to a large extent—the Indian working class was already
politically aware before he arrived; in fact, passive resistance would turn out to
be ineffectual in the violent South African context.[9] Consequently, forty years
later, Dara's elder son, Jake, will reject the Gandhian tactics of his father's generation, as there "comes a time when you have to start shoving back. We talk,
they thrive. Let's see how they like a bit of their own medicine" (211).

Firebrands like Jake may have been few and far between in the early part of
the twentieth century, as the South African Indians had to strive to keep together and improve their living conditions on their own. The old generation built
up their community with no help from the outside and instead were obliged to
rely on ethnic philanthropy to make them an autonomous community:

---

fissures in the Indian community and the ruthless exploitation of the more disadvantaged by
the more affluent members.

8 Samuelson, "Making Home on the Indian Ocean Rim," 306.

9 Maureen Swan, *Gandhi: The South African Experience* (Johannesburg: Ravan, 1984).

> Yahya and Madhoo, together with scores of their contemporaries, con-
> tinuously and with monotonous repetition handed over their meagre
> savings towards the construction of clinics, hospitals and whatever other
> facilities the community needed and which the government should nor-
> mally have provided.
>
> *The Lotus People*, 77

As has occurred among many diasporic communities throughout history, nostalgic attachment to the ancestral homeland gradually fades and the emotional longing to return to one's roots loses its hold. *The Lotus People* chronicles
the slow death of the values of the old generation and their firm belief in the
strength and righteousness of their worldview. In a conversation with Dara,
Pravin Naran reveals that he is well aware that his death is near and confesses
his regret that their children have become too westernized, "When their time
comes they'll be caught unawares. It is one of the reasons we can no longer
depend on them on matters of importance" (236).

The third generation eulogize their fathers' personal and intrinsically honest way of doing business and helping their less fortunate fellows. Sam knows
he is stepping into big shoes on Dara's death, as his father was very much of the
old school: "A dying breed, perhaps Dara was the last of them" (383). However,
the family endeavors to keep the old values alive despite—or because of—
the increasing outside turmoil and challenging political circumstances. After
Jake's brutal death in police custody, Shaida, Dara's wife, is compelled to tell
Zain, their grandson, about his Indian ancestry.

> You are a Pathan too—the product of a tribe whose heritage is as glori-
> ous as its history. You are the descendant of legendary warriors who bow
> before no man and bend their knees to God alone. ... But do not be misled
> by your militant background. You are an upholder of the rights of man,
> not some kind of savage animal that bares its teeth at every imagined
> insult.
>
> *The Lotus People*, 472–473

The words that Sam overhears from his mother's lips will sink deep into his
own consciousness and will bring about his own awakening. The increased
harshness of the apartheid regime turns moderates into radicals, giving them
back a sense of ethnic pride:

> *Nang* [honour], Jake! Sam shouted to the sky, his fist in the air. You kept
> your faith with honour. What was it ma said to your son? 'Your father

chose to forfeit his life rather than compromise his honour. You can do
no less.' Dammit, *bru*, I've been what *baji* would have called recreant—
I forgot where I came from. How the hell can I know where I'm going?

The Lotus People, 475

Jake's fierce commitment to what he believed was right was forged at an early
age. Shaida attends a women's gathering where an assertive Dr. Goonum steps
out of history to encourage them to attend a mass rally to protest against the
Ghetto Bill.[10] Unknown to his mother, the young Jake reacts strongly to Goonum's words, "his fists clenched till the knuckles shone white with anger" (91).
This precocious encounter with injustice, the reality that the new law clearly
spelled out was aimed specifically at the Indians to ruin them economically,
seals the boy's fate. He will become a well-known and highly respected freedom fighter and member of *Umkhonto we Sizwe* who has "escaped certain
death so often they've nicknamed him 'Aza Kwela'—the man who dances in
and out of the Security Branch's clutches with impunity and mocks them with
devilish abandon" (163), but who uncannily forsees his own demise:

The day those cowards come to my place I'll blow their heads off and to
hell with their fucked up laws.
    That's the day they'll hand your body to us.

The Lotus People, 103

Lest We Forget

The novel is dedicated to the figure of Dr. Goonum, "lest we forget," to recuper-
ate the truth that has remained untold. Hassim thus devotes a great deal of
narrative space to describing Indian resistance:

Rally followed mass rally. Grey Street and the roads leading off it became
the focal point of the Resistance Movement. Throughout the country,
from every Indian area, money poured into the coffers of the Natal Indian
Congress and was utilised towards furthering the cause of the Passive Resistance Campaign.

The Lotus People, 95

---

10   Hassim spells her name "Goonum," whereas her autobiography uses "Goonam" (see *Coo-
     lie Doctor: An Autobiography* [Durban: Madiba, 1991]). I have kept to Hassim's spelling
     throughout this chapter.

The incorporation of historical figures is Hassim's personal tribute to the unflagging efforts of people like Dr. Dadoo, M.D. Naidoo, Fatima Meer, and Dr. Goonum. His fictional characters interact with these fighters and bring the struggle down to grass-roots level. While black leaders do not form the backbone of his narrative, Hassim also connects their struggle to that of the Indians.[11] The anti-apartheid struggle in Durban is focalized around the Grey Street area, the Casbah, a predominantly Indian part of town but where black Africans also plied their trade. The South African Indian community is seen to undergo a steady evolution from the days of zealously preserving their Indianness to joining forces with the other South Africans in a common fight for justice. The allotted Indian areas become an "urban space of idealised desire," a space where Indians are not free to fulfil their dreams, as their past is corrupted permanently by the imposition of colonial rule.[12] However, the apartheid city harbors avenues of resistance and subversion in the area surrounding Grey Street and its street gangs, a topic to which I shall return later.

Hassim captures the prejudice and ignorance of the white population, perceived by the Indians as greedy and inherently unjust, who cannot see beyond the stereotype of the money-grabbing Indian shopkeeper. The whites fail to distinguish between the wealthy merchant class and the poor, working-class Indians who become virtually invisible like the blacks and Coloureds, who live in appalling conditions, with the result that the traders are seen as typical Indians and the plight of the poor is completely overlooked. This upward leveling does little to improve the white view of the community, as prejudices against Indians are based on the latter's acute business sense, with which they compete fiercely with the whites. Moses Renton, a Coloured school principal, explains white greed to Sandy and Jake:

> Why are the whites trying to break the back of the wealthy Indian? After all, eighty percent of our people live below the poverty line. Those are their statistics, not mine
> That's an easy one, my boy. Your wealth is a threat to them.
> *The Lotus People,* 118

Contact with Coloureds during the apartheid years was more intense than with blacks or whites, particularly with Muslims or Christians, who "might share a

---

11   Steve Biko and Nelson Mandela are both mentioned, and the fourth generation of South African Indians are described as being "the product of the '76 Soweto Uprising" (507).

12   Sara Upstone, *Spatial Politics in the Postcolonial Novel* (Farnham & Burlington VT: Ashgate, 2009): 87.

bond of faith with them."[13] Mr. Renton harbors no illusions about Indian privileges despite their higher racial ranking above Coloureds and blacks. In fact, he argues that the racist legislation harms the Indians much more deeply than the Coloured group:

> I'm not saying the Ghetto Act won't affect us. It will. When they take you out of your home and hand it to a white, do you think that white will tolerate a coloured neighbour for more than a few days? But the Indians are property owners, the coloured is a tenant. When he is pushed out he can move on without any great financial loss.
>
> *The Lotus People*, 118

Nithin Vania, one of Jake's close friends and known as the fixer, features as the focalizer of Chapter 7, set in 1950. In this way, Hassim narrates the humiliations and restrictions that the Indian community were subjected to from various viewpoints. One night, Nithin inadvertently finds himself outside the Indian area and is savagely beaten up by a group of white thugs for having trespassed in a white suburb. The "vicious grin and the thin lips stretched over gleaming teeth" (290) points to the sadistic pleasure of the dominant group fueled by the power they wield over their peers who happen to be the wrong color. The collective revenge taken by his friends, mostly Coloureds and Indians, for the attack was part of the never-ending racial feud fostered by what Edward Said calls "geographical violence":[14] the institutionalized physical separation of South Africa's population groups. For Nithin, black unity is still a future possibility in 1950; he is not deceived by the apparent ethnic solidarity:

> his beating was incidental to the prime motivation. At different times each of the others had been victims of similar acts; he was merely the spur that had goaded long-suppressed emotions. When the night was over he would be forgotten. He commanded no loyalty and was not deceived into any illusions of belonging.
>
> *The Lotus People*, 293

Although Nithin's colleague John Farley claims that "We don't lend to whites [...] And we don't go near an Af [...]. We stick to our own, the Indians and

---

13   Bill Freund, *Insiders and Outsiders: The Indian Working Class of Durban 1910–1990* (Scotsville: U of Natal P, 1995): 40.

14   Edward W. Said, *Culture and Imperialism* (1993; New York: Vintage, 1994): 225.

coloureds" (325), the Durban underworld followed its own laws and race meant little where money was concerned: "the white boys are beginning to line up in our territory [...] They think black, talk and act like any of us" (233). Outside the gangster world, however, the whites have no relationship with the Indians—"What the hell do we know about the *wit ous* anyway? They're all in their ivory towers, so far removed from us that I don't even know if they catch a crap" (455). Curiously, the Afrikaners are rated higher than the Anglo whites: "At least the Afrikaner is honest. He doesn't bulldust you. He believes in the separation of the races and he says it, loud and clear" (404). Some individual Afrikaners show their ignorance of apartheid horrors, but Shaida spells it out clearly to Van Herden, who is indirectly responsible for bringing Jake's dead body back home for burial:

> If you and all your people—you who voted these *dakus* into power—
> cannot face God with a clear conscience what salvation can insignificant
> people like my family offer? The power to change things is in your hands,
> not ours. My people do not have the vote.
>
> *The Lotus People*, 469

She fails to grasp how "you can empathise with us as individuals and yet, collectively, hate us so much?" (470). That a certain number of liberal whites existed during the apartheid era is borne out by Barbara Homan, one of Nithin's bosses. She laughs at Nithin's angry response and refusal to be a toady at the firm's segregated Christmas party for the Indian staff. Nithin expresses his admiration for her attitude but warns her not to "ever repeat what you did today. They'll break you so fast you'll never recover if you live to be a hundred" (365). In general terms, however, the image that the non-whites have of the whites is far from flattering. Renton's experience as a school principal has shown him that the young Indians of the 1950s are "far wiser than those of [their] age a generation ago" (117). He admires their political awareness:

> I can guarantee there's not one white kid as politically advanced as those
> I meet in the Casbah. And your command of the language, I doubt any
> English-speaking boy of your age can even come close to you. Must come
> from all the reading you do.
>
> *The Lotus People*, 117

As far as cross-racial interaction is concerned, one of the most dramatic moments in the novel is the description of the Zulu–Indian riots in Durban in

1949, when 87 Africans and 50 Indians were killed and 503 injured.[15] The young Jake is immersed headlong in random and unforgettable violence:

> Yacoob [Jake] was pushed back into the alley by a group of Indians as they sought refuge from the sheer mass of Africans who had descended on them. Using his shoulders and his elbows he shoved his way forward, tripped over a young woman lying on the pavement, her sari almost torn off her shoulder, the deep cut of a panga running diagonally across from her neck and disappearing into her waist.
>
> *The Lotus People*, 149

Anthony Lemon attributes to the leaders of the Indian Congress the understanding that "the causes of the riots were deep-rooted, and that the hatred exhibited was partly due to frustration and partly due to the fact that the 'privileges' enjoyed by Indians, such as freedom from the pass laws, were not shared by Africans."[16] In *The Lotus People*, however, Hassim makes a far more serious claim. The killings were instigated by the whites following the well-worn policy of divide and rule:

> Everything is almost in place. It's time we blasted these coolies to hell
>   You're sure it can't be traced back to us?
>   Not a chance. It will be put down to a spontaneous uprising by the kaffirs. All it needs is a catalyst and it will snowball on its own after that. Our recruits are well paid and there will be rich pickings for them.
>
> *The Lotus People*, 141

The Durban riots remain a painful memory for South African Indians, whoever the ringleaders were, as they put paid to the racial harmony of areas like Grey Street where Indians traded alongside Africans and seriously delayed for several years any joint action by Indians and Africans.

The Real Fighters

Hassim's re-creation of the Casbah shows the subversion of colonially demarcated spaces being transformed into resistance "offering new perspectives, new

---

15   For more details on the riots, see Bill Freund, *Insiders and Outsiders*, 57–58.

16   Anthony Lemon, "The Political Position of Indians in South Africa," in *South Asians Overseas: Migration and Ethnicity*, ed. Colin Clarke, Ceri Peach & Steve Vertovec (1990: Cambridge: Cambridge UP, 2009): 137.

sites of imagination and creativity, from which the colonial representation of territory can be excised and, perhaps, overcome."[17] The author's depiction of the area reinforces the notion of the Casbah as a chronotope for understanding the history and evolution of the South African Indian community:

> In the late forties Grey Street, and the roads bisecting it, were a miniature replica of a major city in India. [...] the Casbah, as it was often referred to, was inhabited almost exclusively by Indians, with a fair sprinkling of coloureds.
>
> *The Lotus People*, 168–169

Govinden argues that place is an inescapable denominator in South African writing, as living in a particular place was the result of who one was in racial terms and this also determined one's personal experience and identity. Referring to *The Lotus People*, she writes:

> Reading the novel you imagine yourself constantly walking in and out of this intricate grid of streets. And we appreciate Hassim's own peripatetic imagination, both in time and space, throughout the novel.[18]

The interracial harmony in Hassim's Casbah cannot conceal the poverty and oppressiveness. Just a few streets away, as Nithin discovers to his disadvantage, the white area of Berea is, literally, another world. The areas of subversion in the apartheid city are encapsulated in the street gangs in which Jake plays an active role:

> The Casbah, in the early forties, had been in the grip of a crime wave initiated by a wild bunch with a reputation for quick violence and little respect for either the law or the rights of the ordinary citizen.
>
> *The Lotus People*, 195

The underworld life lurks just beneath the surface of the "vibrant and energetic community that was representative of the second and third generations of the early settlers" (169). Hassim's memories of the Grey Street of the 1940s may owe a great deal to the nostalgic memory of an impressionable teenager—like his character Jake, in fact: "there was no other area of under one square mile that could equal it for the intensity of its emotions and its pursuit of justice" (109).

---

17   Upstone, *Spatial Politics in the Postcolonial Novel*, 13.

18   Govinden, *A Time of Memory*, 27.

The novel subtly implies that the gangster world of the Casbah is a toned-down version of the crimes of the apartheid regime. The laws that sought to control and intimidate the Indians made their everyday lives far more unbearable than any of the ruthless business deals carried out by the local *dakus*. The tensions surrounding the forced removals enshrined in the Group Areas Act of 1950 and the humiliations inflicted upon the Indians by the white officials push the younger generation to breaking point. During the visit of Botha, an investigator charged with delivering an eviction notice, the Afrikaner's overbearing attitude and utter contempt for Indians seals his fate. In a well-orchestrated act of revenge, Jake murders the investigator for dishonoring his sister Ayesha: "his hand reached out and, seemingly by accident, his palm enveloped Ayesha's breast. It remained there for a second, then, incredibly, began to fondle her" (207). Jake, pretending to deliver some flowers at the investigator's house, speaks Afrikaans perfectly, sounding "more like a Boer than a Boer himself would have sounded" (213). Botha is murdered in cold blood but Sam cannot but condone his brother's action. After all, the apartheid state had brought such acts of violence on its own shoulders through the colonial—and therefore inherently unfair—divisions of territory:

> Men like the investigator enjoyed terrorising simple people and didn't deserve to live. Whilst he himself would never have been able to pull the trigger, there was no way he could condemn Jake for his actions. How a man died was often the result of his own choosing. The investigator should have known that one of his victims would someday turn on him.
> *The Lotus People*, 214

The irony of the incident is that Botha's wife was convinced that it was an Afrikaner, one of her own people: "I'll never forget that voice as long as I live" (215).

The narrative suggests that the *daku* style of life is the only sensible option left to South African Indians if they wish to overcome white injustice. Sam's friend Sandy reminds him that "there is no better university than the gutter. The education system's geared to keeping us down in the gutter" (222). There is a common denominator between the two worlds, as Sam claims: one finds out what people want, then supplies it. "The only difference is in how society perceives the two methods of operation" (231). In this respect, Jake is clearly a *daku* but also a true hero. In the words of the veteran journalist Mrs. Bramdaw: "People in this town used to think he was a gangster. My husband and I subscribed to the view that he was the most moral person we had ever met" (514). Sandy confides in his friends that "I used to think there was an anger in him, that he was acting on hate alone. Only now do I realise that he was motivated by justice" (520).

The revenge taken for the insult to Ayesha underlines two significant points in this novel. First, the family's *izzat* must be reinstated and this can only be achieved through male intervention; second, women in general terms play entirely passive roles in *The Lotus People*. It is true that Hassim grants the women characters some agency. but this tends to be when marriages have to be arranged and the stubborn attachment of the menfolk to village customs is clearly inappropriate to urban South Africa. The women's thoughts, fears, and hopes are submerged beneath the highly masculinized public business world, run by both *dukans* and *dakus*. One of the rare female characters who stands out for her assertiveness and courage is Dr. Goonum, who is, of course, a real-life person. The novel does not deviate from many other male-centered diasporic narratives that tend to universalize migrant experiences without taking into consideration the constraints of gender and, of course, class.[19] That women's experiences differ considerably from men's is borne out by the following observation by the British sociologist Avtar Brah, in which she describes how diaspora experiences are determined by considerations of gender:

> Clearly the relationship of the first generation to the place of migration is different from that of subsequent generations, mediated as it is by memories of what was recently left behind, and by the experiences of disruption and displacement as one tries to reorientate, to form new social networks, and learns to negotiate new economic, political and cultural realities. Within each generation the experiences of men and women will also be differently shaped by gender relations.[20]

The women in the novel tend to hover in the background. Occasionally they step out of the shadows, as is the case with Jake's wife Hannah, who is also imprisoned for sedition, or his mother, Shaida, who occasionally is allowed to stand up for what she believes is right. By contrast, one of the few women to be granted a sizeable amount of textual space, Kamla Vania, follows the dutiful path of the Indian wife. Nithin's mother's ambition "revolved around the need to endure stable marriages for her girls and a homely environment for her son. Whatever other dreams she may have had were abandoned years ago" (298). When the wives of the third generation take part in the dialogues in the

---

19   See Felicity Hand, "Impossible Burdens: East African Asian Women's Memoirs," *Research in African Literatures* 42.3 (Fall 2011): 100–116.

20   Avtar Brah, *Cartographies of Diaspora* (London: Routledge, 1996): 194.

Goodwill Lounge or the Club Lotus, the talk becomes laborious, almost trivial, and could easily have been omitted. The women are represented as being excessively manipulative and unpleasantly scheming. The real action is carried out by the men, and the women are almost a hindrance to the progress of the Indian community. The iconic historical figures of Fatima Meer and Dr. Goonum shine through the text, but Hassim fails to provide memorable fictional women in what is an unbalanced male-centered narrative. It is true that in the sphere of gender relations, strict adherence to cultural—in other words, patriarchal—values has served as a source of social cohesion, so that women like Dr. Goonum were unusual and a host of feisty Indian women characters would probably not reflect the reality of the times. However, the novel would have gained in depth if one of the women had been the focalizing character of at least one chapter. In a 525-page novel which sets out to chronicle the lives of three generations of South African Indians, one might have expected a more balanced portrait of the women in the family. As Jake says, "They're the real fighters. Put them in the front line and the war" (415). Significantly, his sentence remains unfinished, as the clandestine prison visit is abruptly curtailed.

Hassim's project in his debut novel is to commemorate the early struggles of the South African Indians, and his sympathies clearly lie on the side of those who actively fought or resisted the many affronts to their dignity. For Nithin, the Indian who "not only imitates his oppressors but actually outclasses them in his effort to emulate their behaviour" (356) is the most despicable. Indian subservience is regularly punished in the novel for effectually being the worse crime an Indian is capable of. Nithin remembers the day at school when he refused to defer to the established racial hierarchy and punches a white boy. When the father of the injured boy went to the school to complain, the formmaster shows himself to be an authentic white clone. "He sounded like a white man, even more so […] and looking at the visitor submissively" (321). Nithin settles the score when he calls on Mr. Barsu's house a year later and the former teacher is so scared of his former pupil's rage that he urinates in his trousers. Nithin warns him: "Keep thinking about me, creep. I might decide to come back and finish the job, when I can find your balls" (324). Likewise, Hassim has no mercy for stooges and toadies. Zain, Jake's son, politely but firmly, throws out of his father's funeral the Special Branch spy:

> "You, lady," Zain said, "You desecrate the sanctity of my father's funeral and violate the privacy of our house. You are a disgrace to every person of colour in this country. It is good that you are standing, that everyone here can see the Judas in you and point you out to their friends in the streets. My father will rest in peace, you are damned for ever. Now go! Get out of

here and tell your white masters what I said and then find a hole to creep into."

The Lotus People, 444

Zain takes on a much more aggressive stance against those favored by the repressive state, "unlike Jake, who had no time for the white man but differentiated between the State and the man in the street, Zain makes no such allowances. To him they're all the same—the enemy" (491).

Conclusion: An Integral Part of the Country

The novel carefully maps the evolution of the Indian community in political terms and its gradual realization that they have a part to play in the forging of a truly democratic state. The tactics change; Jake tries to show his former boxing trainer that there are no better options, that defeat has to be acknowledged by the passive resisters. "You, Uncle Lou, are like my father and my grandfather. You're all dreamers. Your way has failed. It's time you accepted it and stood aside" (378). Nithin, Sandy, Karen, and Sam acknowledge their half-hearted participation in the struggle: "When it came to the bottom line we simply took a walk, like it wasn't any business of ours" (488). Karan confesses that "I guess we've always had the convictions, what we lacked was the courage," while Nithin reflects that "perhaps it was a commitment, a failure to totally involve ourselves" (497). The fourth generation, the great grandchildren of the two patriarchs, Yahya Ali Suleiman and Pravin Naran, have no doubts about their loyalties. The inspiration of the Goonums and the Naickers—"a hundred like them lost everything they possessed but stood their ground and refused to compromise" (508)—has forced the youngsters to move on, embrace more militant tactics, and become members of the ANC. The legend of Aza Kwela—Jake—lives on in his son, nephews, and nieces. Sam had once said to his father that they were "an integral part of this country. All of us, including yourself, were born here. It's the only life we know" (285), but his compromise with the anti-apartheid struggle stopped there. Even when he could barely speak after the sustained torture inflicted on him in police custody, Jakes begs his brother:

> tell the old man ... to hang in there. Too many good people ... have died in ... this struggle. If he takes the family out now ... it'll be ... like a betrayal, of everything ... we fought for ... like....
>
> *The Lotus People,* 415

For Jake and for the fourth generation, Indians are as much a part of the anti-apartheid struggle as blacks or Coloureds, and South Africa is their home.

The history of the gangs is presented as part of the history of Indian indenture and colonialism and as part of the anti-apartheid struggle. By highlighting the political activities of the gangsters, Hassim forces the reader to rethink his or her definitions. as the apartheid government is often revealed to be the authentic gangster. The insertion of historical—and heroic—figures into the narrative raises it to epic proportions and forces the reader to rethink the silences and half-truths surrounding the Indian contribution to the anti-apartheid movement. Sam muses on the decision his father forced him to make so many years ago:

> *daku* or *dukan*, for now and forever. He didn't fully appreciate the limitations in that statement. There was no contradiction there—he was simply missing the big picture. The real decision I should have been making was either death or survival.
>
> *The Lotus People,* 523

Finally the choice is made, neither *daku* nor *dukan*, as the Indian community was and is much more complex and heterogeneous than this duality might suggest; *The Lotus People* uncovers the forgotten history of South African Indians and makes a solid claim for the recognition of the role they have played in the making of South Africa.

Works Cited

Brah, Avtar. *Cartographies of Diaspora* (London: Routledge, 1996).

Freund, Bill. *Insiders and Outsiders: The Indian Working Class of Durban 1910–1990* (Scotsville: U of Natal P, 1995).

Goonam, Dr. (Kesaveloo Goonam). *Coolie Doctor: An Autobiography by Dr. Goonam* (Durban: Madiba, 1991).

Govinden, Devarakshanam Betty. "Healing the Wounds of History," in *SA Lit. Beyond 2000,* ed. Michael Chapman & Margaret Lenta (Scotsville: U of KwaZulu–Natal P, 2011): 287–302.

Govinden, Devarakshanam Betty. *A Time of Memory: Reflections on Recent South African Writings* (Durban: Solo Collective, 2008).

Hand, Felicity. "Impossible Burdens: East African Asian Women's Memoirs," *Research in African Literatures* 42.3 (Fall 2011): 100–116.

Hassim, Aziz. *The Lotus People* (Johannesburg: STE, 2002).

Hassim, Aziz. *Revenge of Kali* (Johannesburg: STE, 2009).

Hofmeyr, Isabel. "The Black Atlantic Meets the Indian Ocean: Forging New Paradigms of Transnationalism for the Global South—Literary and Cultural Perspectives," *Social Dynamics* 33.2 (2007): 3–32.

Lemon, Anthony. "The Political Position of Indians in South Africa," in *South Asians Overseas: Migration and Ethnicity*, ed. Colin Clarke, Ceri Peach & Steven Vertovec (1990; Cambridge: Cambridge UP, 2009): 131–148.

Rastogi, Pallavi. *Afrindian Fictions: Diaspora, Race, and National Desire in South Africa* (Columbus: Ohio State UP, 2008).

Said, Edward W. *Culture and Imperialism* (1993; New York: Vintage, 1994).

Samuelson, Meg. "Making Home on the Indian Ocean Rim: Relocations in South African Literatures," in *Indian Ocean Studies: Cultural, Social, and Political Perspectives*, ed. Shanti Moorthy & Ashraf Jamal (London: Routledge, 2010): 298–317.

Stiebel, Lindy. "'Last Stop Little Gujerat': Tracking South African Indian Writers on the Grey Street Writers' Trail," *Current Writing* 22.1 (2010): 1–20.

Swan, Maureen. *Gandhi. The South African Experience* (Johannesburg: Ravan, 1984).

Upstone, Sara. *Spatial Politics in the Postcolonial Novel* (Farnham & Burlington VT: Ashgate, 2009).

CHAPTER 4

The Reception of Ahmed Essop in Spain

Or, the Race Factor in the Comparative Literary Reception of Contemporary South African Writers in Spain

Juan Miguel Zarandona

World Literature and Translation

Since the time when Johann Wolfgang von Goethe (1749–1832) proposed it in several of his essays and gave it the name *Weltliteratur*, the concept of 'world literature' has always been subject to great controversy as far as its definition and scope are concerned. In recent years, with the upsurge in interest in postcolonial literature and the advent of the twenty-first century, this debate has staged a comeback. For example, in 2003, the American scholar David Damrosch published his now well-known book *What Is World Literature?*, the title of which is self-explanatory. For him and current trends in the study of literary theory, the object of interest of world literature has ceased to be the sum total of the world's national literatures, especially, or even only, the past masterpieces of Western European literature. Instead, we have witnessed the circulation of works into the wider world beyond their country of origin, and an unprecedented expansion of the range of works—including those from the margins of national literary canons—from around the world that contemporary readers have *access* to thanks to the phenomenon of globalization.

Consequently, David Damrosch defines and establishes a difference between the blanket term 'literature,' which serves to express the sum total of the world's literatures, and 'world literature,' a subset of the plenum of literature that encompasses all works of literature that circulate beyond their culture of origin, either in translation or in their original language,[1] or, in its most expansive sense, any work that has ever reached beyond its home base.[2] And how does a work enter into world literature? It does so by a double process: first, by

---

1 For example, literary works written in Latin America when read in Spain, or postcolonial African literature in English when read in Britain, Ireland, or by any non-native reader of English texts the world over.

2 David Damrosch, *What Is World Literature?* (Princeton NJ: Princeton UP, 2003a): 4.

© KONINKLIJKE BRILL NV, LEIDEN, 2018 | DOI 10.1163/9789004365032_005

being read as literature; second, by circulating out into a broader world beyond its linguistic and cultural point of origin.[3]

And, as has been mentioned, this access happens mainly thanks to the continuous and devoted practice of an ancient art, *translation*. David Damrosch confirms, in his introductory pages, that he will be chiefly concerned with tracing what is lost and what is gained in translation, looking at the intertwined shift of language, era, region, religion, social status, and literary context that a work can incur as it moves from its point of origin out into a new cultural sphere;[4] and that he will do so because today more and more translations are being made from and among an unprecedented range of literary worlds; and that, when well done, these multiple translations can give us a unique purchase on the scope of the world's cultures, past and present.[5]

Consequently, this emphasis on the circulation of texts and global contexts instead of national ones, and on what texts gain (or lose) in translation, brings about a space of fruitful collaboration between the field of literary theory and that of translation studies. World literature examines what happens when national literary works cross borders by means of translation, become international, change in the process, and develop different meanings in different settings.

This chapter will hopefully benefit from this hybrid approach by focussing its attention on the translated corpus of contemporary postcolonial South African literature in Spain. In doing so, these pages will also help us to understand how this very specific crossing of cultural and literary borders has had an impact, however small, on building this immense corpus of world literature based on spatial and temporal circulation and the translation of literary works.

The Race Factor and South African Literature in Spain

In this regard, the database on African Literature in Spanish translation BDÁfrica,[6] compiled by a team of researchers from the University of Málaga, Spain, includes 170 entries for South African writers. The following table summarizes their findings. For the purposes of this chapter, a column stating the ethnic origin of the writers has been added:

---

3 Damrosch, *What Is World Literature?*, 5.

4 *What Is World Literature?*, 34.

5 *What Is World Literature?*, 36.

6 María Fernández Ruiz, Gloria Corpas & Míriam Seghiri, "BDÁfrica: diseño e implementación de una base de datos de la literatura poscolonial africana publicada en España," *Hermēneus* 18 (2016): 427–450.

TABLE 4.1

Writer	N° of entries	Racial group[a]
Achmat Dangor (1947–)	3	Indian
Alan Paton (1903–88)	4	White
André Brink (1935–)	4	White
Bessie Head (1937–86)	1	Coloured
Breyten Breytenbach (1939–)	1	White
C.M. van den Heever (1902–57)	1	White
Deon Meyer (1958–)	3	White
J.M. Coetzee (1940–)	41	White
J.R.R. Tolkien (1892–1973)	55	White
James McClure (1939–2006)	7	White
John Conyngham (1959–)	2	White
Nadime Gordimer (1923–2014)	37	White
Nelson Mandela (1918–2013)	4	Black
Nicholas Mhlongo (1973–)	1	Black
Pauline Smith (1882–1959)	1	White
Peter Abrahams (1919–)	1	Coloured
Roy Campbell (1901–57)	1	White
Tony Eprile (1955–)	1	White
William Plomer (1903–73)	1	White
Zakes Mda (1948–)	1	Black

a   These race-based groups correspond to those formerly established by the apartheid regime.
    They are still in use in post-apartheid South Africa. Whites have not been subclassified into
    their English, Afrikaner or Jewish backgrounds. The same applies to blacks: Xhosa, Zulu, etc.

The number of white writers clearly outperforms those corresponding to other race groups: 159 entries out of 170. There is only one Indian writer, with one entry, Achmat Dangor; there are only two Coloured authors, with two entries, Bessie Head and Peter Abrahams; and there are only three black authors, Nelson Mandela, Nicholas Mhlongo, and Zakes Mda, with another six entries. To write in English is also a very useful asset to get some kind of reception in Spanish, as there is only one translation from a text originally in Afrikaans, that written by C.M. van den Heever,[7] and none from any autochthonous South

7   C.M. van den Heever, *Verano: Clásico sudafricano en lengua afrikáans*, tr. Santiago Martín &
    Juan Miguel Zarandona (Disbabelia 6; Valladolid: Universidad de Valladolid, 2002).

African language. To be a Nobel Prize winner is very convenient, too (Gordimer, Coetzee), or a legendary President (Mandela). Despite writing in English, belonging to the Indian South African community does not seem to be a real asset or guarantee any kind of successful reception outside South Africa, at least in Spain.

It must also be taken into account that BDÁfrica does not and cannot cover everything. It does not include translations into the other official languages of Spain (Catalan, Galician, Basque, etc.), for example. And, above all, it only covers full translated volumes, not other possible, but probable, shorter translations published in periodicals, anthologies, etc. On the other hand, it includes writers who were born in South Africa in colonial times, but who can hardly be regarded as South Africans (Tolkien, Campbell). Likewise, being an immigrant nation has meant that there are a large number of fully committed South African writers who were not actually born in South Africa, which is quite typical among the Indian community.

What is wholly true is the fact that, in South Africa, race used to determine who got published and who would develop a successful literary career. To a great extent this is still true, which, it can be argued, plays against the reception of those works written by South Africans with roots in the Indian subcontinent. And race also determined who got translated and joined 'world literature' according to the criteria mentioned above. To prove and study it in some detail, we have chosen three South African writers, all of whom are alive but of a certain age: i.e. one that enables them to have witnessed apartheid and post-apartheid times, and who belong to different communities. In other words, the white J.M. Coetzee (1940–), with forty-one entries; the black Zakes Mda (1948–), with one entry; and the Indian Ahmed Essop (1931–), with no entries in this database. Essop, chosen to represent the South African Indian literary world, was in fact born in the state of Gujarat (India) but moved to Johannesburg with his family as early as 1934. This chapter will focus on the reception of his works in Spain, and compare it with that of his national counterparts mentioned above as the perfect tool with which to assess an unsatisfactory reality.

A New National Literature for the New South Africa

The first all-inclusive elections in South Africa took place in 1994; and the first Constitution for all South Africans was approved and enacted in 1996. These two key dates put an end to a number of infamous laws that only promoted inequality, segregation, division, and hatred, the so-called foundations of apartheid.[8] In tune with the times, a number of pioneering and enthusiastic South African academics and (wo)men of letters set about the task of establishing an inclusive national literature for the New South Africa, something that the country had been lacking.

Longman, the world-class publisher, offered international readerships the volume *Southern African Literatures*, by Michael Chapman, professor at the former University of Natal. The approach was wholly different from what had been the rule in apartheid South Africa. Because of this, Chapman emphasizes that his study contains his (new) view of the diverse but interrelated literatures of southern Africa, and that his selections range from the expression of the stone-age Bushmen (San) to that of modern voices in the independent states. He also reminds his readers that in South Africa there was little consensus (in 1996) on how a single South African literature might be constituted, and that South Africa, where ethnicity was both encouraged and enforced by apartheid, possibly presented an extreme case of literary linguistic division; and he claims that the Xhosa bard and the settler journalist, for example, despite being divided by language, literacy, race, and probably sentiment, were both part of the same story.[9] Shared space and encounters are the key factors:

> We might want to ask ourselves whether Xhosa literature would have taken the direction it did had there been no colonial settlement in Xhosa space; obversely, whether early South African literature in English would have followed its particular course had it not encountered indigenous people around its early settlements.[10]

The new national literature for the whole of southern Africa (South Africa included) was going to be one, a single one, in clear opposition to previously separated branches of non-national traditions. And it had to cover all races, cultures, languages (San, Bantu, European, others); pre-colonial, colonial, and postcolonial; independence and post-independence; oral and written. The book was written according to these criteria, and the world knew it. The unifying factor was the shared territory which facilitated the construction of a whole network of interrelationships that they, all the artificially separated branches, could not avoid.

---

8   Prohibition of Mixed Marriages Act (1949), Group Areas Act (1950), Population Registration Act (1950), Immorality Act (1950), Reservation of Separate Amenities Act (1950), Bantu Education Act (1953), Natives Resettlement Act (1954), etc.

9   Michael Chapman, "Introduction: Writing Literary History in Southern Africa," in *Southern African Literatures* (London & New York: Longman, 1996): xv–xvi.

10   Chapman, "Introduction: Writing Literary History in Southern Africa," xvii.

The year 1996 also saw the publication of a local South African volume entitled *Rethinking South African History*, originating in the former University of Durban-Westville's Centre for the Study of Southern African Literature and Language (CSSALL), founded in 1994. The approach was the same and it was shared by its different chapter contributors. Jean-Philippe Wade, for example, wrote that the CSSALL therefore had committed itself to overcoming this damaging legacy, by calling for an integrated study of South African literature which simultaneously overcame the dominance of the literatures of Afrikaans and English and the consequent marginalization of the literatures of the African languages, and added that the CSSALL was aware that—remarkably—no integrated encyclopedia of South African literature existed, and therefore committed itself to producing one.[11] C.T. Msimang claimed that after a long history of separate development, the time had come for the three streams to converge and flow as one big river and that the three systems of African, Afrikaans, and English literatures should form three branches of one big tree: a South African national literature.[12] Johan van Wyk commented that during the apartheid years not only were the literatures in the different languages institutionalized as disconnected fields of study with separate literary histories, but that oral traditions had been seriously neglected. He argued that in a society where oral practices exist side-by-side with the printed book, it was impossible to arrange material exclusively around books, authors, oeuvres, and dates, as the authors of oral lore were usually not known, and this lore was impossible to date.[13]

The Arrival of This New National Literature in Spanish Translation

According to the BDÁfrica database, this commitment to try and look across the barriers of language, race, and culture,[14] or to merge African-language literature with South African literary history in order to build a New South African

---

11   Jean–Philippe Wade, "Introduction: Disclosing the Nation," in *Rethinking South African Literary History*, ed. Johannes A. Smit, Johan van Wyk & Jean–Philippe Wade (Durban: Y Press, 1996): 3.

12   C.T. Msimang, "The Status of African Literature in South African Literary History," in *Rethinking South African Literary History*, 67.

13   Johan Van Wyk, "Towards a South African Literary History," in *Rethinking South African Literary History*, 33, 35.

14   Michael Chapman, "Writing Literary History in Southern Africa," in *Rethinking South African Literary History*, ed. Johannes A. Smit, Johan van Wyk & Jean–Philippe Wade (Durban: Y Press, 1996): 40–49.

national literature really deserving the name,[15] has not reached Spain and
its national literary system of translated texts. This is clearly a phenomenon
worth studying.

As stated above, the three examples that we will study in this chapter are
the South African writers J.M. Coetzee (1940–), Zakes Mda (1948–), and Ahmed
Essop (1931–), representing the white, black, and Indian communities respectively. Essop and the literature of the South African Indian community will
enjoy very special treatment in order to validate its seemingly very poor reception by means of Spanish translation, as well as to speculate on its causes.

An Integrated Case Study: Coetzee, Mda, and Essop in Spain

To begin with, we will present data about the comparative reception of our
three writers from two sources, the Archive of the Barcelona newspaper *La
Vanguardia* and the Spanish ISBN Agency database of books published in
Spain, both available online.

The *La Vanguardia* Archive

La Vanguardia (www.lavanguardia.com) is a national Spanish newspaper that
has been published in Barcelona since 1 February 1881. From 3 May 2011 on-
ward, a second edition has also been published in Catalan. Consequently, it is
not only one of the oldest Spanish newspapers, but it offers free access online
to its complete archive including all its issues since 1881 (http://hemeroteca
.lavanguardia.com). The search by means of the keywords 'J.M. Coetzee,' 'Zakes
Mda,' and 'Ahmed Essop' produced the following results (consulted on 19 July
2016):

TABLE 4.2

South African writer	*La Vanguardia* entries
J.M. Coetzee	411
Zakes Mda	48
Ahmed Essop	0

---

15   C.F. Swanepoel, "Merging African-Language Literature into South African Literary His-
      tory," in *Rethinking South African Literary History*, ed. Smit, van Wyk & Wade, 20–30.

Coetzee is very well represented. He is mentioned for the first time on 1 October of 1987 on the occasion of the first translation of one of his novels, *Vida y época de Michael K. (Life and Times of Michael K)*, into Spanish. Since then, his many appearances in the pages of *La Vanguardia* have faithfully traced his literary career and many aspects of his personal life. They also inform readers about, and review, what, when, and how his texts were translated in Spain, or what happened when he was awarded the Nobel Prize for Literature. There are interviews where his personal views about many topics are expressed. His emigration to Australia is also covered.

Although forty-four matches may seem a lot for Zakes Mda, a writer relatively unknown in Spain, the figure may be misleading. His first appearance was on 30 August 1988, when an article reported how a Catalan stage director, Teresa Devant, had presented a play by him, *And the Girls in Their Sunday Dresses*, at the Edinburgh Festival Fringe, a section of the Edinburgh International Festival. However, most appearances occur in the years 1998 and 2007, when the same Teresa Devant presented in Barcelona two plays by Zakes Mda in Catalan translation: *La romàntica història d'una monja* (1998) (*The Nun's Romantic Story*) and *I les noies vestides de diumenge* (2007) (*And the Girls in Their Sunday Dresses*). These two events will be studied in more detail below.

Ahmed Essop has otherwise never caught the attention of *La Vanguardia*, which, unfortunately, is just what we expected. As we will see, the total absence of data is sometimes as meaningful as full data about a given phenomenon.

The Spanish ISBN Agency

The Spanish Agencia del ISBN (www.mcu/es/libro/CE/AgenISBN.html) was established in 1972, when it became compulsory by law to publish commercial books with the ISBN code in Spain. Since then it can be regarded as the perfect catalogue of Spanish translated books for research purposes and the study of the reception of foreign literary works. As far as Coetzee, Mda, and Essop are concerned, the following are the likewise unequal results yielded by this catalogue (consulted 15 July 2016):

TABLE 4.3

South African writer	Spanish ISBN entries
J.M. Coetzee	77
Zakes Mda	1
Ahmed Essop	0

The Race Factor

The race factor that used to determine the fortunes of South African (wo)men of letters still seems to have a great impact not only in the South African nation but also when the nation's literature is translated into other languages, such as Spanish, and becomes part of circulated world literature. This claim requires further discussion.

J.M. Coetzee

The chronicle of the privileged reception of J.M. Coetzee in Spain is beyond all doubt a success story. In spite of his enigmatic, experimental, and difficult literary texts, almost all his works—fiction, autobiography, essays, speeches, and research—have been translated into Spanish, and many of them also into the other main regional languages of Spain: Catalan, Galician, and Basque. In particular, his novels have been published and reprinted repeatedly in different formats: hardback, paperback, audio. With the sure help of its film adaptation, premiered in 2008, *Disgrace* (1999) has been the leader of this success: it has been published and reprinted often (2000, 2002, 2003, 2004, 2005, 2008, and 2009 [twice]) by different publishing houses and with two differently rendered titles: *Desgracia* and *Deshonra*. The Nobel Prize for Literature, awarded to him in 2003, does not explain the whole phenomenon, as the following earlier publication dates for his novels show:

· *Vida y época de Michael K* (1987)
· *Foe* (1988)
· *Esperant els bàrbars* (1988) (2000) (2003) [Catalan]
· *Esperando a los bárbaros* (1989) (2003)
· *El maestro de Petersburgo* (1996) (2001)
· *La edad de hierro* (2002)
· *L'Edat de ferro* (2002) [Catalan]
· *A vida e o tempo de Michael K* (2003) [Galician]
· *Vida i época de Michael K* (2003) [Catalan]
· *Desgracia* (2000) (2002)
· *Desgràcia* (2003) [Catalan]

One of Coetzee's later novels, *The Childhood of Jesus*, was published in 2013. The very same year, three translations of this novel were available in Spain:

La infancia de Jesús, in Spanish, by Miguel Temprano; *La infantesa de Jesús*, in Catalan, by Dolors Udina; and *Jesusen haurtzaroa*, in Basque, by Aritz Gorrotx-ategi. This can only be termed instant circulation. And the phenomenon shows no sign of abating yet: 2016 saw the publication, in two volumes, of another collection of essays by Coetzee, entitled *Las manos de los maestros*.[16]

A sequel to this allegorical treatment of a 'Jesus' namesake, *The Schooldays of Jesus*, appeared in 2016 in the UK with Harvill Secker, and was published in the USA with Viking in early 2017. And the reception of this book confirms the trend: it was available in Spanish, translated by Javier Calvo, *Los días de Jesús en la escuela*; and in Catalan, again by Dolors Ubina, *Els dies d'escola de Jesús*. Both translations appeared promptly in 2017.

Zakes Mda

Mda is a South African writer with a long and successful national and international literary career. Among his most celebrated titles are, at the very least, the following novels: *The Heart of Redness* (2000), *The Madonna of Excelsior* (2002), *The Whale Caller* (2005), *Cion* (2007), *Black Diamond* (2009), and *The Sculptors of Mapungubwe* (2013). He is also a poet and a playwright. Only one of his early works, *Ways of Dying* (1995),[17] has been translated into Spanish, as *Formas de morir*.[18] This can only be seen as affording very limited access in Spain to Zakes Mda's narrative talents.

However, apart from this translation, and as already indicated, two plays by Mda, *The Nun's Romantic Story* (1991) and *And the Girls in Their Sunday Dresses* (1988/1993), have enjoyed some reception in Spain. Teresa Davant, the previously mentioned stage director, met Zakes Mda in Botswana while he was in exile there, and they have been friends ever since. She presented the first play at the Muntaner Theatre, part of the Barcelona Summer Festival Teatre Grec, in 1998. The new title was *La romàntica història d'una monja*, as the text was translated into Catalan by Carme Serrallonga. It was only presented once, on 26 June, and this translation has not been published. Some years later, the second play was staged at the Barcelona Versus Theatre, 4–29 April 2007. Teresa Davant was again the stage director and she also translated the text, in collaboration with

---

16   J.M. Coetzee, *Las manos de los maestros*, tr. Javier Calvo (Barcelona: Literatura Random House, 2016).

17   Zakes Mda, *Ways of Dying* (Cape Town: Oxford UP Southern Africa, 1995).

18   Zakes Mda, *Formas de morir*, tr. Bianca Southwood (Barcelona: Barataria, 2001).

Mercè Vallejo, into Catalan as *I les noies vestides de diumenge*. This translation has not been published, either.[19]

This poor reception should come as no surprise; it is the most typical reception accorded black African writers and colonial and postcolonial African literature in Spain. Even celebrated masters such the Nigerian Chinua Achebe (1930–2013) and the Kenyan Ngũgĩ wa Thiong'o (1938–) have had a very poor reception in Spain and in Spanish translation, as I was able to study in my research papers. What has happened to Mda had happened before both to Achebe[20] and Ngũgĩ.[21] Literature by black African writers are only partially translated, or not translated at all. When they are translated, this tends to happen very late, or never. Also, when they are translated, or retranslated, they never reach large audiences or become really popular, as only minorities read them, if at all. This is not what Achebe, Ngũgĩ or, of course, Mda deserve. The obvious question is why this situation is as it is.

Paul Bandia, for example, has studied the extreme difficulties involved in the complex process of translating hybrid postcolonial African texts into European languages. First of all, the original language text is indeed an interpretation, or first-level translation, of former oral texts in an African language, plus the postcolonial experience in that language. Then, if translated into a second European language without that background (second-level translation), Spanish, for example, the difficulties only increase, as both the orature and postcoloniality must be reproduced.[22] García de Vinuesa has also claimed that the problem with African literature in Spain is that it is always classified as exotic, minority, marginal, etc. Only publishing houses devoted to this kind of texts, or with specific collections for lesser known writers, become interested in this literature. Consequently, these authors, with the possible exception of writers from Spain's former colony of Equatorial Guinea (particularly writers now resident in Spain or the USA) are never regarded as mainstream or valued as they deserve.[23]

---

19   Gloria Montero, "I les noise vestides de diumenge, de Zakes Mda." *Assaig de teatre: Revista de l'associació d'investigació i experimentació teatral* 59 (2007): 177–178.

20   Juan Miguel Zarandona, "*A Grain of Wheat* (1967/1986), de Ngũgĩ wa Thiong'o, en español: *Un grano de trigo* (2006) y algunas reflexiones sobre la traducción de literatura africana," *Afroeuropa: Journal of Afroeuropean Studies* 2.3 (2008), online: 1–18.

21   Juan Miguel Zarandona, "El corpus de traducciones españolas de Chinua Achebe (1930–): traducción sincrónica y diacrónica comparada de los traductores," *Afroeuropa: Journal of Afroeuropean Studies* 4.1 (2010), online: 1–22.

22   Paul Bandia, *Translation as Reparation: Writing and Translation in Postcolonial Africa* (Manchester: St. Jerome, 2008): 159–174.

23   Maya García de Vinuesa, "La construcción de la literatura africana anglófona en el ámbito editorial español y su traducción al castellano," in *Literaturas hispanoafricanas: realidades y contextos*, ed. Inmaculada Díaz Narbona (Madrid: Verbum, 2015): 198–212.

But the problem of this cultural distance and misunderstanding between Spain and African letters is probably deep-rooted in history, as a volume published by the University of Valladolid research group Afriqana (www.afriqana .org) tried to demonstrate some years ago. *Cultura, literatura y cine africano: acercamientos desde la traducción y la interpretación* (African Culture, Literature, and Cinema: Approaches from Translation and Interpretation) is partly a collection of research papers on African literature, and partly an anthology, in Spanish translation, of some of the earliest texts written in Africa in European languages (English, French, Portuguese, Italian, German, and Afrikaans).[24] The introduction details the historical events that account for this aloofness between Spain and Africa. Spain always specialized in the Americas and never had but a marginal presence in the African continent.[25]

Ahmed Essop

Essop is a prolific writer who has published three novels, *The Visitation* (1980), *The Emperor* (1995), and *The Third Prophecy* (2004), and four collections of short stories. *The Hajji and Other Stories* (1978), *Noorjehan and Other Stories* (1990), *The King of Hearts and Other Stories* (1998), and *Narcissus and Other Stories* (2002). He is also the author of a number of titles comprising research, essays, and poetry: *Suleiman M. Nana: A Biographical and Historical Record of His Life and Times* (2002), *The Universe and Other Essays* (2010), *History and Satire in Salman Rushdie's "Satanic Verses"* (2009), *Exile and Other Poems: And A Commentary of a Selection of Verses from the Ruba'iyat of Omar Khayyam* (2010), *The Garden of Shahrazad and Other Poems* (2011), and *The Moors in the Plays of Shakespeare* (2011). His long career, typical of an independent observer, has gained him a leading position in the canon of the South African Indian community, whose exploits, weaknesses, and lifestyle he has chronicled as nobody else has done, both in apartheid and post-apartheid times.[26] His unique sense of humor, among the worst life difficulties, has been praised very frequently.

---

24   *Cultura, literatura y cine africano: acercamientos desde la traducción y la interpretación*, ed.
      Juan Miguel Zarandona (Soria: Diputación de Soria—Universidad de Valladolid, 2011).

25   Juan Miguel Zarandona, "España y África o la necesaria construcción de puentes mediante la cultura, la literatura, el cine y la traducción e interpretación," in *Cultura, literatura y cine africano* (2011), ed. Zarandona, 3–9.

26   Further reading: Pallavi Rastogi, "Introduction: Are Indians Africans Too, or: When Does a Subcontinental Become a Citizen," in *Afrindian Fictions: Diaspora, Race, and National Desire in South Africa* (Columbus: Ohio State UP, 2008): 1–22; Singh, Jaspal K. "Transformations in Ahmed Essop's Political Ethos," *Research in African Literatures* 42.3 (Fall 2011), special issue on Asian African literatures, special guest editor Gaurav Desai: 46–55.

Is the fact that *La Vanguardia* keeps no record and the Spanish ISBN Agency
has no entry of his work in translation something surprising or something
logical? It is, in fact, no great surprise; even in its native country, South African
Indian literature goes practically unnoticed. This is an old and enduring phenomenon. For example, in 1989, it was still claimed that in the field of creative
literature Indians had not distinguished themselves as other South Africans
had, that only a handful of writers have had their work published, that no
major writer had emerged so far, and that it was logical to wonder why this was
the case, in view of the fact that Indian creative talent was manifest, although
rarely developed to its full potential.[27] Years later, post-apartheid South African
Indian scholars finally found in the rebirth of South Africa an opportune moment for examining the real and complete literary wealth of the country, to
vindicate a space, hitherto resisted, in which to excavate the nation's suppressed literary heritage in all its diversity and to discover a local topography
that had been ignored.[28] The neglect of South African Indian women writers
is even greater: "Some of the recent critical discussions and surveys of South
African literatures proceed as if writing by South African Indian (women)
simply does not exist."[29] And all this has many international consequences, as
Spain proves:

> The way South African literary critics and anthropologists represent
> South African literature to themselves has ramifications in the interna-
> tional community. There is almost total ignorance of the existence of
> South African Indian (women's) writings at this level.[30]

Fortunately, however, sources such as BDÁfrica, *La Vanguardia* and the ISBN
Catalogue do not tell the whole story. The journal *Hermēneus*, published by the
Soria School of Translation and Interpretation of the University of Valladolid,
Spain (www5.uva.es/hermeneus), included a translation of Essop's short story
"Two Sisters" (1978)[31] in its 2010 volume (issue 12). The Spanish title was, logically,

---

27   Y.G. Reddy, "Cultural Perspective: Literature," in *The Indian South Africans: A Contempo-
        rary Profile*, ed. Antony J. Arkin, Karl P. Magyar & Gerald J. Pillay (Pinetown, S.A.: Owen
        Burgess, 1989): 201.

28   Devarakshanam Govinden, *A Time of Memory. Reflections on Recent South African Writing*
        (Durban: Solo Collective, 2008): 343.

29   Devarakshanam Govinden, *A Time of Memory*, 4.

30   Govinden, *A Time of Memory*, 19.

31   Ahmed Essop, "Two Sisters," in *The Hajji and Other Stories* (1978; Johannesburg: Picador
        Africa, 2004): 32–38.

"Dos hermanas."[32] Finally, and wholly unexpectedly for a South African Indian, Essop made his first appearance in Spanish. The rarity of this translation was also the origin of a research paper published in 2016.[33] But this will not be the end. The Hermēneus Project not only publishes the aforementioned journal, but a series of exotic and unknown translations named Disbabelia. The University of Valladolid Press has made a commitment to publishing, in its series Ediciones de la Universidad de Valladolid, a volume featuring a selection of short stories by Essop in Spanish translation in 2018. His entry into the space of world literature may be near, as well as the end of the long period of discrimination suffered. Essop clearly deserves it, as all readers who approach him and his work can always enjoy fully entertaining, witty, satirical, symbolic, committed, and critical fictions. He never disappoints.

This can only be made possible after a long life devoted to letters. Although he was published before in different journals, his literary career officially started in 1978 with his first volume of short stories, *The Hajji and Other Stories*, which was widely acclaimed: it won the prestigious Olive Schreiner Award in 1979, and it was prescribed for first-year students of English at the formerly Indian-only University of Durban–Westville in 1985 and 1986, for example. Johannesburg was said to have found a new voice. The expectations have been fulfilled nearly forty years later.

His rich pages are written from a unique viewpoint, his and that of the South African Indian community that he represents. His fiction allows those interested to see present-day South African affairs from the different perspective of the Indian community, the least vocal one, always caught between white power and black majority, and from that of a very talented member of the same community. Essop's texts also display extraordinary coherence. His main object of literary interest and creative inspiration is the Johannesburg Indian community, when it inhabited the largely Indian suburbs of Newtown and Fordsburg, and when they were made to resettle in the distant, apartheid-created township of Lenasia, where Essop himself moved in 1963. Because of this, he can be regarded as the most eminent chronicler of the day-to-day lives and aspirations of his Johannesburg community. His work testifies to the resilience and vitality of a small world of human beings squeezed between the interests of dominant racial groups and prone to traumatic experiences,

---

32   Ahmed Essop, "Dos hermanas," tr. Sabrina Solar Solórzano, *Hermēneus* 12 (2010): 337–345.

33   Juan Miguel Zarandona, "South African Indian Ahmed Essop in Spanish Translation: 'Dos hermanas' (2010), a Story of Many Linguistic and Cultural Barriers," in *Continental Shifts, Shifts in Perception: Black Cultures and Identities in Europe*, ed. Sharmilla Beezmohun (Newcastle upon Tyne: Cambridge Scholars, 2016): 151–175.

both in the apartheid and post-apartheid periods, and their cultural and his-torical traces. However, he does not limit himself to the Indian community; his works present a complete tapestry of apartheid and post-apartheid South Africa, where formerly impossible relationships and connections between the different individuals and communities (white, black, Indian, Coloured) of the nation are now possible and can be analyzed in detail and from a fully ironical viewpoint. Some things never change.

There is always strong criticism of the old and new South Africa, Essop's only commitment being to truth, but always with a rich sense of humour, typical of his Indian community. Essop presents the reader with a moving understand-ing of the weak human condition, and an empathy that only real knowledge of human affairs can provide. And, finally, he always displays a unique artis-tic use of the English language that can only come from his community, the largest diasporic Indian community outside India, and one that has created a hybrid culture whose contribution to South African letters deserves more attention.

All these merits make him a perfect candidate to have his works circulated in the realm of world literature and translated into other languages, which is something that has not happened so far, apart from the Spanish example mentioned above. The UNESCO Index Translationum bibliographical database does not have any record of Ahmed Essop in translation into any language. Neither do different key national libraries such as the Bibliothèque National de France, the Biblioteca Nazionale Centrale di Roma, the Deutsche Nation-albibliothek, the Biblioteca Nacional de Portugal, the Nationale Bibliotheek van Nederland, the Bibliothèque Royale de Belgique, or the National Library of India. The search pages of the different national branches of Amazon (Australia, Germany, Brazil, Canada, China, the USA, France, India, Italy, Japan, Mexico, the Netherlands, the UK, and Spain) store no record on Ahmed Essop except the original South African editions in English. Indeed, the National Library of South Africa catalogue includes thirty-one entries under the key word 'Ahmed Essop.' It seems highlyy probable that Essop has never been translated into any other language, with the recent exception of Spanish.

And What About the Coloured Community?

Before heading to the final conclusions, I would just like to claim that the South African Coloured community is also waiting for a more balanced recep-tion in other languages and cultures. This necessary vindication also prompted the aforementioned journal *Hermēneus* to publish a short story in 1999 by the

South African Coloured writer S.P. Benjamin, "'n Verdwaalde engel,"[34] translated as "Ángel errante."[35] The positive consequence of this translation project
is that it brought into the Spanish canon of translated literary texts not only
the work of a Coloured author but also a text originally written in Afrikaans,
something that does not happen very often.

Conclusion

The first undeniable finding can be worded as follows: Spanish reception of the
new national literature of South Africa, by means of translation, is very incomplete and unsatisfactory. It is conspicuously unequal and discriminatory, and
does not honor the inclusive values of the New South Africa as established by
the democratic Constitution of 1996. In other words, it is still very negatively
marked by the previously dominant race-based social and cultural policies of
the formal national political regime known as apartheid. White writers, even
today, are much more likely to have international resonance and readership,
and it seems much easier for them to enter the transnational canon or space of
well-established world literature. Old habits die hard.

Among the many communities that make up the South African rainbow nation, the Indian community is by far the least popular among international
readers, both lay or expert, as is clearly exemplified by the Spanish cultural
scenario, as part of an international domain sharing the same characteristics.
It is the one most in need of a consciously applied translation policy to be
able to conquer international markets. It is the one that requires a stronger ap-
plication of cultural affirmative action. Ahmed Essop, the "Grand Old Man of
South African Indian Literature" according to Pallavi Rastogi,[36] and our most
representative prototypical example, deserves, without question, a leading position in the South African national canon, in the translated literature system
belonging to the Spanish national literary polysystem, and in the comprehensive multilingual complex canon of world literature, a fact which would make
room for many different translations of his singular works into Spanish, its

---

34   S.P. Benjamin, "'n Verdwaalde engel," in *Die Lewe is 'n halwe roman* (Cape Town: Queillerie,
      1999): 17–25.

35   S.P. Benjamin, "Ángel errante," tr. Santiago Martín & Juan Miguel Zarandona, *Hermēneus*
      8 (2006): 253–264.

36   Pallavi Rastogi, "Essop's Fables: Strategic Indianness, Political Occasion, and the Grand
      Old Man of South African Indian Literature," in *Afrindian Fictions: Diaspora, Race, and
      National Desire in South Africa* (Columbus: Ohio State UP, 2008): 47–69.

close linguistic allies, and many other world languages. It is a matter of justice that, to my mind, the wrongs of the South African past be mended in the field of literature and world literature as well.

Besides, his compatriot South African Indian writer Achmat Dangor (see Table 4.1) has already proved that it is possible for a writer from their community to get translated and enjoy a reception in Spain. Dangor, novelist, poet, playwright, short-story writer, etc., from Johannesburg, and CEO of the Mandela Foundation (2007–13), has already seen the translation of three of his novels into Spanish: *La maldición de Kafka* (1999) (*Kafka's Curse*, 1997), *Fruta amarga* (2004) (*Bitter Fruit*,[37] 2003), and *Trilogía de Z Town* (2009)[38] (*The Z Town Trilogy*, 1990). It is thus indeed possible.

References

Arkin, Antony J., Karl P. Magyar & Gerald J. Pillay, ed. *The Indian South Africans: A Contemporary Profile* (Pinetown, S.A.: Owen Burgess, 1989).

Bandia, Paul. *Translation as Reparation: Writing and Translation in Postcolonial Africa* (Manchester: St. Jerome, 2008).

Benjamin, S.P. "Ángel errante," tr. Santiago Martín & Juan Miguel Zarandona, *Hermēneus* 8 (2006): 253–264.

Benjamin, S.P. "'n Verdwaalde engel," in *Die Lewe is 'n halwe roman* (Cape Town: Queillerie, 1999): 17–25.

Chapman, Michael. "Introduction: Writing Literary History in Southern Africa," in Chapman, *Southern African Literatures*, 1–13.

Chapman, Michael. *Southern African Literatures* (London & New York: Longman, 1996a).

Chapman, Michael. "Writing Literary History in Southern Africa," in *Rethinking South African Literary History*, ed. Johannes A. Smit, Johan van Wyk & Jean-Philippe Wade (Durban: Y Press, 1996b): 40–49.

Coetzee, J.M. *The Childhood of Jesus* (London: Harvill Secker, 2013a).

Coetzee, J.M. *La infancia de Jesús*, tr. Miguel Temprano García (Barcelona: Mondadori, 2013b).

Coetzee, J.M. *La infancia de Jesús*, tr. Miguel Temprano García (Barcelona: Debolsillo, 2014).

Coetzee, J.M. *La infantesa de Jesús*, tr. Dolors Udina (Barcelona: Edicions 62, 2013c).

---

37   This volume was shortlisted for the Booker Prize in 2004.

38   This translation opened the literary series of Casa África, the Spanish government organization responsible for the nation's African cultural relations.

Coetzee, J.M. *Jesusen haurtzaroa*, tr. Gorrotxategi Mujika (Donostia–San Sebastián: Meettok, 2013d).

Coetzee, J.M. *Las manos de los maestros*, tr. Javier Calvo (Barcelona: Literatura Random House, 2016a).

Coetzee, J.M. *The Schooldays of Jesus* (London: Harvill Secker, 2016b).

Coetzee, J.M. *Los días de Jesús en la escuela*, tr. Javier Calvo Perales (Barcelona: Literatura Random House, 2017a).

Coetzee, J.M. *Els dies d'escola de Jesús*, tr. Dolors Udina (Barcelona: Edicions 62, 2017b).

Damrosch, David. "Introduction: Goethe Coins a Phrase," in Damrosch, *What Is World Literature?* (2003a), 1–36.

Damrosch, David. *What Is World Literature?* (Princeton NJ: Princeton UP, 2003b).

Essop, Ahmed. "Two Sisters," in *The Hajji and Other Stories* (1978; Johannesburg: Picador Africa, 2004): 32–38.

Essop, Ahmed. "Dos hermanas," tr. Sabrina Solar Solórzano, *Hermēneus* 12 (2010): 337–345.

Fernández Ruiz, María R., Gloria Corpas & Míriam Seghiri. "BDÁfrica: diseño e implementación de una base de datos de la literatura poscolonial Africana publicada en España," *Hermēneus* 18 (2016): 427–450.

García de Vinuesa, Maya. "La construcción de la literatura africana anglófona en el ámbito editorial español y su traducción al castellano," in *Literaturas hispanoafricanas: realidades y contextos*, ed. Inmaculada Díaz Narbona (Madrid: Verbum, 2015): 198–218.

Govinden, Devarakshanam Betty. *A Time of Memory: Reflections on Recent South African Writing* (Durban: Solo Collective, 2008).

Mda, Zakes. *Formas de morir*, tr. Bianca Southwood (Barcelona: Barataria, 2001).

Mda, Zakes. *Ways of Dying* (Cape Town: Oxford UP Southern Africa, 1995).

Montero, Gloria. "I les noise vestides de diumenge, de Zakes Mda," *Assaig de Teatre: Revista de l'Associació d'Investigació i Experimentació Teatral* 59 (2007): 177–178.

Msimang, C.T. "The Status of African Literature in South African Literary History," in *Rethinking South African Literary History*, ed. Johannes A. Smit, Johan van Wyk & Jean-Philippe Wade (Durban: Y Press, 1996): 51–70.

Rastogi, Pallavi. *Afrindian Fictions: Diaspora, Race, and National Desire in South Africa* (Columbus: Ohio State University Press, 2008a).

Rastogi, Pallavi. "Introduction. Are Indians Africans Too, or: When Does a Subcontinental Become a Citizen," in *Afrindian Fictions: Diaspora, Race, and National Desire in South Africa* (Columbus: Ohio State UP, 2008b): 1–22.

Rastogi, Pallavi. "Essop's Fables: Strategic Indianness, Political Occasion, and the Grand Old Man of South African Indian Literature," in *Afrindian Fictions: Diaspora, Race, and National Desire in South Africa* (Columbus: Ohio State UP, 2008c): 47–69.

Reddy, Y.G. "Cultural Perspective: Literature," in *The Indian South Africans: A Contemporary Profile*, ed. Antony J. Arkin, Karl P. Magyar & Gerald J. Pillay (Pinetown, S.A.: Owen Burgess, 1989): 195–213.

Singh, Jaspal K. "Transformations in Ahmed Essop's Political Ethos," *Research in African Literatures* 42.3 (Fall 2011), special issue on Asian African literatures, special guest editor Gaurav Desai: 46–55.

Smit, Johannes A., Johan van Wyk & Jean-Philippe Wade, ed. *Rethinking South African Literary History* (Durban: Y Press, 1996).

Swanepoel, C.F. "Merging African-Language Literature into South African Literary History," in *Rethinking South African Literary History*, ed. Johannes A. Smit, Johan van Wyk & Jean-Philippe Wade (Durban: Y Press, 1996): 20–30.

Van den Heever, C.M. *Verano: Clásico sudafricano en lengua afrikáans*, tr. Santiago Martín & Juan Miguel Zarandona (Disbabelia 6; Valladolid: Universidad de Valladolid, 2002).

Van Wyk, Johan. "Towards a South African Literary History," in *Rethinking South African Literary History*, ed. Johannes A. Smit, Johan van Wyk & Jean-Philippe Wade (Durban: Y Press, 1996): 31–39.

Wade, Jean-Philippe. "Introduction: Disclosing the Nation," in *Rethinking South African Literary History*, ed. Johannes A. Smit, Johan van Wyk & Jean-Philippe Wade (Durban: Y Press, 1996): 1–9.

Zarandona, Juan Miguel. "El corpus de traducciones españolas de Chinua Achebe (1930–): traducción sincrónica y diacrónica comparada de los traductores," *Afroeuropa: Journal of Afroeuropean Studies* 4.1 (2010): 1–22, http://journal.afroeuropa.eu/index.php/afroeuropa/article/view/158 (accessed 15 August 2016).

Zarandona, Juan Miguel. "España y África o la necesaria construcción de puentes mediante la cultura, la literatura, el cine y la traducción e interpretación," in *Cultura, literatura y cine africano* (2011a), ed. Zarandona, 3–9.

Zarandona, Juan Miguel. "*A Grain of Wheat* (1967/1986), de Ngugi wa Thiong'o, en español: *Un grano de trigo* (2006) y algunas reflexiones sobre la traducción de literatura africana," *Afroeuropa: Journal of Afroeuropean Studies* 2.3 (2008): 1–18, http://journal.afroeuropa.eu/index.php/afroeuropa/article/view/118 (accessed 15 August 2016).

Zarandona, Juan Miguel. "South African Indian Ahmed Essop in Spanish Translation: 'Dos hermanas' (2010), a Story of Many Linguistic and Cultural Barriers," in *Continental Shifts, Shifts in Perception: Black Cultures and Identities in Europe*, ed. Sharmilla Beezmohun (Newcastle upon Tyne: Cambridge Scholars, 2016): 151–175.

Zarandona, Juan Miguel, ed. *Cultura, literatura y cine africano: acercamientos desde la traducción y la interpretación* (Soria: Diputación de Soria—Universidad de Valladolid, 2011b).

CHAPTER 5

The Madman in the Garden

Or, Achmat Dangor's Search for the Common Literary Origins of the Distinct Muslim Communities of South Africa in Kafka's Curse (1997)

Salvador Faura

We spring our heroes on you when you least expect it, conjure them up from dusty townships, make them walk across shark-infested waters, bring them old and wizened to your doorstep in order to defeat you with their wisdom.[1]

..

The title of this chapter is a reference to one of the verses in *Leyla and Mejnun* and a follow-up on the concluding lines of *Regarding Muslims* (2014). In fact, it is precisely in the concluding lines of *Regarding Muslims* that Gabeba Baderoom affirms that South Africa "allows us to consider the ways in which Islam, slavery, sexuality and race are imbricated, as well as the place of Muslims as a minority in a secular democracy."[2] In other words, in *Regarding Muslims*, Baderoom analyzes how Islam can be rendered ordinary and, at the same time, be made exotic in a number of cultural manifestations of the South African nation. To complement Baderoom's research, I first refer to Fuzuli, the great Muslim poet of the Orient and the author of *Leyla and Mejnun*. I then analyze *Kafka's Curse*, written in the late-twentieth century by the South African author Achmat Dangor. To conclude, I link *Leyla and Mejnun* to *Kafka's Curse* because these two narratives use a genuinely Eastern tale that moves away from the picturesque and that approaches true Islamic tradition as a way to describe nations and captivate audiences:

As jewels are gathered throughout the land
And, one by one, into pearls are wrought,

---

1 Achmat Dangor, *Kafka's Curse* (New York: Vintage, 2000): 22.
2 Gabeba Baderoom, *Regarding Muslims* (Johannesburg: Wits UP, 2014): 160.

© KONINKLIJKE BRILL NV, LEIDEN, 2018 | DOI 10.1163/9789004365032_006

So let the words of the Gardener fall
From the Garden of Speech in a tale to enthrall.[3]

Fuzuli's famous work, written in 1536 in the Muslim regions of the Indian Ocean, is the story of a man maddened by love for a woman who represents all that he desires but who is also, de facto, unattainable for him. The problem with Fuzuli's madman is that his beloved cannot be read as a real person but only as an abstract rendering of his religious ideals. Beyond this, the problem with Fuzuli's madman is that idealizations are often unreachable for human beings as well as for the social groups they represent. In *Leyla and Mejnun*, in other words, Fuzuli describes the love of a Muslim man for—and his pilgrimage toward—a woman who represents sixteenth-century Islam in the Orient. Interesting for us here is that, by doing so, Fuzuli is also constructing the story with which Dangor explores the conditions of the Muslims of South Africa four hundred years later.

The structure of my essay is thus: I commence by dealing with Fuzuli's long poem as part of the shared roots of the distinct Islamic communities of South Africa. Secondly, I argue that Dangor's novel can read as a postcolonial 'reply' to Fuzuli's narrative; thirdly, I maintain that Dangor's version of Mejnun's love for Leyla unifies the distinct Muslim groups of the South Africa of the 1990s. Further, I argue that the shared 'Muslim space' that Dangor re-creates in *Kafka's Curse* enriches the literature of the South African nation at large.

My idea is that the distinct Islamic communities of South Africa can recognize—and identify with—Dangor's version of *Leyla and Mejnun* because they have all inherited this tale from their ancestors: as Dangor writes "what are the real origins of the legend?" Dangor's answer is simultaneously vague and clear: Mejnun's legend, which Dangor defines in psychological terms as "a coping mechanism," may have originated after "a trivial incident, sentimentalised and exaggerated to heroic proportions by slaves from India or Java or Malaysia." Yet—Dangor suggests—this legend could also be African, for this continent "is fecund [...] with the kind of foliage which gives birth to the secret lives that are the [...] substance of magical parable."[4] Other passages in *Kafka's Curse*, however, offer other explanations of the genesis of Mejnun's tale: "*In Arabia, I think—where else would he set his beginnings?*"[5] Dangor's imprecise guesses point to the fact that his version of Fuzuli's romance belongs to none

---

3   Fuzuli, *Leyla and Mejnun*, tr. Sofi Huri, intro. & notes Alessio Bombaci (London: George Allen & Unwin, 1970): 151.

4   Dangor, *Kafka's Curse* (New York: Vintage, 2000): 30.

5   Dangor, *Kafka's Curse* (New York: Vintage, 2000): 22; emphasis in the original.

of the Islamic communities of South Africa in particular and, at the same time, to all of them without exception. One thing is certain—Dangor explains—and that is that the story of the man who goes crazy waiting for his unattainable beloved is a "Muslim," and "whoever passed on [the tale to him] made a very firm point of that" (31).

Leaving aside the shared Muslim origins of Dangor's variant of Leyla and Mejnun, the fact is that the Islamic communities of the nation can also identify with Dangor's characters because of their South African setting. In particular, Dangor treats his Muslim hero as a believer who is confronted with the social norms of the racist regime of the 1990s, and his female figure as the only means to save this character from racist marginalization. Dangor's version of Fuzuli's tale is, thus, genuinely South African—and justifiably connected to South African history.

One way or another, the presence of Islam in the Rainbow Nation can be traced back to the seventeenth century—when the colony was under the control of the Dutch East India Company. At that point, the Muslim community of the country was made up of a handful of influential personalities who had been exiled from their native lands for political reasons. Among the faithful of those days was the Javanese Sheikh Yusuf of Bantam, who helped establish the first cohesive group of believers in the nation, and Prince Abdullah Kadi Abu Salaam of Tidore, who became famous for writing a copy of the Qur'an from memory.[6] The majority of the Muslims who entered the country—or who converted to Islam—in that period set up home in Cape Town. Actually, the Muslims who inhabit that area at present are still often referred to as 'Cape Malays.' Cape Muslims often speak Afrikaans and English though they usually prefer the former over the latter. As Henriette Roos explains, this preference has a foundation, and that is that some of the earliest texts in Afrikaans were written there in order to teach the Qur'an. Surprising though it may seem, this is the case because the local authorities of that period prohibited the sale of baptized Christians and encouraged "the spread of Islam among convicts and slaves."[7]

The second wave of South African Muslims arrived in the country from the British Raj between the 1860s and the early twentieth century. During that period, many Muslims were set to work in sugarcane fields, or entered the nation

---

6 See Anon. "Sheik Yusuf" and "1700–1799" in "South African History Online: Towards a People's History," http://www.sahistory.org.za/people/sheik-yusuf and http://www.sahistory.org.za/archive/1700-1799 (accessed 12 July 2016).

7 Henriette Roos, "Torn Between Islam and the Other: South African Novelists on Cross-Cultural Relationships," *Journal of Literary Study* 21.1–2 (2005): 50.

as passenger Indians who expanded their businesses beyond the seas. Large numbers of this second wave of Muslims settled in KwaZulu–Natal. From a linguistic viewpoint, the Muslims who set up house in that area have always considered themselves to be different from the 'Malay' inhabitants of Cape Town. Today, for example, most KwaZulu–Natal Muslims are English-speakers even if some of them are also fluent in several Indian tongues.

Last but not least, the third wave of Muslims who migrated to South Africa is made up of North African and South Asian workers who settled in the nation after the end of Separate Development. The majority of the members of this community established themselves in the most prosperous areas of the country, for, leaving politics aside, what they wanted most was to improve their financial status.[8] Most of the members of this community can use English, but many have Arabic as their mother tongue.

According to statistical data, Islam (wrongly regarded as a monolithic block) is often considered the fastest-growing religion in South Africa. As explained above, however, the Muslim communities of the country can be split into at least three different groups, depending on their geographical origins, on the languages they speak, and on the different traditions with which they identify. If there is one cultural element that can unite all South African Muslims, this is Fuzuli's romance. As I see it, this is the case because the story of Leyla and Mejnun has been handed down historically to all of the Islamic communities of the nation. Besides, Fuzuli's romance presents a combination of South African essentials and Muslim exoticism that can fascinate both its Muslim readership and its broader South African audience.

Fuzuli's real name was Muhammad ibn Suleyman. He was born in Iraq, which was then part of the Ottoman Empire. 'Fuzuli' actually means 'presumptuous.' Thanks to its unpleasant connotations, Muhammad ibn Suleyman's pseudonym was never copied by any other poet, which was his main intention when he chose it. Fuzuli's biographer, Ashiq Chelebi, who wrote in the sixteenth century, explains that Fuzuli's poems were highly praised in the Muslim regions of the Indian Ocean, and that his work was further promoted by and translated at the court of the Mughal emperors of the subcontinent, where he ended his days.

As was customary in his time, Fuzuli wrote in Turkish, Arabic, and Persian. This could be one reason why Fuzuli is acclaimed by the Muslim communities of South Africa as well as in the regions of the Indian Ocean from where

---

8   For further information, see Pali Lehohla, *Documented Immigrants in South Africa, 2013* (Pretoria: Statistics South Africa, 2014) 36–53.

their ancestors come.[9] Whatever the case, South Africa's Muslims regard Leyla and Mejnun as the Islamic equivalents of what Romeo and Juliet have stood for culturally, and literarily, in the West. Just as Shakespeare's characters tend to be represented psychologically as established in the original play but with often vastly different sociocultural settings, Leyla and Mejnun have often been modified by the different epochs, diverse languages, and numerous contexts in which they have sojourned.

In these circumstances, what happens is that, even if all the versions of Mejnun present him as an icon of love driven to madness, and even if all the variants of Leyla see her as an ideal, there is no standard version of them to think of whenever their legend is mentioned. I analyze Fuzuli's poem here because of its spread in the regions of the Indian Ocean from where the Muslim communities of South Africa come. Most importantly, I examine the poem because I consider that *Kafka's Curse* 'replies' to Fuzuli's work rather than to any of the other versions of this account in circulation.

My use of the word 'reply' to refer to *Kafka's Curse* does not imply that Dangor adjusts to the South African setting two characters who already existed in the collective imagination of the Muslim regions of the Indian Ocean. On the contrary, my use of 'reply' suggests that Dangor's novel can be read as a postcolonial development of Fuzuli's narrative, just as Fuzuli's account is often studied as a religious answer to Nizami of Ganja's twelfth-century romance. My hypothesis implies that Dangor's main characters were actually born in the Muslim regions of the Indian Ocean, that they traveled to the Indian subcontinent, and that they reached the changing South Africa of the 1990s via *Kafka's Curse*.[10]

The theory that Fuzuli's poem comes from Nizami's verses is best demonstrated by referring to its opening lines, which present a "fluent throng of chatterers" asking Muhammad ibn Suleyman to translate Nizami's tale into their language.[11] The stanzas that take up this request, however, do not repeat Nizami's plot literally. For Alessio Bombaci, there is one significant divergence between Fuzuli's version of the narrative and that of Nizami. In Bombaci's

---

9   See "Fuzuli" in Selcuk Aksin Somel, *Historical Dictionary of the Ottoman Empire: Ancient Civilizations and Historical Eras* (Lanham MD: Scarecrow, 2003). 94.

10   For further information about the historical versions of *Leyla and Mejnun*, see Alessio Bombaci's comments on Abulfaraj al-Isfahani's *Kitab al-Aghani* in his introduction to Fuzuli's poem. Written in AD 967 and in Arabic, Abulfaraj al-Isfahani book is often unfortunately overlooked by English-speaking critics. Hilary Kilpatrick's *Making the Great Book of Songs* (2003) is a welcome attempt at correcting this neglect.

11   Fuzuli, *Leyla and Mejnun* (London: George Allen & Unwin, 1970): 150.

view, Fuzuli's male protagonist is a Muslim on his way to a woman who represents al-Mubdi.[12] Nizami's protagonist, meanwhile, is a real man directing his feelings at his earthly female beloved.[13] In other words, Fuzuli's 'reply' changes Mejnun, his beloved, and the nature of their love, which is another way of saying that he 'replies' to, rather than adapts, his Persian sources.

The 'reply' is a common practice in the Muslim nations of the Indian Ocean. From olden days, the poets of this geographical realm have written compositions that have the same characters as—and similar themes to—the texts that they emulate. In these circumstances, Dangor's postcolonial version of *Leyla and Mejnun* can be analyzed as a 'reply' to Fuzuli's text, just as Fuzuli's poem is considered to have 'replied' to Nizami. To connect Dangor's novel to Fuzuli, I can refer to Muhammad ibn Suleyman's closing verses, where the latter challenges a rival writer, or would-be writer, to "re-create" his narrative. "If thy ability," he says,

> Is equal to thy great humility
> Go, write an equal to my verses here;
> Show critic's art comes of creation clear.
> Speak but of goodness, failing this, my friend
> Remain in silence. Here my words have end.[14]

In 1997, in other words, *Kafka's Curse* "shows critic's art" and re-writes a story of insane love that, from a postcolonial point of view, seems to me to 'reply' to Fuzuli's *Leyla and Mejnun*. As I see it, the main convergence between Dangor's novel and the poem it emulates is related to the way in which Dangor appropriates the most famous lovers of the Indian Ocean. Its main divergence, conversely, is related to the fact that Dangor does not set his romance in any territory of the Muslim world but in the South Africa of the last decade of the twentieth century. In these circumstances, Dangor's account offers more than a postcolonial home to a myth that unites the Afrikaans-, English-, and Arabic-speaking

---

12   Al-Mubdi, the Originator is one of the ninety-nine appellations of Allah. For a complete list see https://www.youtube.com/watch?v=TMXGo_JuiAM (accessed 1 August 2015).

13   In his introduction to Fuzuli's poem, Bombaci defends that Nizami's madman could be based on a real man (Qays ibn Mulawwah) who lived in the Umayyad Caliphate during the seventh and eighth centuries, and who maddened for the love of a real woman. This hypothesis, published in 1946 in a still undisputed article was initiated by Ignatii Iulianovich Krachkovski, who followed the wanderings of Nizami's Mejnun among the Banu Amir tribe of the Arabian Peninsula.

14   Fuzuli, *Leyla and Mejnun*, 332.

Muslims of his country; Dangor's text grants the Islamic communities of his native land a space in which they can reflect upon their country and share their conclusions with the rest of their compatriots.

Dangor's version of Mejnun is called Oscar. In Dangor's words, Oscar is "just another play-white whose hidden life is being exposed" (66) in the 1990s. In my view, though, Oscar, often referred to as Majnoen, the madman, is also—and primarily—a Muslim. I suggest that Majnoen can be seen as a symbol uniting all of the Islamic groups of South Africa before 1994 because, apart from being discriminated against for racial reasons, he is also scorned for his religion. Oscar's story can be summarized in the following way: his father, a rich Muslim, had powerful enemies—people who could not forgive him his Dutch mother. Thus, Oscar's family's businesses and houses were expropriated. When that occurred, Oscar could only move forward by taking "advantage of his fair skin" and by hiding his faith. "I was fair" he says at one point, and "this oppressive country had next-to-Nazis in government, yet had a place, a begrudged place but a place nevertheless, for Jews [...] Because they were white" (32–33).

As a Muslim in South Africa, Oscar is in a truly desperate situation. If he changed his religion, opportunities would open to him. For him:

> It was a matter of life or death [...]. Not being able to study, to go to university, became an architect, being forced to remain Omar Khan, the son of a newly impoverished township entrepreneur, was a form of death! I changed from Omar Khan to Oscar Kahn [...]. It was like leaving one dimension of the world for another, where time and place remained the same, but their surfaces had different textures.
>
> *Kafka's Curse*, 33

By substituting his true self for a persona that could be more accepted by the 'normative' South Africa of the early 1990s, though, Oscar became prey to a malady that compelled his body to breathe abnormally, so much so that he finally turned into a tree. In a way, *Kafka's Curse* is the postmodern story of why Oscar Kahn became a tree, and the surreal narrative of how this tree grew in his South African house. On one occasion, for example, Dangor's madman defines himself as an architect who designs houses that "make functional other people's dreams and fantasies" (30). This is perhaps the reason why Oscar developed an exaggerated feeling for his residence, and metaphorically "repaired and restored, obsessively battling the effects of the house's [...] decline" (12). "We bought this old house near the park" he says:

> This house of gnarled character, floors of wood polished to a gleaming
> smoothness like ageing skin, mottled veins in its grain and knots of his-
> tory which recorded the bruised passage of naked feet.
>
> *Kafka's Curse*, 48–49

Unluckily, though, Oscar's "house had an air of audacious illicitness" (48) and
he "sometimes imagined that the sound of the wind in its old-fashioned eaves
was a lament." He and his white South African wife were perhaps "too conventional" to satisfy "its garish instincts or perpetuate the subtle, aberrant history"
which they had inherited (49).

To round out the idea that houses are a symbol of the Muslim communities in South Africa, Dangor describes his brother's dwelling as well. Unlike
Oscar's, Malik's home had not changed, instead resisting all attempts to violate
its shape. Malik had actually expanded his residence, saved it from the ruins
of time, and added a little sanctuary to it. Obliquely, Dangor's explanation reminds us that Malik never changed his name, passed as white, or abandoned
the religion of his forefathers. Without doubt, Malik's house is different from
Oscar's because of the way these two brothers relate to their Islamic roots.
"It struck me," Dangor's narrator writes, "that our history is contained in the
homes we live in, that we are shaped by the ability of these simple structures
to resist being defiled" (52).

The culminating moment of the novel occurs when Anna—Dangor's ap-
pealing version of Leyla and the impersonator of the 'normatively racist' South
Africa of the 1990s—returns to her husband's house after their divorce. It is
there that Anna discovers the true origins of her spouse in the Muslim regions
of the Indian Ocean, that she understands the suffering of the Islamic communities of her country, and that she learns that her husband had metamor-
phosed from Omar to Oscar only to end as Majnoen—the madman. It is also
in Oscar's house—and garden—that the ordinary as well as exotic elements of
Dangor's fragmented narrative fuse to represent Islam's postmodern adaptation to the South African setting.

I entirely agree with Elaine Young when she affirms that this writer compos-
es the first and the last chapter of his novel as if they were part of a fairy tale.
As Young sees it, in fairy tales, a male hero is made to journey through several
obstacles—or to travel to foreign lands—until he discovers his true identity.[15] Dangor's Muslim character journeys to white Anna: on the one hand, to

---

15   For further information on the structure of *Kafka's Curse*, see Elaine Young, "Cursing and
       Celebrating Metamorphosis: Achmat Dangor's 'Kafka's Curse'," *Current Writing: Text and
       Reception in Southern Africa* 12.1 (2000): 27–29.

exemplify the difficulties that he is made to overcome in the 'normative' South Africa of the early 1990s that she represents; on the other, to illustrate how Oscar's social circumstances have gradually driven him mad. One way or another, what is clear to Dangor's audiences at the close of *Kafka's Curse* is that Oscar's madness has helped him evade apartheid, but that it has also compelled him to confront his Islamic roots with his present condition. Moreover, what is clear to Dangor's audiences is that Oscar's narrative can proudly form part of South Africa's national literature.

The main difference between Mejnun's journey and Oscar's is that *Kafka's Curse* 'is' and, at the same time, 'is not' a traditional folktale. The idea, as Young explains, is that the identity of the hero of a fairy tale is resolved at the end of his pilgrimage, when he can meditate on the wisdom that he has acquired.[16] What happens in *Kafka's Curse*, meanwhile, is that Dangor's male protagonist gains wisdom not at the close of his adventures but in the second chapter of his book. In point of fact, it is precisely in the second chapter of Dangor's novel that the structure of traditional folktales collapses. This is the case because it is there that Oscar voices his surreal reflections.

The process that changes Omar into Oscar and the reflections that turn him into Majnoen can be defined as 'degeneration.' This is not only because, in order to improve his economic status, Dangor's male protagonist 'degenerates' his Muslim self in the midst of Dangor's text but also because, following Nietzsche in *Human, All Too Human* (1878), the presence of what the latter calls 'degenerate' types can—and actually does—change societies. For Nietzsche, 'degenerate' types are formed by socially marginalized individuals who are in fact freer that the 'normative' citizens of the society that imprisons them. In this manner, 'degenerate' types can weaken and transgress established social structures. Bearing Nietzsche's theory in mind, in *Kafka's Curse*, Oscar's 'degenerate' version—Majnoen—can be said to act as an agent of social change in the sense that he allows 'normative' Anna to grasp the situation of her Muslim compatriots.

Young's theory—that *Kafka's Curse* follows and at the same time distances itself from the structure of a traditional fairy tale—is reinforced in Dangor's last chapter. There, Oscar's madness deepens, spreading to the other personae of the novel. At this stage, then, Majnoen's insanity transgresses the 'normative' country through which he journeys and this transgression may end up integrating him.

Pursuing this idea of Oscar's 'degenerating' journey, I now wish to comment on the very first sentence of *Kafka's Curse*: "In the end, Anna left her husband

---

16   Elaine Young, "Cursing and Celebrating Metamorphosis," 21.

Oscar because he breathed down her neck" (3). Apart from Dangor's use of the verb 'leave,' the fact that his narrative begins with the idea of 'inhaling' and 'exhaling' air is also significant. In this passage, Dangor links the act of 'breathing' to the idea of 'being born': i.e. to Oscar's origins. In turn, Dangor also compares the idea of birth to the notion of 'journeying to death.' Along the same lines, the concept 'journeying to death' is associated with Oscar's symbolic (re)turning to his Muslim roots in an indeterminate region of the Indian Ocean.

Dangor strategically initiates his version of Mejnun's love story by speaking of Oscar's breathing on Anna and by referring to the end of their romance first because, in this way, Anna is forced to reflect on her husband's journey across the South Africa that drove him mad. Perhaps Oscar would not have become 'degenerate' Majnoen if he had symbolically stayed in the land of his ancestors; if he had kept his true Muslim identity among 'normative' South Africans, or if he had not helped strengthen the oppressive society that drove him crazy—as when he designed a tower in Durban: "Apartheid with its balls up" (45). Anna's problem is that it is now too late to confront her discovery: Oscar has already mutated into a tree, standing tall in what had been their alcove.

In the passage below, Dangor shows how the story of Oscar's journey to Anna converges enough with, and at the same time diverges sufficiently from, *Leyla and Mejnun*:

> You see, Anna said, [Oscar] remembered his beginnings [...] And told me the story of Leila and Majnoen. Now Majnoen is both a name and a madness [...]—there lived a beautiful princess named Leila whom everybody wanted to marry. That's what people want from princesses. Marriage ...
>
> But she fell in love with her father's gardener Majnoen, a gifted man, but strange. He talked to trees and whispered to flowers and could make things grow just by breathing on them. Of course, no princess could freely marry a gardener, so they agreed to run away. They were to meet in the forest which Majnoen knew like no one else [...]. Majnoen promised his beloved that he would wait for her, no matter what. But the inevitable happened ...
>
> *Kafka's Curse*, 22–23

... He turned into a tree! It is at this moment of the narrative that Anna uncovers who the real 'Madman in the Garden' is in her life. The same terms that Dangor uses to define *Leyla and Mejnun* are now also used to refer to Majnoen and his beloved. Majnoen is "both a name and a madness":

[...] A fairy tale of course, embellished [...] until it became a myth [...] It
is noble I suppose to use the gift of storytelling [...] to create a whole way
of life from a strand of fact, a mundane incident quickly observed.

Kafka's Curse, 29

The power of "the madness of Majnoen, or is it [...] Majnoen the madness?"
over Oscar is finally acknowledged by Anna (31). In like manner, the title of
Dangor's novel is also clarified. 'Kafka's Curse' is

an insanity that strikes those who dare to stray from their "life's station,"
that little room which you are told at birth is yours. You may expand it a
bit, add a loft or a garden, build a bigger fence than the one you inherited.
But you leave it at your peril. In fact, you are punished for leaving.

Kafka's Curse, 31

Following this definition, 'Kafka's Curse' is a name for Oscar's madness and the
spiral around which Dangor 'replies' to Fuzuli. Beyond that, 'Kafka's curse' is
also a 'degenerative' malady that lets 'normative' Anna uncover her country's
treatment of her husband and of her Muslim compatriots.

As expected, Anna's lonely walk—and epiphany—inside Oscar's house and
garden, metaphorically covered by the forests of his dementia, has a parallel in
Leyla's wandering in her garden of speech:

One day when thus the season was unkind,
To ease her of her load of heavy grief,
Distressful Leyla to the garden passed
And saw no sign of rose or tulip left.
[...]
She saw the garden as the House of Death
And all her soul burned up with tenderness.
And now in anguish of her burning heart
She told her grief to all the garden bare.[17]

Just as Leyla's walk brings Mejnun to the idealized terminus of their story, Anna's
penetration of her husband's garden significantly sheds light on the origins of
his madness, too. Dangor's mixing of what is ordinary in the South Africa of the

---

17   Fuzuli, *Leyla and Mejnun*, 315.

1990s with Fuzuli's exotic tale finally exposes a Muslim South Africa that had remained veiled for too long.

To conclude, I maintain that Dangor alters the structure of fairy tales to 're-ply' to Fuzuli's version of *Leyla and Mejnun*. Oscar's power to initiate change in South African society has a parallel in Nietzsche's theory of the 'degenerate' type. Last but not least, Anna's discovery of Oscar's story allows her to reflect on the relationship between her country and the Muslim communities it contains in the context of the 1990s. Above all, Dangor's 'madman in the garden' contributes to the creation of a literary space for Muslims in a South Africa that is now culturally richer and socially more inclusive.

Works Cited

Anon. "Leyla Majnun—One of S'pore's Earliest Malay Feature Films," http://eresources .nlb.gov.sg/history/events/8413c59a-9d05-4574-b979-19eb513d8e4e (accessed 12 June 2016).

Anon. *The Ninety-Nine Beautiful Names of Allah*, https://www.youtube.com/watch?v= TMXG0_JuiAM (accessed 1 August 2015).

Baderoom, Gabeba. *Regarding Muslims: From Slavery to Postapartheid* (Johannesburg: Wits UP, 2014).

Brodie, Nechama. "Religion (They Say) Is on the Rise," http://mg.co.za/article/2016-03 -23-religion-is-on-the-rise-say-researchers (accessed 8 July 2016).

Dangor, Achmat. *Kafka's Curse* (New York: Vintage, 2000).

Desai, Ashwin, & Goolam Vahed. *Inside Indian Indenture: A South African Story, 1860–1914* (Cape Town: HSRC Press, 2010).

Fuzuli. *Leyla and Mejnun*, tr. Sofi Huri (London: George Allen & Unwin, 1970).

Kettani, Houssain. "Muslim Population of South Africa 1950–2020," http://www.ijesd .org/papers/27-D436.pdf (accessed 18 July 2016).

Kilpatrick, Hilary. *Making the Great Book of Songs: Compilation and the Author's Craft in Abu I-Faraj al-Isbahani's Kitab al-Aghani* (Richmond: Curzon, 2003).

Krachkovski, Ignatii Iulianovich. *Among Arabic Manuscripts: Memories of Libraries & Men*, tr. Tatiana Minorsky (*Nad Arabskimi Rukopisiami: Listki Vospominanii o Knigakh i Liudiakh*, 1946; Leiden: E.J. Brill, 1953).

Kritzinger, Johan Jakob. "Christians in South Africa: the Statistical Picture" in http:// www.hts.org.za/index.php/HTS/article/viewFile/2573/4386 (accessed 18 July 2016).

Lehohla, Pali. "Permanent Residence Permits" in *Documented Immigrants in South Africa, 2013*—Statistical Release P0351.4 (Pretoria: Statistics South Africa, 2014): 36–52.

Nietzsche, Friedrich. *Human, All Too Human: A Book for Free Spirits*, tr. Marion Faber (Lincoln: U of Nebraska P, 1996).

Nizami of Ganja. *The Story of Layla and Majnun*, tr. Rudolf Gelpke (New Lebanon NY: Omega, 2011).

Roos, Henriette. "Torn Between Islam and the Other: South African Novelists on Cross-Cultural Relationships," *Journal of Literary Studies* 21.1–2 (2005): 48–67.

Shakespeare, William. "Romeo and Juliet," in *The Illustrated Stratford Shakespeare* (London: Bath Press, 1991): 701–728.

Shawqi, Ahmad. *Quais & Laila*, http://www.mafhoum.com/press/egyman17.htm (accessed 22 August 2014).

Singh Rawai, Harnam. *Laila Majnu*, http://youtu.be/p6RPs6tUP1c (accessed 12 June 2014).

Somel, Selcuk Aksin. *Historical Dictionary of the Ottoman Empire. Ancient Civilizations and Historical Eras* (Lanham MD: Scarecrow, 2003).

Young, Elaine. "Cursing and Celebrating Metamorphosis: Achmat Dangor's 'Kafka's Curse'," *Current Writing: Text and Reception in Southern Africa* 12.1 (2000): 17–30.

CHAPTER 6

Transformation and Transnationalism in Post-Apartheid South Africa

Farida Karodia's Boundaries *(2003)*

Isabel Alonso-Breto

South African fiction produced between the end of apartheid and the turn of the century was categorized as 'transitional,' a mode characterized by the confessional narrative, either fictionalized or presented as autobiography or memoir.[1] According to Emily Davis, in the post-transitional phase, a movement away from this dominant type gave way to an emphasis on difference and the diversity of experience, and on the complexity of identities modeled not only on issues connected to race and national politics but also on gender, sexuality, and, importantly, in Davis's words, "new forms of politics and sociality, particularly transnational ones."[2] For this scholar, transnational connections are paramount in the post-transitional phase, so much so that she brands it the era of the transnational turn, "because of the increasingly global nature of the topics represented in fiction."[3]

Boundaries, Farida Karodia's latest novel to date, was published precisely at the turn of the century, in 2000, the year which marks the divide between one mood—the memoir or autobiography connecting the past to the present—and the other: namely, the transnational turn.[4] *Boundaries* can be seen to encompass both tendencies. On the one hand, it is concerned with past injustices and present legacies of apartheid, and with the necessity to face and overcome them; on the other, the novel recounts the opening of South Africa to a new era of transnational realities. In this polyphonic narrative, the novelties brought

---

1   See Isabel Hofmeyr & Liz Gunner, "Introduction: Transnationalism and African Literature," *Scrutiny2* 10.2 (2005): 3–14, Leon De Kock, "Does South African Literature Still Exist? Or: South African Literature is Dead, Long Live Literature in South Africa," *English in Africa* 32.2 (2005): 69–83, and Meg Samuelson, "Scripting Connections: Reflections on the 'Post-Transitional,'" *English Studies in Africa* 53.1 (2010): 113–117, among others.

2   Emily S. Davis, "New Directions in Post-Apartheid South African Fiction and Scholarship," *Literature Compass* 10.10 (2013): 801.

3   Davis, "New Directions in Post-Apartheid South African Fiction and Scholarship," 801.

4   Davis is quick to note, however, that "such designations function more as scholarly conveniences than neat chronological divisions" (Davis, "New Directions," 801).

about by the incorporation of the nation into the ranks of transnationalism and globalization are seen to affect the life of a very traditional place in South Africa, in a passage-into-modernity tale that, again, needs to be read metonymically as the incorporation of the modern, post-apartheid nation in the global scene.

However, when it comes to political transitions, change is not as abrupt in the social and economic realms as the new political configuration would suggest. Such is the case in South Africa. *Boundaries* is set quite a few years after the first democratic elections held in the country. Yet from the opening pages the novel gives access to a world where not much has changed in the new post-apartheid era. The setting is the traditional South African town of Vlenterhoek, located somewhere in the Eastern Cape. Vlenterhoek works as a prototypical chronotope of the situation of the country at that time. It is a small provincial town where the relations between blacks and whites have not yet been normalized: significantly, we read, early in the text, that "the main street was part of the national road. It was twelve blocks long and formed the boundary between the *whites* and the *blacks*."[5] The situation in this Afrikaner stronghold thus remains anchored to a past which, unfortunately, is still not so distant. Although at present children of all skin colors are allowed to attend the local school together, there is still a great divide in the population, and black pupils tend to be abused by white ones, who are in the majority, since they are the ones who can afford an education. Nothing has changed much here in spite of the spinning of the world around:

> In spite of changes elsewhere in the country since the first democratic elections, and changes in the world at large—like the Berlin Wall coming down, which they had seen on television, and Nelson Mandela walking out of prison to international acclaim—transformation had not yet reached the small town.
>
> Boundaries, 7

After this disheartening opening, *Boundaries* portrays, precisely, the story of a transformation. This transformation reads in two different ways. On the one hand, the topical change from modernity to tradition becomes in this story a change from mores still tethered to the politics of apartheid to the mindset of a more veritably democratic and egalitarian regime. And in order for this to happen, a previous healing process needs to take place—such as the one embodied, on a national scale, in the Truth and Reconciliation Commission.

---

5   Farida Karodia, *Boundaries* (Cape Town: Penguin, 2003): 2. Further page references are in the main text.

On the other hand, this access to modernity and to post-apartheid social mores takes an unequivocal transnational turn. The implication seems to be that globalization affects the lives of literally everybody in the world, including members of those societies which, for a variety of reasons (in this case geographical but more emphatically political), have remained isolated from the rest for a longer period.

The narrative in *Boundaries* is sparked by the irruption of several elements from the outside world into the monotonous life of the self-absorbed town, elements which, in different ways, disrupt its stagnant social and economic order and hasten it toward a new, *worldly* status. To begin with, a couple of travelers who happen to pass through the town (suggesting that Vlenterhoek seldom receives any deliberate visit) notice that the townspeople look extremely healthy, and soon learn that the reason is that all the city locals drink water from the nearby Hemelslaagte springs. It immediately awakens in them the idea that exploiting this source of water, a globally esteemed and increasingly expensive good, might well become extremely profitable. From there on, they start making moves towards the acquisition of the totality of the lands occupied by the springs. In the same days, two further persons happen to pass through Vlenterhoek—scouts of a film company in search of locations for a documentary film which is to be shot partly in India and partly in South Africa. Mesmerized by the local landscape, they decide to shoot here. These serendipitous findings coincide, finally, with the return to Vlenterhoek of three locals who had left the town years earlier. They are Leah, who quit both the town and South Africa when she married forty years earlier and has spent most of her life in Canada; Rebecca, a Coloured woman who has become a successful and outspoken opposition MP in Cape Town; and Frikkie, a young Afrikaner man who met fame and success as a baseball player but suffered a terrible accident which crippled him for life, and, refusing to return as a failure, has stayed away like the others.[6]

Another noteworthy intrusion comes about in the opening pages, when an unidentified corpse in an advanced state of decomposition is found in the veld. Finding out who this murdered person was occupies a prominent part of the narrative, until it is eventually disclosed that the body is that of Ivan, the illegitimate child of Hendrick Jouvert, the rich white local landowner, and a black woman, and that he was killed by his father when he decided to ask

---

6   Herself a returnee from Canada after the end of apartheid, Karodia has explored the topic of return in other works, such as *A Shattering of Silence* (London: Heinemann, 2003) and several short stories, among them "Against an African Sky," in *Against an African Sky and Other Stories* (Cape Town: David Philip, 1995).

for recognition of his ignored filial rights. The metaphorical implications of these findings—of the rotting corpse, of the person it belonged to, and of the circumstances—are enormous. To begin with, the fact that the corpse was abandoned half-buried obviously recalls the many crimes committed during apartheid which were occulted, silenced, or denied. Then, the fact that Ivan was of mixed race and unacknowledged by his father echoes decades of the racist fear of miscegenation and the systematic oppression and exploitation of the majority of South Africans at the hands of white people. Finally, that this unfortunate young man should have been killed by his own father resonates ominously with the immorality of the white South Africans' behavior. The recurrent emergence of this unnamed corpse in the narrative, together with the final vindication of Ivan's ruthless murder, appear as an uncanny intrusion of the past into the lives of Vlenterhoek's citizens, and obviously recalls the work of the TRC in the period of South Africa's reconstruction and development since 1996, when the attempt was made "to heal the wounds of the past,"[7] given that there was "a need among South Africans other than those most severely victimized by Apartheid to recount their suppressed histories."[8] Thus, we can read the narrative thread of the corpse's retrieval and subsequent investigation as a variant within the genre of confessional narrative which, as mentioned above, dominated the transitional period of South African literature, a genre which Karodia, an exiled writer, chooses to explore in fictional terms.

The different subplots in *Boundaries* are intertwined in subtle ways, and together make up a collage of stories and events which result in the transit from a regime anchored in the past and entrenched in its long unquestioned racial class and economic boundaries to a new society where things are slowly beginning to change, and where, importantly, racial barriers have started being questioned. Through a narrative technique which emphasizes the ordinary preoccupations of citizens,[9] a more promising future is inaugurated after this obscure town becomes, in the course of the novel, a point of confluence of peoples of different origins, ethnicity, classes, and occupations who effectively interact with one another. Pointing towards the entry of the New South Africa into the ranks of globalization, Vlenterhoek will increasingly free itself from the grip of the past, until in the end the town will see itself "thrown into the

---

7   Devarakshanam Betty Govinden, "Healing the Wounds of History: South African Indian Writing," *Current Writing* 21.1–2 (2009): 288.

8   Govinden, "Healing the Wounds of History: South African Indian Writing," 288.

9   See Njabulo S. Ndebele, "The Rediscovery of the Ordinary: Some New Writings in South Africa," *Journal of Southern African Studies* 12.2 (1986): 143–157.

international press" (258). Thus this transition, set in the specific context of a small post-apartheid South African town, is one of cataclysmic proportions. Combining personal and psychological alignments with cultural and economic aspects of renewal, the events taking place in the settlement in such a brief period indeed illustrate "how a variety of conditions and parallel processes combine to bring about large-scale patterns of transformation,"[10] or, in other words, that "large scale patterns of transformation come about through a constellation of mutually conditioning factors and parallel processes."[11] Huge transformations, as Gandhi famously proclaimed, are made of small changes. Also, as Neil Smelser remarks,

> profound social transformations [...] develop out of both individual and collective short-term actions within immediate environments: these accumulate in often unexpected ways to constitute fundamental changes in societies.[12]

This is precisely what happens in Vlenterhoek, where transformation is brought about by a myriad of combined elements.

The elements which disturb the placidity of life in the town and which, as a whole, bring about such fundamental transformation can be arranged into three categories: individual, sociocultural, and economic. It cannot be overemphasized that each of these categories necessarily impinges on the other two. As Arjun Appadurai remarked some years ago, when he coined the operative concepts of ethnoscapes, technoscapes, finanscapes, mediascapes, and ideoscapes, current global flows occur "in the growing *disjunctures*" between these domains.[13] This means that it is precisely the complex and nuanced interplay between these ranges of experience that results in the shifting and swiftly evolving flux of contemporary globalization.[14]

---

10   Steven Vertovec, *Transnationalism* (London & New York: Routledge, 2009): 23. Vertovec
      is referring here to ideas presented in David Held, Anthony McGrey, David Goldblatt &
      Jonathan Perraton, *Global Transformations: Politics, Economics and Culture* (Cambridge:
      Polity, 1999).

11   Vertovec, *Transnationalism*, 23.

12   Neil J. Smelser, "Social Transformations and Social Change," *International Social Science
      Journal* 156 (1998): 173–178, cited in Vertovec, *Transnationalism*, 22.

13   Arjun Appadurai, "Disjuncture and Difference in the Global Cultural Economy" (1990),
      in *Theorizing Diaspora: A Reader,* ed. Jana Evans Braziel & Anita Mannur (London:
      Blackwell, 2006): 35.

14   Of Appadurai's categories, ethnoscapes, mediascapes, and finanscapes feature promi-
      nently in *Boundaries*, as the categories of change chosen for analysis show.

Individual Transformation: The Returnees

On a personal level, many things happen in the span of intradiegetic time in *Boundaries*, but three are particularly significant: those connected to Rebecca, Frikkie, and Leah. Rebecca and Frikkie have some aspects in common, and are complementary characters in a way. They are two relatively young persons who left the town when they were younger, in different circumstances. Rebecca left for two reasons, as her flight from her father's tyrannical attitude towards his family resonated with her wish to join the civil movements fighting apartheid in Cape Town. She was full of resentment at her father, and for years she never went back, not even to attend her mother's burial. After the change of regime, she became an opposition MP after the 1994 election, a service she still renders at present. Rebecca eventually decides to pay a visit to her home place when she is asked to do so by the city clerk, Danie Venter, who sees the potential advantage of having an MP interested in local issues. Rebecca's return to Vlenterhoek will have a double outcome. For one thing, she will end up forgiving her father for the past years of abuse, including the suspicion that he may have precipitated her mother's death. What Rebecca learns in her visits to Vlenterhoek and through her own personal process of reconciliation is that her father's aggressive attitude is actually grounded in his own frustration at being a virtual slave to the town's richest white landowner, Hendrik Jouvert, who furthermore fathered his wife's son Ivan. Rebecca's former fear of her own father was thus a collateral effect of the state of submission which the Coloured and black populations were forced to undergo through apartheid. The social repression articulated through racialist and racist policies was transferred into patriarchal abuse and gender violence, exerted by Rebecca's father as a means to compensate for the humiliation he was a victim to, as a worker and as a husband, in the political setting of everyday life. But in the new South Africa there should no longer be any room for such feelings, hence the fact that Rebecca eventually decides to forgive her father for his past sins, symbolically reproducing the intended effect of the TRC. Moreover, she does so after learning that he has terminal cancer, the suggestion being, perhaps, that lifelong exploitation, which has been a scourge for decades in the country, is bound to come to an end. Thus, as Sissy Helff remarks in discussing another work by Karodia, when Rebecca arrives in Vlenterhoek she is "initiating a process of reconciliation within and beyond the novel."[15] Remarkably, the second outcome of Rebecca's return to her birthplace, as will be discussed later on, is her

---

15   Sissy Helff, *Unreliable Truths: Transcultural Homeworlds in Indian Women's Fiction of the Diaspora* (Cross/Cultures 155; Amsterdam & New York: Rodopi, 2013): 58.

becoming a spokesperson for the community when the time comes. The narrative thus celebrates the advent of a new era in which Coloureds can become socially visible and fulfill prominent social responsibilities which had formerly been denied to them.

Frikkie Jouvert is in some way Rebecca's counterpart. Like her, he left his birthplace and family in a desire to get as far away as possible from his father, in this case the Afrikaner landowner Hendrik Jouvert. Both in the social and in the private sphere, Jouvert is a resolute tyrant; the patriarchal model spanned the whole spectrum of South African society. However, Frikkie left his home town in a far more advantageous position than that of Rebecca, since he became part of the national rugby team, thus making his family and the whole of Vlenterhoek proud of his achievements. But Frikkie's fortune turned when he was shot in the knee in a violent attack in the street, after which he became a cripple, losing his privileged status. This shooting plays again as a metaphor for the doomed fate of his ethnicity and class in the new, post-apartheid South Africa; the vicious episode also illustrates the endemic state of violence still looming over the country and society. Humiliated after losing the full use of his leg, Frikkie at first rejects the idea of going back home to Vlenterhoek, choosing, like Rebecca, to remain in Cape Town. He doesn't return until thirteen years later, after the springs of healthy water have been discovered by two colleagues working for the same transnational company as himself. Frikkie immediately realizes the springs' huge economic potential, and becomes the company spokesperson. On the personal level, Frikkie's transformation and redemption is connected less to the figure of his father, as is the case with Rebecca, than to that of his former girlfriend, Suzette, who bore his child while he was absent and chose not to tell him. An astonished Frikkie learns of the existence of this child, his son, and will eventually decide to renew his relationship with Suzette. This process and gesture appear to suggest the need for the South African family-nation to be reassembled out of its fragments, and also the need for South Africans to assume responsibilities connected with their troubled past.

Rebecca's and Frikkie's personal transformations thus echo different aspects of the nation's dynamics, while that of Leah, the main character in the story, suggests the leap of the country into globalization, into a transnational world where nations can no longer be considered in isolation but, rather, need to be seen as part of an extended web of human, sociocultural, economic, and political global relations which have more prominence than they ever did in the past.

Leah's parents were two English immigrants who bore three daughters on South African soil. The youngest, Leah, was a beautiful and ambitious girl anxious to leave this stifling provincial town at any cost—a psychological pattern that we see repeated in several characters of the younger generation, especially young women, but also young men. In order to leave, Leah made the wrong decision (as it turned out) to marry an English engineer working at the same mining company as her father, and who was twice her age. She and her new husband first moved to Zimbabwe and then to other countries, before settling in Vancouver after he suffered a work accident which obliged him to retire. The novel begins years afterwards, after Leah has become a widow and is slowly finding her way around in her new status. Remarkably, she does not regret her husband's death at all. At this point we learn of the silent ordeal that living with that man for more than three decades has meant for this woman. Always mean and possessive, in the last years he had grown increasingly paranoid about any kind of social relation that Leah might entertain; quite irrationally, he refused to give her any money or food, which he kept hidden in remote parts of the house or on his person. He had not allowed Leah to travel to South Africa even for her parents' funeral. Their only child, Erica, had quit the family home as soon as she could, leaving Leah even more miserable. Leah is unforgiving—as her husband lies dying she whispers in his ear, "I hope you rot in hell, you bastard" (63), such is her resentment. Since he dies bankrupt, as a widow Leah is forced to build a new life from scratch, with only the support of the Canadian welfare system. All in all, Leah's experience points to the precariousness in the lives of women relegated to the domestic sphere, including those living in Western countries, who do not make a living by themselves yet whose function cannot be overlooked.

Not long after her husband's death, Leah meets DiDi, a thirteen-year-old girl who, a victim of abuse at home, left her family when she was ten and has lived in the street ever since. Slowly Leah overcomes DiDi's mistrust and wins her over, until DiDi starts living at her place more or less regularly. The two women create what can be called an affiliative type of family,[16] completely successful in replacing their respective miscarried familial relations. This new type of family can be connected to the imperatives of globalization, with the dispersion of once locally contained communities and the dissolution of traditional family values. A free woman, Leah can now make the longed-for trip to South Africa her husband would not allow. She even convinces DiDi to travel with her, feeling nervous about going back on a visit after all those years. The two women's arrival in Vlenterhoek will cause a commotion in the small town, particularly DiDi's bizarre looks and her streetwise idiom. A new sense of belonging in the world at large is embodied by this young Canadian woman, who for

---

16   Edward W. Said, *The World, The Text, and the Critic* (London: Faber & Faber, 1984): 19.

her part remains fascinated by the townspeople's provincialism. She becomes friends with the group of Rebecca's and Frikkie's younger siblings, a racially mixed small gang which it is easy to see as the ideal embodiment of the future South Africa.[17]

Although her visit to Vlenterhoek is a great source of joy for her, in the end Leah decides not to remain in South Africa, and she returns to Vancouver with DiDi. Leah embodies that contemporary South African subject whose sense of attachment to a particular place is unsteady, showing the "ambivalent affiliations" which Amin Malak has defined as "a diffuse loyalty that exceeds an attachment to a single territory, a weddedness to an idea of 'home' rather than to real places."[18] In the end, Leah resumes her transnational identity, acknowledging that she cannot remain in Vlenterhoek but that she does not fully belong in Vancouver either, and that both places are equally and extremely important for her.

Sociocultural Transformation: The Film Crew

Cultural change is bound to occur in one way or another in a world where transport and media have gained vertiginous speed and reach into every corner of the earth. The world is rapidly changing and South Africa is not left behind. Indeed, although Iain Chambers refers here to urban conglomerations of greater size than Vlenterhoek, his reflections on the rapid spread of what he terms "world culture" apply well to the changes that are about to occur in Vlenterhoek after the arrival in the area of the filmmakers' crew:

> Urban life is being transformed under the impact of a global formation. If we are to talk of globalism, it is a globalism which refers not only to the powers and movement of capital and the international division of labor, but also to institutions, relations and ideas.[19]

Circulating through these channels as if it were the blood of the social organism, culture is indeed the strong force capable of effecting mental opening

---

17   Karodia shows childhood as a period relatively free of (post-)apartheid restrictions in several works, most notably in *Boundaries* and in the long short story "Against an African Sky."

18   Amin Malak, "Ambivalent Affiliations and the Postcolonial Condition: The Fiction of M.G. Vassanji," *World Literature Today* 67.2 (Spring 1993): 242.

19   Iain Chambers, *Migrancy, Culture, Identity* (London & New York: Routledge, 1995): 109.

and precipitating social change. And cultural change is precisely what the town, like the nation, needs in order to move forward. Cultural change is the key to a shift in the people's attitudes, which is seen as imperative: "It was easy to legislate change, but it was not so easy to change attitudes and that was where the real challenge in the country lay" (82–83).

The arrival of the film crew in Vlenterhoek means that all the population has a chance to enjoy the possibilities offered by a multicultural society in miniature. This is a novelty, since although diversity runs deep in the making of South Africa, from the nation's inception in 1910 strong efforts have always been made to keep the different communities separate.[20] The sense of a gulf between the different groups has been embedded in the town psychology, where "the whole concept of hyphenating people was still an unknown phenomenon … people were either black or white" (29). The arrival of the film crew is an opportune reminder that we all "exist within an inter- and transnational system of differentiated but global reference,"[21] and as such it is remarkable that the film should be about a dancer of Indian origin who had managed to infuse in her art a number of heterogeneous influences, namely a fusion of "Gypsy, Rajastani and Middle Eastern traditional dance styles" (152). This dancer's artistic feat echoes the literary achievements of the author herself, Farida Karodia embodying the hybrid, diasporic, and transnational identity characteristic of contemporary global Indianness also explored in other chapters of this collection and in a number of critical studies elsewhere.[22]

There is no apparent reason for the film producers to choose to shoot some scenes in South Africa except for the seeming appropriateness of the landscape, which can yield the right colours in the film, and the economic advantage that shooting in this place might mean—a pecuniary resonance which should not go unnoticed in a work so concerned with the advent of globalization. In any event, as a sort of poetic counterpoise to the conventional and long-established separation of races in this part of the world, the film crew brings in not only a completely multicultural group of people but also an ideology of cultural blending more in tune with the contemporary world than the outdated views of the locals. This has an effect. The most ample example of

---

20   See, in this regard, Cynthia Lytle, "DeraciNation: Reading the Borderlands in the Fiction of Zoë Wicomb" (doctoral dissertation, University of Barcelona, 2015).

21   Chambers, *Migrancy, Culture, Identity*, 109.

22   See *Indian Writers: Transnationalisms and Diasporas*, ed. Jaspal K. Singh & Rajendra Chetty (New York: Peter Lang, 2010); *Indian Diaspora and Transnationalism*, ed. Ajaya Kumar Sahoo, Michiel Baas & Thomas Faist (New Delhi: Rawat, 2012) and *Global Indian Diaspora: History, Culture, and Identity*, ed. Ajaya Kumar Sahoo & Laxmi Narayan Kadekar (New Delhi: Rawat, 2012), among many.

this cultural—or ideological—evolution is provided by the change of attitude of an elderly lady who initially acts quite disgracefully. When the crew first arrive in the town, this woman bluntly refuses to hire her room to an African American man, simply because of his skin color. This may sound outrageous, yet it is not perceived as racist by most of the townspeople. Nevertheless, after the experience of living alongside the crew in the same locality, the second time the crew visits the city when the film is going to be premiered, the very same lady explicitly makes a telephone call to offer this black man a room in her house. Change on a small scale has been effected through mere human contact, and from now on it can only reverberate and grow. This is, however, not an entirely altruistic development: the locals are aware that their only way to escape economic stagnation is by opening themselves up to the world. And this necessitates readjustment toward difference and otherness, as entailed by impending globalization and the emerging transnational order.

The film premiere is an important occasion for the town's inhabitants—the vast majority—who attend it to sit and feel close to one another. This happens in the closing pages of the novel, and while they are indiscriminately applauding the accomplishment and gorgeous mise-en-scène of their place in the film, the implication is that they are actually celebrating their being together, symbolically leaving behind the long trail of apartheid, and their having been put "on the map" (273) together. A new epoch, open to change and to cultural and racial fusion, is thus felicitously inaugurated.

Economic Transformation: The Hemelslaagte Springs

As the socially conscious Rebecca reflects, "something had to be done to save the town. There were no industries to sustain it. Most of the people in the district were farmers and pensioners. Others worked as laborers or domestics. It was a pitiful situation" (240). The town is stagnating not only socially but also economically. Indeed, economic interest is the most prominent drive moving the narrative forward, since it is the need to expand the citizens' economic horizons that prompts the town clerk, Danie Venter, to visit Rebecca Fortuin in Cape Town, thus sparking her desire to return after all those years. It is also out of economic interest that Frikkie Jouvert returns after thirteen years, which he does in his capacity as representative of the powerful company intending to invest in the area. We have seen that both these characters have family feuds to resolve with their respective fathers, which they do by emulating the TRC in processes of forgiveness and reconciliation. But by going beyond the personal to enter the realm of financescapes, Rebecca and Frikkie position themselves very differently when economic transformation reaches Vlenterhoek through the commercialization of the Hemelslaagte water springs. Surely responding to their respective upbringing in apartheid South Africa, as a non-white and a white person respectively, Rebecca and Frikkie assume different and even opposite roles in the upcoming confrontation between interests of the company and the townspeople.

For one thing, Frikkie works for this transnational company, and it bears repeating that his interest in exploiting the springs is purely economic. He represents a neoliberal approach—he does not want to harm the community, if possible, but is not keen on shareholding at all. His conviction is that the professional management of this lucrative business by the company he is part of may, in the short and long term, be more profitable to the town's economy than any other possibility. This means that he is not keen on allowing the citizens to participate in such a lucrative business except as passive observers and, possibly, employees of some kind. By contrast, Rebecca is genuinely interested in improving the life conditions of the majority of the people, but not at the expense of their losing their agency and their decision-making capacity and rights, and she is ready to give up anything to achieve this end. Therefore, in alliance with Leah—who, crucially for the narrative, owns the last plot of land surrounding the springs and is, with her sisters, unwilling to sell—Rebecca will become the ordinary people's representative, strongly defending the principle that, if the springs are to be industrially exploited, as is the case and appears convenient, control of water production and distribution should remain, partially at least, in the hands of the community.

The tension between Frikkie and Rebecca's opposing attitudes with regard to this issue represents two different aspects of the Janus-faced processes of transnationalism. Globalization and transnationalism are in themselves politically ambiguous; it is the kind of practices deriving from them that shape different political positions. Indeed, on the one hand one might think that these processes open up new possibilities for most people, in the form of access ('access' being a crucial concept in our times) to information, travel, jobs, social relations, and organization—in a nutshell, the possibility of improving the economic well-being of the majority. This idea of redistribution would seem to go along with a necessary softening of oppressive ideologies such as homophobia or racism. Thus understood, globalization and the rapid increase of transnational processes would certainly point to processes of boundary weakening[23] which, all in all, should be generally welcome. On the other hand,

---

23   See Jan Neverdeen Pieterse, "Hybridity, So What?" *Theory, Culture & Society* 18.2–3 (2001): 219–245.

however, and on a more practical level, it is impossible not to acknowledge that this ideal redistribution and release of constrictive boundaries is far from being a reality, and that social and economic inequalities have actually been exacerbated with the advent of transnational practices and globalization. Thus, in themselves these labels remain politically empty, and can be used to various ends. As Smith and Guarnizo have warned,

> the liminal sites of transnational practices and discourses can be used for the purposes of capital accumulation quite as effectively as for the purpose of contesting hegemonic narratives of race, ethnicity, class and nation.[24]

Transnationalism, in fine, is neither good nor bad per se; it is the use we make of the advantages and disadvantages that accompany it that becomes decisive with regard to its ultimate benefit or damage.

In Vlenterhoek, once the bounty for human health of the Hemelslaagte Springs water is discovered, an unstoppable process of land commercialization begins. The company which employs Frikkie, IRH, later found to be a filial of American Resorts Inc., is said to be "an international company with vast holdings throughout the world" (254). When IRH starts buying all the terrain surrounding the springs, they do so in a very discreet manner, in a ghostly movement intended to forestall any early reaction on the part of the citizenry. This corresponds to what Smith and Guarnizo refer to as "transnationalism from above,"[25] including not only transnational companies but also global media and supranational political institutions. The category shows a type of transnationalism masterminded by a relatively small global group. The transnational practices derived from these institutions nonetheless impinge on people's individual lives; soon the area surrounding Vlenterhoek becomes full of signs reading "No trespassing" (152). This is a return of the old racial and class boundaries, now in the guise of unbounded transnational capitalism, which has the same effect as apartheid—the curtailing of people's freedom.

---

24   See Michael Peter Smith & Luis Eduardo Guarnizo, "The Locations of Transnationalism," in *Transnationalism From Below*, ed. Michael Peter Smith & Luis Eduardo Guarnizo (New Brunswick NJ: Transaction, 1998): 3–31. As these scholars remark, the political nature of globalization is not always evident: there are minority groups which do not necessarily resist the economic order of the world, even if they may represent minorities disrupting the 'grand narratives' of the nation-state.

25   Smith & Guarnizo, "The Locations of Transnationalism."

This example goes to show that we should not speak of transnationalism as something aseptic or ethereal, at a distance from real human lives and needs. On the contrary, transnational practices frequently impinge materially on people's daily existence, often resonating with other types of oppression.

The establishment of a tourist health resort or spa intended to exploit the springs eventually meets with resistance, however. On the very day construction work is begun, Leah suddenly decides to throw herself on the ground to obstruct the IRH bulldozers' progress. She is immediately followed in her heroic gesture by DiDi, Rebecca, and a handful of other women. Eventually, all the people gathered for the event become engaged in the confrontation with the intrusive bulldozers, and succeed in stopping them. This turn of events illustrates what Smith and Guarnizo refer to as transnationalism "from below," and which involves local forms of resistance to the abuses of transnational capitalism, in the informal economy, through ethnic nationalism, and through grassroots activism. The community's resistance succeeds in halting the works, in an unexpected tour de force which encapsulates a whole global tendency whereby a *politics of place* is put into practice, one that, while recognizing the formal diversity of globalization, proposes alternative forms of understanding it.[26] The novelty resides in seeing place and the local as invested with power to confront the global, and as a refusal to be merely its passive recipients.[27]

We can hardly ignore the fact that it is a group of women who spark this rebellion 'from below' against the indiscriminate forces of globalization as well as against transnationalism 'from above.' As Arturo Escobar and Wendy Harcourt contend,

> In rethinking political responses to modernity and global capitalism it is important to build on the creativity, knowledge and experience of women's groups engaged in place-based politics.[28]

Indeed, emphasized in the story is the paramount role of women and of a specifically female sensibility (but in no way exclusive to women) in confronting modes that are associated with practices that are conventionally male, hierarchical, segregative, and/or exploitative.

---

26   Wendy Harcourt & Arturo Escobar, "Women and the Politics of Place," *Development* 45.1 (March 2002): 8.

27   María Angélica Garzón, "El lugar como política y las políticas de lugar: Herramientas para pensar el lugar," *Signo y Pensamiento* 27/53 (2008): 102.

28   Harcourt & Escobar, "Women and the Politics of Place," 13.

> The conflicts that women are experiencing within the different domains
> (body, home, environment and social public space) usher in new forms
> of cultural and political relations.[29]

In this way, Leah sets an example of a proactive attitude through her renun-
ciation of a life of subservience to a tyrant husband, a sea-change that started
with her emotional adoption of DiDi and her decision to return to South Africa.
Leah's gradual rejection of passive acceptance becomes plainly evident in her
courageous initiative against the bulldozers at this later point in her life, a gesture which manages both to symbolically redress the systematic oppression
she silently accepted through her married life and to stop an insidious abuse
of the Vlenterhoek people's rights. Through her act of defiance, Leah gains
political and economic control of her future; thanks to this timely intervention, the locals will eventually succeed, as had been Rebecca's purpose, in gaining access to the shareholding benefits of the commercial exploitation of the
springs. Thus Leah becomes part of a contingent of women who, "as actors in
their own lives," are "working together towards greater equity, respecting and
working with cultural and other differences."[30] Through Leah's, Rebecca's, and
the other women's impulse to risk their lives against the impending menace of
a grim type of transnationalism imposed 'from above,' the whole set of male
neoliberal values represented by Frikkie and IRH is challenged, to be replaced
by more respectful and less hierarchical and oppressive systems of resource
exploitation, wealth distribution, and social relations.

Conclusion

Through the political intervention initiated by the Vlenterhoek women, this
Eastern Cape South African town definitely loses its provincial character, to
become what could be called a 'glocality' in the sense established by Harcourt
and Escobar, who explain that "glocalities are simultaneously global and place-
based, and their specific configuration will depend on their cultural content as
well as on the power dynamics at play."[31] These scholars go on to define these
places as rife with political potential:

---

29   "Women and the Politics of Place," 13.
30   Harcourt & Escobar, "Women and the Politics of Place," 13.
31   "Women and the Politics of Place," 13.

Glocalities ought to be understood as descriptive of all places because today no place is constituted wholly by local or global factors. At the same time glocal spaces, understood as strategic, have tremendous potential as a base for new and transformative politics and identities. Glocalities, the places and spaces produced by the linking together of various social movements in networks [...], or by the connection of places to global processes, are therefore both strategic and descriptive, potentially oppressive and potentially transformative.[32]

Such is the case with Vlenterhoek, which acts as a site of oppression where different types of boundaries still hold sway yet provide hitherto unexplored possibilities for transformation. Indeed, the specific political configuration of Vlenterhoek and its connection to the long-lasting, harmful regime of apartheid, whose deep influence will not vanish overnight, cannot be disregarded. Rather, throughout the narrative, slow processes of post-apartheid transformation are seen to be taking place all around, which gradually make the old town values and prejudices disappear, making room for new social configurations. It is not by chance that the aged lady displayed in the news media as an example of good health and a lure for potential investors should die by the end of the novel. Her passing away symbolizes the death of an epoch, and consequently the birth of a different time: "Life as the residents of Vlenterhoek had known it –for better or worse– was never to be the same again. Their sleepy little town had finally come of age" (279).

The resentments of apartheid are slowly subsiding, as seen, among other examples, in the reconciliation of Rebecca and Frikkie with their respective fathers, and the complex processes of mutual forgiveness-cum-redemption they undergo. Responsibilities connected with past wrongs are also being accepted, as demonstrated by Frikkie's acknowledgment of Martin, his illegitimate son by Suzette, and by Hendrick Joubert's final tacit admission that he was responsible for murdering Ivan, his own Coloured son whom he had refused to acknowledge. More generally, the social mores and cultural values are changing, albeit slowly; the stark racism and rejection of cohabitation that were the infamous mark of apartheid are being left behind, in an unstoppable march towards the future hastened, in the case of this particular glocality, by the providential visit of the multiracial film crew. Last but not least, not only socially and culturally but also economically the town, an epitome of the South African nation, is seen to be entering the ranks of transnationalism and globalization.

---

32   "Women and the Politics of Place," 13.

Against apolitical understandings of current global processes, through the character of Leah and the kind of transnationalism that she introduces in the narrative, Karodia makes effective a critique of watered-down, politically empty understandings of globalization and transnational practice and foregrounds instead what Jan Nederveen Pieterse has termed 'critical globalism': i.e. the acknowledgment that since globalization is here to stay and we cannot overlook it, precisely for this reason we should critically engage with globalization processes, "neither blocking them out nor celebrating them, but being alert to their evolution and being critical of them."[33] The transnational connections which affect life in Vlenterhoek take on different dimensions: individual and strongly personal, cultural, and ideological, economic, and definitely political. The novel finally demonstrates the claim by Escobar and Harcourt that qualifies the systematization provided by Smith and Guarnizo: namely, the suggestion that "globalization does not really happen 'from above' or 'from below,' but always 'in between.'"[34]

In sum, Karodia's novel foregrounds "the value of imaginative writing as a site of discursive resistance to authoritarian attitudes and practices."[35] In this particular case, the authoritarian attitudes and practices emanate, on the one hand, from the resilient remnants of apartheid and, on the other, from careless neoliberal policies which allow invasive and harming transnational capitalist practices.

Works Cited

Appadurai, Arjun. "Disjuncture and Difference in the Global Cultural Economy" (1999), in *Theorizing Diaspora: A Reader*, ed. Jana Evans Braziel & Anita Mannur (London: Blackwell, 2006): 27–48.

Chambers, Iain. *Migrancy, Culture, Identity* (London & New York: Routledge, 1995).

Davis, Emily S. "New Directions in Post-Apartheid South African Fiction and Scholarship," *Literature Compass* 10.10 (2013): 797–804.

---

33   Jan Nederveen Pieterse, "Development of development theory towards critical globalism," ISS *Working Papers* (1995), http://EconPapers.repec.org/RePEc:ems:euriss:18935 (accessed 13 August 2015).

34   Harcourt & Escobar, "Women and the Politics of Place," 13.

35   Graham Huggan, "'Greening' Postcolonialism: Ecocritical Perspectives" (2004), in *Literature and Globalization: A Reader*, ed. Liam Connell & Nicky Marsh (London & New York: Routledge, 2011): 171.

De Kock, Leon. "Does South African Literature Still Exist? Or: South African Literature is Dead, Long Live Literature in South Africa," *English in Africa* 32.2 (2005): 69–83.

Frenkel, Ronit. *Reconsiderations: South African Indian Fiction and the Making of Race in Postcolonial Culture* (Pretoria: U of South Africa P, 2010).

Garzón, María Angélica. "El lugar como política y las políticas de lugar: Herramientas para pensar el lugar," *Signo y Pensamiento* 27/53 (2008): 92–103.

Govinden, Devarakshanam Betty. "Healing the Wounds of History: South African Indian Writing," *Current Writing* 21.1–2 (2009): 287–302.

Harcourt, Wendy, & Arturo Escobar. "Women and the Politics of Place," *Development* 45.1 (March 2002): 7–14.

Held, David, Anthony McGrey David Goldblatt & Jonathan Perraton. *Global Transformations: Politics, Economics and Culture* (Cambridge: Polity, 1999).

Helff, Sissy. *Unreliable Truths: Transcultural Homeworlds in Indian Women's Fiction of the Diaspora* (Cross/Cultures 155; Amsterdam & New York: Rodopi, 2013).

Hofmeyr, Isabel, & Liz Gunner. "Introduction: Transnationalism and African Literature," *Scrutiny2* 10.2 (2005): 3–14.

Huggan, Graham. "'Greening' Postcolonialism: Ecocritical Perspectives" (2004), in *Literature and Globalization: A Reader*, ed. Liam Connell & Nicky Marsh (London & New York: Routledge, 2011): 171–176.

Karodia, Farida. *Against an African Sky and Other Stories* (Cape Town: David Philip, 1995).

Karodia, Farida. *Boundaries* (Cape Town: Penguin, 2003a).

Karodia, Farida. *A Shattering of Silence* (London: Heinemann, 2003b).

Kumar Sahoo, Ajaya, Michiel Baas & Thomas Faist, ed. *Indian Diaspora and Transnationalism* (New Delhi: Rawat, 2012).

Kumar Sahoo, Ajaya, and Laxmi Narayan Kadekar, ed. *Global Indian Diaspora: History, Culture, and Identity* (New Delhi: Rawat, 2012).

Lytle, Cynthia. "DeraciNation: Reading the Borderlands in the Fiction of Zoë Wicomb" (doctoral dissertation, University of Barcelona, 2015), http://www.tdx.cat/bitstream/handle/10803/285583/Cynthia_Lytle_THESIS.pdf?sequence=1 (accessed 13 August 2015).

Malak, Amin. "Ambivalent Affiliations and the Postcolonial Condition: The Fiction of M.G. Vassanji," *World Literature Today* 67.2 (Spring 1993): 277–282.

Ndebele, Njabulo S. "The Rediscovery of the Ordinary: Some New Writings in South Africa," *Journal of Southern African Studies* 12.2 (1986): 143–157.

Pieterse, Jan Nederveen. "Development of development theory towards critical globalism," *ISS Working Papers* (1995), http://EconPapers.repec.org/RePEc:ems:euriss:18935 (accessed 13 August 2015).

Pieterse, Jan Nederveen. "Hybridity, So What?" *Theory, Culture & Society* 18.2–3 (2001): 219–245.

Said, Edward W. *The World, The Text, and the Critic* (London: Faber & Faber, 1984).

Singh, Jaspal K., & Rajendra Chetty, ed. *Indian Writers: Transnationalisms and Diasporas* (New York: Peter Lang, 2010).

Smelser, Neil J. "Social Transformations and Social Change," *International Social Science Journal* 156 (1998): 173–178.

Smith, Michael Peter, & Luis Eduardo Guarnizo. "The Locations of Transnationalism," in *Transnationalism From Below*, ed. Michael Peter Smith & Luis Eduardo Guarnizo (New Brunswick NJ: Transaction, 1998): 3–31.

Samuelson, Meg. "Scripting Connections: Reflections on the 'Post-Transitional'," *English Studies in Africa* 53.1 (2010): 113–117.

Vertovec, Steven. *Transnationalism* (London & New York: Routledge, 2009).

CHAPTER 7

At the Crossroads of Nowhere and Everywhere

Home, Nation, and Space in Shamim Sarif's The World Unseen

Esther Pujolràs-Noguer

Border Space, Diaspora Space, and Cartographies of Desire

Set in the early 1950s, Shamim Sarif's *The World Unseen*, published in 2001, invites the reader to witness the devastating effects of a national territory *perfectly* compartmentalized into racial spaces. As a consequence of the institutionalization of apartheid in 1948 and the Population Registration Act of 1950, the South African space became a network of racial boundaries where whites, Indians, Coloureds, and blacks—these were the formalized racial groups—had to, paradoxically, cohabit separately. But what did apartheid and the Population Registration Act of 1950 mean in terms of 'nation building'? Or, to put it differently, what kind of nation was imagined–to use Benedict Anderson's terminology–under apartheid?[1]

I claim that the national space imagined under apartheid laws was a 'border space'—the national territory that is configured as a consequence of internal colonialism. The nation that results from this internal colonialism is imagined as essentially 'white,' simultaneously instituting 'whiteness' as the norm and relegating the non-white to the category of deviations. If 'white' is constituted as the self, then what follows is that non-white ethnicities are assigned the label 'Other,' but in internal colonialism, this 'Other' is, ironically, also an intrinsic and, I would add, intimate component of the nation. As Avtar Brah notes, borders, in general, are imbued with an inner sense of contradiction, since their agonizing will to prohibit hides, in truth, an appetite for transgression where, in the fear of the Other, there abides a fear of the self.[2] Henceforth, in the border space concretized as apartheid South Africa, the level of intimacy reached by the prohibition/transgression, self/Other dyads produces geographical demarcations that are social and cultural dividing lines and which are subjected to a consistent psychic tension, creating national

---

1 See Benedict Anderson, *Imagined Communities: Reflections on the Origin and Spread of Nationalism* (London: Verso, 1983).

2 See Avtar Brah, *Cartographies of Diaspora: Contesting Identities* (London & New York: Routledge, 1996): 198.

paranoia. However, it is Brah's provocative connection between borders and metaphors that I find particularly engaging in an analysis of border space. In her own words:

> Borders are arbitrary constructions. Hence, in a sense, they are always metaphors. But, far from being mere abstractions of a concrete reality, metaphors are part of the discursive materiality of power relations. Metaphors can serve as powerful inscriptions of the effects of political borders.[3]

Therefore, following Brah, I propose a reading of Sarif's *The World Unseen* geared to an understanding of borders or, to be more precise, of border space, as a metaphorical inscription. As befits such an inscription, the text is built upon the arbitrariness of borders, and so it is eager to disclose 'the world unseen'—the acts of trespass lurking behind the prohibitions set up by the law, the Other that surreptitiously but confidently defines its stature as self. In the world depicted in Sarif's text, it is clear that metaphors, in their condition as discursive participants in the game of power relations, can serve as potent inscriptions of the effects of political borders; also, I argue, they can forge a site of contention where the arbitrariness of borders is brought to the fore.

The World Unseen is conceived as an act of memory. Sarif is a British citizen, currently based in London, whose South African Indian heritage stands at the core of her narrative. The world she recovers in her novel is a compendium of stories told to her by her family. Thus, to the border space concept previously delineated, I would add Brah's 'diaspora space,' one in which multiple journeys converge into one journey "via a *confluence of narratives* as it is lived and re-lived, produced and reproduced and transformed through individual as well as collective memory and re-memory."[4] Crucial to the specific history—and, therefore, narrative—of the South African Indian diaspora is the notion of 'Indianness.' Considering how, as Brah suggests, the concepts of "border and diaspora reference a politics of location,"[5] two interrelated questions arise: (1) where is 'Indianness' to be situated in this narrative, this act of memory, that unites past and present, apartheid and post-apartheid South Africa, home and homeland?, and (2) how does *The World Unseen* contribute to configuring the New South Africa? At the intersection of the above questions, there surfaces an interrelated concern: namely, how race, nation, gender, and sexuality are

---

3 Brah, *Cartographies of Diaspora*, 198.
4 *Cartographies of Diaspora*, 183; italics in original.
5 *Cartographies of Diaspora*, 204.

reconceptualized in the New South Africa. It all seems to indicate "the inherent blurring of boundaries" that Frenkel acknowledges as a common trait of South African Indian fiction.[6] This blurring of boundaries, this border-crossing, engenders a space which, I claim, is generated, following the work of the geographer Doreen Massey, in relational terms.

Massey's conceptualization of 'space' originates as a reaction to the understanding of time and space which sustains traditional geography. In the latter, time, as Massey points out, is equated with movement and progress, whereas space is apprehended as stasis and reaction. This division of time and space, on the one hand, and the equation time=movement / space=stasis, on the other, give rise to a definition of a sense of place, of belonging, of rootedness which is constructed upon the notions of 'stability' and 'unproblematical identity.'[7] When 'nation' is understood as a geographical, cultural, economic, political, and linguistic reality, we assume that stability and identity purport this space. And yet, when 'race' enters this national reality, as is the case of South Africa, the notions of 'stability' and 'unproblematical identity' are unceremoniously destabilized and problematized.

Massey proposes a reexamination of space and time based on the inseparability of both terms, thus contradicting the uncontested belief held in the field of geography which conceives of space and time as separate entities. As she quietly puts it, "space and time are inextricably interwoven."[8] Undoubtedly influenced by Einstein's theory of relativity, Massey advocates for an underlying reality which consists in a four-dimensional space-time in clear opposition to the three-dimensional space and one-dimensional time that a traditional perspective supports. This four-dimensional space-time does not preclude a disappearance of space and time as independent entities; rather, it calls for a treatment of space and time as mutually dependent even if this dependence is felt as frictional. In Massey's own words:

> It is not that we cannot make any distinction at all between them but that the distinction we do make needs to hold the two in tension, and to do so within an overall, and strong, concept of four-dimensionality.[9]

---

6 See Ronit Frenkel, "Reconsidering South African Indian Fiction Postapartheid," *Research in African Literatures* 42.3 (Fall 2011): 2. See also Ronit Frenkel, *Reconsiderations: South African Indian Fiction and the Making of Race in Postcolonial Culture* (Pretoria: U of South Africa P, 2011): 1.

7 Doreen Massey, *Space, Place and Gender* (Cambridge: Polity, 1994): 151.

8 Massey, *Space, Place and Gender*, 152.

9 *Space, Place and Gender*, 261.

The consequence of envisaging space-time as inseparable, mutually dependent entities—even if in tension—forming a four-dimensionality is that space can no longer be sustained as absolute, in tune with stasis, but relational and therefore in tune with movement. Space is delineated by social relations and because of this, space cannot be static; it is necessarily dynamic in its very inception, not perceived as an appendage of time, but *in* time. What follows is Massey's definition of space:

> Space is not a 'flat' surface in that sense because the social relations which create it are themselves dynamic by their very nature. It is a question of a manner of thinking. It is not the 'slice through time' which should be the dominant thought but the simultaneous coexistence of social relations that cannot be conceptualized as other than dynamic. Moreover, and again as a result of the fact that it is conceptualized as created out of social relations, *space is by its very nature full of power and symbolism, a complex web of relations of domination and subordination, of solidarity and co-operation.*[10]

This powerful and symbolic space woven from relations of domination and subordination, solidarity and co-operation, a space that lurks behind the static national demarcations of apartheid, is none other than the space captured textually in *The World Unseen* and laid out by cartographies of desire. Recognition of this space both acknowledges and reinforces the defiant mappings of desire unveiled by queer theory. Sarif's novel invokes 'desire' as a strategic tool with which to discursively counter the national space of apartheid South Africa.

This relational space is arranged around the relationship between Amina and Miriam. Love, in its most metaphorical sense, and not for this reason any less powerful, is the weapon employed to initiate border crossing. Their relationship is the vortex of this particular cartography of desire which will orchestrate the other love stories, racial border-crossings. From Amina, there issues forth the story of Jacob and Miss Smith, a Coloured man and a white woman, and from Miriam, the story of Rehmat and James, an Indian woman and a white man, on the one hand, and of Jehan, an Indian woman, with an unnamed black man, on the other. The lines that divide and secure blackness, whiteness, and Indianness are systematically menaced by love relationships that persistently cross racial barriers, hence undermining the border space that frames the nation. What is interesting to highlight is how these racial border-crossing stories emanate from a gender border-crossing story, thus allowing homoeroticism

---

10   Massey, *Space, Place and Gender,* 265; italics mine.

to enter this relationally constructed narrative. To add yet another layer of nuance to this 'world unseen,' the cartography of desire that Amina and Miriam reproduce is located within the parameters of 'Indianness.' Hence, not only does Amina and Miriam's cartography of desire challenge the South African border space but it also queries the closed-in character of 'Indianness.' Nevertheless, the ultimate question emerging from Amina and Miriam's cartography of desire is connected to their capacity to transform the border space of apartheid South Africa into a 'home.' Taking into account that 'home' is a discourse organized in terms of 'inclusion' and 'exclusion,' and that any diaspora entails a 'homing desire,' Amina's overtly feminist agency and Miriam's more attenuated one, should be inscribed as an expressive moment of belonging, as a significant episode in the nation-building project of the New South Africa.[11] Their own border-crossing experience—same-sex desire—demands to be recorded alongside the other racial border-crossing experiences that emanate from them, and accounted for as indispensable chapters for understanding the challenge posed by the Rainbow Nation.

Female Genealogies: Beyond Violence and Blood

The World Unseen is eminently a text en-gendered under the unique parameter of hope; Amina and Miriam's desires are orchestrated by an inveterate optimism to move beyond survival. But the grammar of hope of *The World Unseen* is concurrently encapsulated in a grammar of violence. How the great destructive energy that permeates Sarif's text is utilized *productively* to engender a cartography of desire wherein love is nurtured constitutes, to my mind, the narrative ethos of *The World Unseen*. The violence that initiates the world unseen and gives rise to the narrative is the one perpetrated against Begum,

---

11   See Rosemary Marangoly George, *The Politics of Home: Postcolonial Relocations and Twentieth-Century Fiction* (Berkeley: U of California P, 1996). In *Cartographies of Diaspora*, Brah, from the perspective of diaspora studies, offers an approach to 'home' that is very similar to that elicited by George, who affirms that "the question of home [...] is intrinsically linked with the way in which processes of inclusion and exclusion operate." She also pinpoints how home and belonging are constituent of the diasporic condition, which, in its turn, operates under the auspices of a 'homing desire,' whereby 'home' is imagined as a mythic place of desire, not to be confused with a desire for a 'homeland.' I believe that Amina and Miriam's ambivalent relationship with their alleged motherland, India, and South Africa, and their capacity to move beyond the national constraints of Indian and South African citizenship, should be registered as an instantiation of 'homing desire.' See Avtar Brah, *Cartographies of Diaspora*, 190–197.

Amina's grandmother, whose picture proudly presides over the Corner Café—
Amina's and Jacob's property[12]—stubbornly resisting the invisibility the Indian
community has woven around her.

That Begum stands as a target of violence is evinced in the very first pages
of the novel when, upon the violent intrusion of the white officers into the
Corner Café, Amina notices with chagrin how her grandmother's photograph
has been broken, "the familiar defiance in her grandmother's eyes distorted by
a crack."[13] Of all the manifestations of violence on the part of the white officers
aimed at distorting the racial borderless space of the Corner Café—blacks,
Coloureds, and Indians are allowed to eat together—by forcing the national
law upon it, the smashing of her grandmother's photo is what "hurt her most"
(7). Hence, the intimate connection between Amina and Begum governs the
whole narrative, embracing Miriam in its textual space and forming a triangu-
lar structure whose nexus—Begum, Amina, and Miriam—configures a female
genealogy which manages to create a sense of family out of sheer violence. But
who is Begum and what does she represent in this South African tale?

Begum arrives in South Africa in the 1890s to be married off to a wealthy
South African Indian. Young, innocent, submissive, self-effacing, and "a prized
asset" (137) because of her fair skin, Begum embodies the perfect Indian wife
while simultaneously enduring the devastating effects of such idealization; all
emotional attachment to her new family—her in-laws and her husband—is
erased for the sake of blind obedience and even fear.[14] This is the reason why,
when she is raped by one of the black workers of the family, she resorts to
silence, for she dreads her in-laws' reaction to this sexual assault. The silence
with which she carefully encloses her rape is ruthlessly unveiled by the birth of
her second child, a girl whose curly hair and dark skin menacingly jeopardize
the paternity of Begum's husband. The condemnation of Begum on the part of
her family and, by extension, the whole Indian community is conveyed through
silence. She is never given the opportunity to render her own account of the
incident; instead, she is severely wounded, "beaten senseless by her in-laws"

---

12   Jacob is Amina's Coloured business partner and a very good friend of hers.

13   Shamim Sarif, *The World Unseen* (2001; Los Angeles: Enlightenment Press, 2009): 7. Fur-
      ther page references are in the main text.

14   The idealization of Indian womanhood has been steadily analyzed and questioned in
      works of literary criticism, such as Jasbir Jain, *Writing Women Across Centuries* (New
      Delhi: Rawat, 2002), and Felicity Hand, "Shaking off Sharam: the Double Burden of British
      Asian Women," in *On Writing (and) Race in Contemporary Britain*, ed. Fernando Galván
      & Mercedes Bengoechea (Alcalá de Henares: Universidad de Alcalá, 1999): 133–138. For a
      sociological perspective on the topic, see Jyoti Puri, *Woman, Body, Desire in Post-Colonial
      India: Narratives of Gender and Sexuality* (London & New York: Routledge, 1999).

(142), and "sent home in disgrace to her family in India" (142). To top it all, she was only "nineteen years old, and all acceptable avenues to a normal, respectable life were now closed to her forever" (142). The violence inflicted on Begum is physical and affective; her back was injured as a consequence of the beating, her bones forever "misshapen" and "bruised" (16), and her memories "battered" (16) by the memory of how her husband, at the railway station, tricked her into leaving her eldest son behind in South Africa.

The situation, in detail, is as follows. Begum, determined to take her eldest son along with her and her daughter to India, engages in a fierce struggle with her in-laws, who want to keep her son with them, until they finally give in to her demands. However, what Begum did not know was that her husband's family had devised a stratagem to keep her son with them. On the day of her departure, while she is already on the train, her husband, standing on the platform, asks her to hand the boy down "so he could kiss him goodbye" (143). Begum agrees, but as "the train was quickening over the track" (144), her husband's grip on the boy tightens and she is forced to release him. Everyone on the station "could hear the screams of the woman on board the train even after it was long out of sight" (144).

Condemnation, Judith Butler observes incisively, "becomes the way in which we establish the Other as nonrecognizable," thus plunging otherness into invisibility and inflicting violence "upon the condemned in the name of 'ethics'."[15] Begum is unmercifully condemned on grounds of her impure, unfemale, un-Indian nature and she must face the ultimate, terrible consequence of condemnation which is formulated as an annihilation of the Other, destroying "the conditions of autonomy" and eroding their "capacity for both self-reflection and social recognition."[16] If the Other is annihilated, its subjectivity does not have to be addressed. Violently condemned though she is, Begum is not annihilated: she is iconically recovered, and her subjectivity addressed, through her granddaughter, Amina, who proudly re-hangs her photo, "carefully mounted and framed" (103), in the Corner Café for everybody to see.

Silenced by both her own family and the Indian community at large, Begum nonetheless learns to articulate her story and pass it on to Amina, instilling in her the knowledge she violently experienced, planting in her the seed of independence and freedom that she herself failed to achieve:

> Amina had learned much from Begum, most of it knowledge or advice that few other women of her grandmother's age had dared to even

---

15   Judith Butler, "Giving an Account of Oneself," *Diacritics* 31.4 (Winter 2001): 31.
16   "Giving an Account of Oneself," 31.

learn themselves, much less impart to an impressionable young girl. Her maternal grandmother spoke to her of pride, of self-reliance, and of courage. These were the things to cultivate, she had told her granddaughter, and not a slavish attitude to duties and traditions that were built on subservience and pain and fear.

> *The World Unseen*, 16

Indeed, Amina's behavior reveals how profoundly she has taken her grandmother's advice, how "entirely lacking in any semblance of the expected attributes of docility and self-effacement" (18) she was. Contravening the Indian female dress code, she wears trousers, she is financially independent, and she refuses to get married; what is more, as Miriam insightfully remarks, she seems to wield power "over those around her" (32). In other words, Amina is forcefully and, regrettably, visible. The Indian community both enjoys and resents Amina's entrepreneurship; after all, there is some particularly Indian trait in her commercial impulse, though, unfortunately, her gender is apprehended as an obstacle to business acumen. Not surprisingly, it is Miriam who best captures Amina's ambivalent status in the Indian community:

> Miriam knew of her, of course; everybody did. For despite her lack of conformity, she was still Indian, still a very young unmarried girl, and her seemingly unlimited freedom and lack of concern for propriety was of great concern to everyone in the Asiatic Bazaar. Her way of dressing, the fact that she had just opened up her own business ('with a Coloured man'), even Begum's photograph hanging proudly in the café—all these facts only fed the interest of those around her. They were appalled and horrified and shocked, but many began to patronize her café because they liked the food, they liked the atmosphere, and they liked the prices.
>
> *The World Unseen*, 28

Nevertheless, Begum has not only bequeathed a fiercely independent spirit to Amina, but also a racial stain that, unlike her own mother, Mrs. Harjan,[17] and very much like her grandmother, she wears with naturalness, dignity, and defiance, thus rejecting its seemingly polluting nature. Once again, it is in Begum's

---

17   Amina's mother resents her hybridity and blames Begum for ruining her life and growing up as an "outcast that nobody wanted" (68). She believes that Begum has also ruined Amina with "her talk of bravery and being smart and looking after yourself" (69). Curiously enough, it is Amina's father who empathizes with his mother-in-law and respects her wish never to return to South Africa while she is still alive.

photograph displayed at the Corner Café that Amina deliberately threatens and, consequently questions, 'Indianness' by granting visibility to this beautiful young woman who protectively holds a little girl with curly hair whose skin is some shades darker than hers. On first contemplating the photo, Miriam's perceptive eyes capture the audacity so adamantly exhibited by this young woman, although only later will she be able to associate the young woman and little girl with Amina, acknowledging her—Amina's—inherited "blackness":

> The setting of the photograph suggested that she was in India, and beside her stood a little girl with cropped curly hair, solemn and sad, barely looking into the camera lens at all. The woman—the child's mother, Miriam presumed—had no such compunction, and stared at those who passed by her photograph with an air that was almost defiant. She was very beautiful and her figure was slender, but she did not stand up straight; she leaned on a chair back with one hand, the other arm held protectively round the little girl.
>
> *The World Unseen*, 103

Amina and Miriam disembark in Durban in the same year, 1946, amidst the political turbulence caused by the Ghetto Bill and the ensuing protests on the part of the Indian Congress. As a seventeen-year-old arriving in South Africa with her family, consisting only of her father and mother, Amina is impressed by the activism exhibited by the Indian community, as is Miriam, a young wife who, like Begum, is taken to South Africa after her marriage to a South African Indian, Omar. Both Amina and Miriam share an instinctive excitement at the new life opening up for them in this new country, and yet, at the same time, they abhor its "terrible new laws" (131) that "take back land from people just because they [are] Indian and not White" (131). However, whereas adolescent Amina assumes an active role, participating in the demonstrations, Miriam adopts the position of a distant observer. Despite the restrictive legislation, Amina does not glance back at India as the forsaken homeland but instead sees South Africa as *her* "new country" (131), *her* "new world" (131), in contrast to the overwhelming homesickness that enfolds Miriam, who cannot imagine "why [her] husband had brought [her] to such a place" (131). As the submissive, self-effacing Indian wife that she represents, she is enslaved to a staggering passivity that stands in clear opposition to the unrelenting agency that envelops Amina. How is it possible for these two plainly divergent women to delineate *their* distinctive cartography of desire under the constraints imposed on them by both the Indian community and the South African national landscape?

Sarif's narrative is sensitively drawing a link between Begum and Miriam; their respective arrivals in South Africa are due to their arranged marriages, their husbands and in-laws treat them as subservient servants, loneliness and silence encircle their existence, and violence is a menacing presence both *outside*—due to apartheid laws—and *inside* the family environment. Miriam is informed by Farah, her abusive sister-in-law, that Jehan, Omar's mad sister, had once dated a black man, a "*kaffir*" (41), a relationship that ended when "the men in the family caught him and almost beat the life out of him" (41). Worse still is the violence vented upon Miriam's other sister-in-law, Rehmat, who was brutally whipped by her own father when he learned of her relationship with James, a white man. Henceforth, the grammar of violence that unstrings the harmony of Begum's life story seems also to govern Miriam's personal experience in South Africa, but, luckily for her, Amina comes to her rescue. Just as Begum *liberates* Amina from a life of subordination, so does Amina *liberate* Miriam from the prospects of such a life. The heteropatriarchal design that institutionalizes violence against women is implacably exposed when Amina tells Miriam the story of Begum. The unveiling of Begum's story forges a female genealogy that demands reassessment of 'blood' relations. Webster's Dictionary defines 'blood' as "parental heritage," "descent from nobility, from pure-bred stock," hence unleashing the patriarchal constitution of the concept. Behind the words 'nobility' and 'pure-bred stock' resides an indubitable desire to preserve the purity of the parental heritage in the event that this heritage is endangered. If women pollute the purity of the paternal heritage through their liaisons with non-Indian men, it is the task of Indian men to restore purity to the paternal heritage by chastizing and silencing them. The sadness, cruelty, and injustice that surround Begum's story draw Amina and Miriam together. Begum's story is Sarif's narrative mechanism to challenge conservative—read: patriarchal—perspectives on 'blood' relations by proposing a female genealogy grounded in empathy and affection that transcends familial ties. In truth, Miriam's family does not assuage but, on the contrary, intensifies her loneliness. As she despondently remarks, "no one had smiled at her for ten whole days" (23), until she goes to the Corner Café and Amina generously smiles at her, hence relieving her homesickness. A grateful Miriam realizes that "her ten days of counting, of watching for some sign of concern or pleasure or kindness, had finally ended with the smile Amina Harjan had given her" (33).

Amina's power resides in her capacity to transform the racial and gender violence that dominates the national South African geography into Massey's relational space, epitomized in the novel by the Corner Café. Not in vain, it is to the Corner Café that Rehmat runs in her escape from the police. Due to the Prohibition of Mixed Marriages Act (1949) and the Immorality Act (1950),

Rehmat's marriage to James, even though they live in Paris and are simply visit-ing South Africa, is nonetheless treated as a criminal offense. They have to flee the country to avoid imprisonment.[18] It is also in the Corner Café that Miss Smith and Jacob can freely interact; in a place where, echoing Miss Smith, "we are all of us losing our dignity as human beings" (230), the café offers them a space where their dignity as human beings can be safeguarded.[19]

Nevertheless, the question of how Amina succeeds in creating this relation-al space out of this border space remains as yet unanswered. I would argue that this question cannot be answered unless another is formulated: what does South Africa offer Amina that India denied her? There is a South Africa that lies beneath the national geography and which is identified as its landscape. The South African landscape provides Amina with the freedom and indepen-dence that will permit her subjectivity to flourish. Her first glimpse of South Africa already suggests that it is the landscape that infuses her spirit with the liberty and absence of restraint she needs and which India, immersed in its social conventionalities, persistently denies her:

> On the morning that they had docked she had stood almost alone on the upper deck at daybreak, and had watched the coastline rise up from nowhere, out of the ocean, as clean and as bright as the edges of a map, and she smiled to see it. She could make out little then except the golden rim of the beaches, but they seemed to be unending, and at once she had felt at home, released, able to breathe, and her innate confidence had combined with this immediate empathy for the country they were now approaching, and had given her a strength of purpose that nobody could

---

18   Rehmat and James return to South Africa for just a quick visit to see the family. Due to the abovementioned laws, and although they married in Paris, they cannot be together; Rehmat remains at her family's house while James stays in a hotel. The police find out about them because Farah, Rehmat's and Omar's sister-in-law, betrays them. Rehmat manages to escape thanks to Amina, who hides her in her café and later drives her to the airport, where she has contacts who help Rehmat go through the usual police controls. Her husband, James, has meanwhile already left the country via Nairobi.

19   Jacob's and Miss Smith's unaccomplished romance complements that of Rehmat's and James's. Whereas Rehmat and James are both young and, in the end, can be together, albeit not in South Africa, Jacob and Miss Smith are older—Jacob is a widower and Miss Smith has a son who lives in London—and their romance is their last chance to build a fulfilling relationship with somebody and so defeat impending loneliness. Unlike Rehmat and James, though, South African laws stand in their way; after a humiliating incident in which Jacob is forced to pretend he is Miss Smith's driver, they both realize that their romance will remain an impossibility.

contain. [...] The cursory, half-hearted attempts they had made in India
to try to make their daughter conform to accepted conventions fell away
completely in South Africa.

The World Unseen, 17

Once she in South Africa, her job as a gardener and taxi driver allows her to discern "the untried and often wild country" that is concealed behind the racially
sectioned national territory and that fits her "like a well-cut suit of clothes"
(17). It is in the immensity of this landscape that her relationship with Miriam
develops. Hired by Omar to make an orchard outside the house and shop he recently bought in Delhof, outside Pretoria, Amina has the opportunity to spend
time with Miriam. Miriam invites Amina to take part in the family routine with
her children while her husband is away, either conducting business or seeing
Farah, their sister-in-law, with whom he is having an affair.[20] Little by little,
Omar's authoritarian place in the family is replaced by Amina's gentle touch.

Amina prompts Miriam's individual development by letting the woman
behind the wife and the mother surface. As Miriam insightfully reveals to
Amina, "you make me think. And that's a good thing, isn't it?" (155). It is this
thinking that impels her to rebel against her abusive husband and accept
Amina's proposition to teach her how to drive in order to cook in her café.
Driving and work mean independence, and Miriam is, at this stage, determined to gain it. Patriarchal violence, once again, besets the narrative. Miriam
had already suffered Omar's outburst of violence the night she helped a black
boy who had been hit by a car driven by a white man:[21]

> She had always dreaded this moment; not out of physical fear, though
> certainly she had been. But because she knew it would be a terrible thing
> to have to understand about your husband, that he would really hit you,
> and she had always thought when she was younger that hitting was the
> one thing that she would never tolerate.
>
> *The World Unseen*, 220

---

20   It is interesting to note how Sarif's narration signals Farah, the sister-in-law, as a betrayer.
      She betrays Rehmat by revealing her marriage to James to the police and she betrays Mir-
      iam by having an affair with her husband.
21   Miriam's sensitive questioning of racist attitudes contrasts with Omar's internalization of
      nineteenth-century racial discourses that place whiteness at the top of the evolutionary
      ladder. As an Indian man, he feels superior to black people, whom he treats with utter dis-
      respect, but his subservient attitude towards white people exhibits his sense of inferiority
      before them.

Miriam knows that Omar will not permit her to work at the Corner Café, but she also knows that he cannot possibly present her with any plausible reason that would explain his negative attitude. His "'I don't like it.' [...] 'If I don't like it, that should be enough'" (343) no longer placates Miriam, who, quietly but confidently, is ready for the fight that she knows will follow. This is Miriam's first overt defiance, as conveyed through the eyes of John, their black servant:

> Outside, John passed before the window on his walk up and down the patio, and was perturbed to see the master and his wife facing each other like two boxers, intent and alert, each waiting for the first strike.
>
> *The World Unseen,* 340

Omar does hit Miriam, but unlike in the previous scene, this time his violence no longer empowers him but, on the contrary, emasculates him. Miriam has already made her decision. Although her love story with Amina is seemingly truncated by Miriam's realization that she cannot possibly abandon her three children, her final acceptance of Amina's job offer tentatively draws a space in which the prospect of a future can be imagined.

Conclusion: From Border Space to Homing Space

In *Cartographies of Diaspora,* Brah illustrates how the concept of diaspora in-scribes a 'homing desire,' not to be confused with the desire for a 'homeland,' and cautions us against the belief that all diasporas "sustain an ideology of return."[22] Amina's and Miriam's personal diasporas are not sustained by an ideology of return but, rather, are buttressed by the fabrication of a 'homing space,' a space modeled after Massey's relational principle, a space, in short, which is impregnated with emotions. Amina's capacity to recover the land-scape behind the border space that apartheid South Africa became should be understood as, essentially, a metaphorical act. Her empathy with the land allows her to metaphorically *home*[23] the space and forge a female genealogy with Begum and Miriam that extends beyond violence and blood.

To understand Amina's and Miriam's allegiance to South Africa, we need to disentangle 'home' from its unidirectional ethos and, rather, approach it through the lens of bell hooks' perception that it is "no longer one place" but

---

22 *Cartographies of Diaspora,* 197.

23 I use 'home' as a verb in an attempt to illustrate the process whereby space, like land, is ploughed, and worked on, to create a sense of 'home.'

"locations."[24] Amina's and Miriam's homing space steps beyond the confines of India and South Africa and lays out the script for a 'home' in which 'gender,' unlike 'national roots,' is allotted a prominent role. Resisting national affiliations, the *world unseen* of Sarif's novel imagines a community at the crossroads of nowhere and everywhere. This at once inclusionary and exclusionary space delimited by the two protagonists' romance evokes the "double-unbelonging"[25] that encompasses the fate of the migrant, placing him and her in a state of constant—sometimes conscious, sometimes unconscious—negotiation of the present with the past. *The World Unseen* offers a post-apartheid look at the past in an attempt to re-member[26]—remember and assemble—the scattered seeds of a present utopian Rainbow Nation by crafting a South-African/Indian network whereby the experiences of alienation, nostalgia, and melancholia of Amina and Miriam are impressed in a profoundly female-oriented text. Thus, the racial and national language that, according to Sandhya Shukla, defines 'Indianness,' encounters, in Sarif's textual space(s), a gender-infused narrative that surpasses national borders.[27]

Works Cited

Anderson, Benedict. *Imagined Communities: Reflections on the Origin and Spread of Nationalism* (London: Verso, 1983).

Brah, Avtar. *Cartographies of Diaspora: Contesting Identities* (London & New York: Routledge, 1996).

Butler, Judith. "Giving an Account of Oneself," *Diacritics* 31.4 (Winter 2001): 22–40.

Daly, Mary. *Gyn/ecology: The Methaethics of Radical Feminism* (Boston MA: Beacon, 1990).

Frenkel, Ronit. *Reconsiderations: South African Indian Fiction and the Making of Race in Postcolonial Culture* (Pretoria: U of South Africa P, 2011).

Frenkel, Ronit. "Reconsidering South African Indian Fiction Postapartheid," *Research in African Literatures* 42.3 (Fall 2011): 1–16.

---

24   See bell hooks, *Yearning: Race, Gender, and Cultural Politics* (Boston MA: South End, 1990): 41–50.

25   See Salman Rushdie, *East, West* (London: Jonathan Cape, 1994).

26   I borrow the term 're-member' and its conjoined meaning as remember and assemble from Mary Daly, *Gyn/ecology: The Metaethics of Radical Feminism* (Boston MA: Beacon, 1990).

27   Sandya Shukla, *India Abroad: Diasporic Cultures of Postwar America and England* (Princeton NJ: Princeton UP, 2003): 9.

George, Rosemary Marangoly. *The Politics of Home: Postcolonial Relocations and Twentieth-Century Fiction* (Berkeley: U of California P, 1996).

Hand, Felicity. "Shaking off Sharam: the Double Burden of British Asian Women," in *On Writing (and) Race in Contemporary Britain*, ed. Fernando Galván & Mercedes Bengoechea (Alcalá de Henares: Universidad de Alcalá, 1999): 133–138.

hooks, bell. *Yearning: Race, Gender, and Cultural Politics* (Boston MA: South End, 1990).

Jain, Jasbir. *Writing Women Across Centuries* (New Delhi: Rawat, 2002).

Massey, Doreen. *Space, Place and Gender* (Cambridge: Polity, 1994).

Puri, Jyoti. *Woman, Body, Desire in Post-Colonial India: Narratives of Gender and Sexuality* (London & New York: Routledge, 1999).

Rushdie, Salman. *East, West* (London: Jonathan Cape, 1994).

Sarif, Shamim. *The World Unseen* (2001; London & Los Angeles: Enlightenment Press, 2009).

Shukla, Sandya. *India Abroad: Diasporic Cultures of Postwar America and England* (Princeton NJ: Princeton UP, 2003).

CHAPTER 8

What Memory Resists

Indenture, Apartheid, and the 'Memory-Work' of Reconstruction in Ronnie Govender's Black Chin, White Chin

Modhumita Roy

As Devarakshanam Betty Govinden observes, "a feature of the post-apartheid literary scene is the way the history of earlier times and of groups which were previously silent is being recalled and recounted."[1] South Africa, she concludes, is "living through a time of memory."[2] What Govinden terms the "time of memory," inaugurated by the formal dismantling of apartheid in 1994, has engendered a flood of new writing, often inspired by the Truth and Reconciliation Commission's catchphrase 'Revealing is Healing.' The process of the Truth and Reconciliation hearings, with emphasis on 'telling' in both its confessional and its testifying variant, opened up a space which Njabulo Ndebele hailed as "the restoration of narrative."[3] Victims and perpetrators came forward to record their stories, which collectively "lifted the veil of secrecy and state-induced blindness" and facilitated the movement from "repression to expression."[4] For Indian South African writing,[5] a second, perhaps more compelling, inspiration was the 150th celebration of the arrival on 16 November 1860 of SS *Truro*, carrying the first wave of indentured Indians to South Africa.[6] The 2010 celebration of this momentous anniversary stimulated writing, much of it focussed

---

1   Devarakshanam Betty Govinden, "Healing the Wounds of History: South African Indian Writing," *Current Writing: Text and Reception in South Africa* 21.1–2 (2009): 286.

2   This is the title of one of Govinden's books: *A Time of Memory: Reflections on Recent South African Writing* (Pretoria: U of South Africa P, 2008).

3   Njabulo Ndebele, "Memory, Metaphor, and the Triumph of Narrative," in *Negotiating the Past: The Making of Memory in South Africa*, ed. Sarah Nuttall & Carli Coetzee (Cape Town: Oxford UP, 1998): 20.

4   Ndebele, "Memory, Metaphor, and the Triumph of Narrative," 20.

5   I have opted to use 'Indian South African' over other variants to emphasize Indian descent as qualifying South African identity, citizenship, and belonging.

6   For the history of Indians in South Africa, see, for example: Ashwin Desai & Goolam Vahed, *Indian Indenture: A South African Story 1860–1914* (Durban: Madiba, 2007); Surendra Bhana & Joy Brain, *Setting Down Roots: Indian Migration in South Africa 1860–1911* (Johannesburg: Wits UP, 1990).

© KONINKLIJKE BRILL NV, LEIDEN, 2018 | DOI 10.1163/9789004365032_009

on indentureship.[7] Indeed, a cursory count of the number of relevant publications shows, according to Lindy Stiebel, that for Indian South Africans this has been an "exceptionally busy" time of memory.[8]

In what follows, I look at Ronnie Govender's *Black Chin, White Chin* as an instantiation of the historical conjuncture produced, on the one hand, by the TRC's "restoration of narrative" and, on the other, the expected 150th anniversary celebration's "time of memory." *Black Chin, White Chin* anticipates the commemorative outpourings of 2010, and like them posits indenture as the "original historical indignity" for Indian South Africans.[9] "Indenture," as Govinden rightly argued, "may be seen as a template for memory among the descendants of immigrants—a memory of suffering, endurance, struggle, and survival."[10] If the "overriding tone is one of pride at the achievements [...and] celebration of their resilience,"[11] in much of this writing the tonal resonance of the "massive communal confessional narrative" of the TRC was melancholia.[12] This dual genealogy of reconstructing the past—apartheid and indenture, melancholia and resilience—I will argue, produce in Govender's novel a certain instability, even an evasiveness, and this instability is evident in the very form of the novel.

Family Saga

Originally titled *Song of the Atman*, Ronnie Govender's *Black Chin, White Chin* is described on the back cover as a "majestic saga that encompasses [...] a family's epic struggle." John Galsworthy, whose three-volume *Forsyte Saga* (1922) remains the most canonical version of the sub-genre of the prose-fiction saga, commented in the Preface, "the word Saga might be objected to on the grounds that it connotes the heroic and that there is little heroic in these pages."[13] He is surely right to express reservations about heroism, as his trilogy emphasizes, with obvious delight, the pettiness, greed, and moral failings of

---

7   See Lindy Stiebel, "Crossing the *kala pani*: Cause for 'Celebration' or 'Commemoration' 150 Years On? Portrayals of Indenture in Recent South African Indian Writing," *Journal of Literary Studies* 27.2 (2011): 77–90.

8   Stiebel, "Crossing the *kala pani*," 78.

9   Govinden, "Healing the Wounds of History," 290.

10   "Healing the Wounds of History," 288.

11   Stiebel, "Crossing the *kala pani*," 83.

12   Susan VanZanten Gallagher, *Truth and Reconciliation: The Confessional Mode in South African Literature* (Portsmouth NH: Heinemann, 2002): 132.

13   John Galsworthy, *The Forsyte Saga* (1922; Oxford & New York: Oxford UP, 1995): 5.

the Forsyte family. Heroic or not, the word "saga" in Galsworthy's title signals a focus on intergenerational family dynamics and, most importantly, on *family* as it both stands in for, and is shaped by, history. Even a cursory reading of Govender's novel confirms that it is indeed a family saga—where the attention is less on the heroic, majestic, or even epic, and more on the representation of a quotidian world. *Black Chin, White Chin* presents an extended Indian South African family and their friends, neighbors, and acquaintances, in a crowded canvas of stories and characters, some drawn in detail, others presented briefly, in passing. The novel's recitation of births, deaths, and marriages catalogues the progress of the community and, along the way, focusses on arrangements and obligations of kinship, and of friendships, with occasional detours into infidelities and betrayals. In this congested staging of stories and characters, it is sometimes difficult to calibrate their relative importance or relevance, especially to the eponymous Chin. Unlike some of the most canonical family sagas—Thomas Mann's *Buddenbrooks* (1901) and Galsworthy's *Forsyte Saga* (1922), for example—which chronicle the decline of merchant families, *Black Chin, White Chin* follows the trials and tribulations of a struggling Tamil-Hindu family in Durban as they rise out of poverty. More importantly, Govender's novel stakes a claim as a historical, even historically accurate, chronicle of Indians in South Africa, from their arrival as indentured laborers to their relative economic success; and this larger, more public history is metonymically presented through the biography of Chin Govender and his family.

The novel is based on the life of the author, Ronnie Govender's "late Uncle Chin Govender," details about whom "were gleaned from conversations with Chin, my mother Chellamma (his own sister), my uncles and brothers, my eldest sister Gonum."[14] In the "Author's Note" appended at the very end, Govender describes the novel as being "as close to a biography as the structure of a novel will allow" (279). He does not explain why a biography in which most events are "true to the last detail" needed to be fictionalized, except to say that it was for "the purpose of constructing a story with a beginning and an end" (279). On the level of narration, then, *Black Chin, White Chin* is more than a simple recounting of an interesting and unique life; the novelized biography is a specific kind of piecing together of collective memory. It is both authentic and true ("gleaned from conversations"); and intentionally fabricated, having used "some license" in introducing imaginary characters (279).

I will return to the question of form raised by the "Author's Note," in particular to the issue of "gleaning" that aids the memory-work of reconstructing the

---

14   Ronnie Govender, *Black Chin, White Chin* (New Delhi: HarperCollins, 2007): 279. Further page references are in the main text.

biography. For the moment, it would be useful to note that the novel is not only the record of a single life, as Govender claims; it is simultaneously about Chin and his family, the Govenders, as it about the larger Indian community in Durban. Though read as a "wide-ranging Bildungsroman of a life filled with vicissitudes against the landscape of twentieth-century South Africa,"[15] *Black Chin, White Chin* is also more than a bildungsroman. While the novel certainly traces Chin's singular life and can be read as a *Bildung*, if anything it is selfconsciously the biography of a family, of an ethnic and social group, and of the changing relations between and among populations in South Africa, under pressure of political and historical shifts. In other words, *Black Chin, White Chin*, in Salman Rushdie's famous description, is "handcuffed to history"—so that the story of the individual is at once the story of the group.[16] Or, put another way, in the more controversial formulation of Fredric Jameson, the novel is an instance of a Third World fiction functioning as a national allegory.[17] In Govender's novel, however, it is not so much the nation *as a whole* that is being allegorized or imagined; apartheid's "official cartography"[18]—its legislated racial separation and displacements—would have rendered the project of generating a unified imagined community problematic, if not impossible. Rather, the "imagined community," reconstructed under the twin historical burdens of indenture and apartheid, is almost exclusively Indian; or, more accurately, Indian South African. In the "Author's Note," Govender makes this very point: "In many ways, Chin's history is typical of the life stories of descendants of indentured labourers whom the British Government brought from India" (280).

To Begin or Not to Begin

What strikes the reader from the outset is the novel's reluctance to begin. After the usual title page and dedication, we read a half-page of acknowledgements

---

15   Govinden, "Healing the Wounds of History," 293.

16   Salman Rushdie, *Midnight's Children* (1981; New York: Penguin, 1991). The novel's beginning connects the individual to the larger history of the nation: "I was born in the city of Bombay [...]. I had been mysteriously handcuffed to history, my destiny indissolubly chained to those of my country."

17   "All third-world texts are [...] necessarily allegorical [...] they are to be read as what I will call *national allegories*"; Fredric Jameson, "Third World Literature in the Era of Multinational Capitalism," *Social Text* 15 (Autumn 1986): 69.

18   I borrow this useful phrase from Duncan Brown, "Narrative Memory and Mapping: Ronnie Govender's 'At the Edge' and Other Cato Manor Stories," *Current Writing: Text and Reception in South Africa* 17.1 (2005): 108–128.

that thank the family without whose support "this story might not have seen the light of day" (ix). This is followed by a letter written to "Devs," dated 1967, which is followed by yet another chapter, which gives the impression of being the 'beginning' but is not. Only then, after these fits and starts, thirty-seven years before the letter to Devs is written, does the novel proper commence— in 1930—in a tumultuous year of political changes, especially for the Indian South African community. It is the year of anti-immigration legislation which restricted property-ownership and mining rights for the Indian community and also had a far-reaching impact on wages and employment. Throughout the decade, a variety of statutes established legal regimes for regulating mobility and residence; that is, they established statutory segregation which would force the inhabitation of particular spaces—geographic, subjective, and psychic. None of this history is directly engaged with in the novel; like its structural reluctance to begin, *Black Chin, White Chin* appears equally loath to attend to, or face head-on, this troubled history, which, nonetheless, is referenced quite pointedly by beginning the narration-proper in 1930.

Along with the reluctance to begin, one also notes the generic instability of the novel—first a short letter, followed by a cryptic "prologue," and then a novel which appears to be a realist family saga but which, too, mutates and changes shape and tone. In the opening pages, we meet the entrepreneurial Baijnath of Baijnath Book-Keepers, whose success is ascribed to his handwriting, which,

> besides being eminently legible, was a thing of beauty. Its symmetry and shape, its swirls, and curls and twirls were so precise that it looked like it came off a printing press.
>
> *Black Chin, White Chin*, 1

Unlike Baijnath's "eminently legible" handwriting, however, the novel's beginning, and especially the letter to Devs, makes a virtue of illegibility, puzzling us with its hieroglyphic beginning, raising questions without answering them: Who is Devs?—and why is he, as the letter writer "Pops" indicates, angry?— "You were angry but you were right." About what is he right? What had Pops done that was "painful, but it had to be that way"?

The "letter"—intriguing rather than illuminating—makes its tantalizing appearance in its entirety at the very beginning and is followed by the "prologue" that is temporally proximate to the writing of the letter, as it describes Chin's journey to Robben Island to deliver it to Devs. This strategically placed, now internationally recognized, toponym, 'Robben Island,' immediately conjures up the history of anti-apartheid resistance without explicitly engaging with it:

we infer, correctly, that Devs is being held there for his political activity. Stomps Diederichs, Chin's friend and senior police officer on Robben Island, emphasizes this association, telling Chin that the place is "only for communists and agitators" (xiv).

Chin knows the letter "was quite innocuous as far as the authorities were concerned," and since we have already read it, we know this to be true. It is not the political but the personal implications that trouble Chin; the letter had the potential "to disrupt the course of his life" (xiv), The authorities, predictably, find and confiscate the letter. Thus, while we get to read the letter, its addressee, Devs, does not. Ironically, the draconian censorship of the apartheid state secures Chin's secret life. His melancholic ruminations about life, his anxiety about intimate secrets being uncovered, his public lies to protect himself, all function as confessions to the reader and build up a certain intimacy. The confiscation of the letter by the authorities shuts Devs out of the circle of communications, so that he remains, as he has always seemed to have been, outside the sphere of Chin's confidences Of greater moment, the aborted communication allows the public lie that he and Devs are not related to remain in place.

Having presented two intriguing snippets in the present—the letter and Chin's journey to Robben Island—the novel proper moves back to the past and begins, as all 'good' (that is, well-behaved) novels should: at the beginning, marked as Chapter 1, page 1. At this point, we seem to be reading a conventional, even formulaic, immigrant novel that faithfully follows the "template for memory" of "suffering, endurance, struggle and survival" that Govinden outlines in her analysis of Indian South African writing.[19] The first pages introduce the enterprising Baijnath, whose father "had come to South Africa from Bihar in India, where he and others like him had been fed stories of gold nuggets being picked on the streets of Durban" (1). From such modest beginnings, Baijnath, with a fortuitous combination of talent, motivation, and diligence, makes something of himself. He becomes the owner of "the first, if not the only Indian business among all the tidily ordered shops and houses" in Umbilo Road (1).

If the two enigmatic opening sections make a virtue of being oblique and mysterious, hesitating to divulge relationships and motives, the beginning of the novel proper fills the pages with dates, names, histories, and political events. We are firmly in Durban, South Africa, in 1930. The history of Indian presence in this area is rehearsed in a condensed if familiar form by strategically invoking the most iconic public moments. The novel lets slip without elaboration

---

19   Govinden, "Healing the Wounds of History," 288.

that Baijnath is a resident of Cato Manor, and as in the case of Robben Island in the opening pages, nothing is made of this toponym either; but its invocation serves as a reminder of the particular history of racial stratification and residential segregation experienced by Indian South Africans.[20] We learn that at this time it is illegal for Indians to have liquor in their possession (4) but that they could "drink at the Indian" bars of white hotels (4); and, of course, the now-obligatory invocation of Gandhi (though not by name) as the "young lawyer from India" who was "a brave man" and who "got kicked out of a train for refusing to move to third class, and he was prepared to go to jail" (5). We further learn of different kinds of Indians—from Baijnath's Standard Four teacher, Mr. Peters, "who spoke much like an Englishman," to Baijnath's family, which did not. The establishment of a separate political entity is also announced: "This Natal Indian Congress is something that [was] needed," as Indians "have a lot of grievances" (5). In other words, under racialism's segregationist pressures, a varied group has been ethnicized under a common signifier, 'Indian,' and, in the early chapters, the novel concentrates on defining this community through their customs, rituals, foibles, and occasional political involvement.

As we read on, we realize that we were mistaken in identifying Baijnath as the central character. He is, instead, a synecdochic presence, a stand-in for the idealized liberal narrative of the Indian community's entrepreneurial ingenuity and success, a narrative staple of the "celebration of resilience" about which Stiebel writes.[21] The actual hero is the "tall and striking" Chin, "a bright lad who'd done well at school" (16), the third son of an extended patriarchal Tamil family in Durban, who are bound to each other by duties and obligations (82). In sharp contrast to the historical year (1930) and its dire consequences, especially for Indian South Africans, which the novel's beginning signals, all the named male characters who crowd the first chapters seem to start humbly but, through perseverance and dedication (and a little help from some wealthy and generous business owners) all flourish. History, defined as momentous events in the life of the nation, occurs, as it were, in the margins, ever-present but adjacent to the main narrative; and, like marginalia, history in *Black Chin, White Chin* is always on the sidelines, never the main text. Politics and political involvement, too, are cast outside the orbit of the familial. Thus, there is Billy Peters, who lived next door to the Govenders and who is "a trade unionist [...] going in and out of jail" (197). Or, later in the novel, it is Michael Mbele, the

---

20   For a history of Cato Manor and an elaboration of 'toponym,' see E. Jeffrey Popke, "Violence and Memory in the Reconstruction of South Africa's Cato Manor," *Growth and Change* 30 (Spring 2000): 235–254.

21   Stiebel, "Crossing the *kala pani*," 78.

hotel doorman, "staunch member of the Communist Party" (104), who reads Marx and demands justice, and is ultimately killed by the police. Chin's claim, of course, is that he "had no idea that Michael had such strong political affiliations and beliefs" (104). Repeatedly in the novel, politics touch *other* lives and livelihoods but almost never stop Chin or inspire him to actively participate. For the most part, he is content to remain aloof and apolitical: "Michael's death drove home to Chin that the lives of his fellow countrymen were shrouded in deliberate anonymity" (103). Although he blames the "single-minded political will" of the state for this disjunction between and among communities, neither the knowledge of Michael's political involvement nor his own experiences of racism politicizes Chin.

The Crisis of Form

The first six chapters trudge along with workmanlike plotting; details of quotidian life are interspersed with some densely referenced accounts of the Indian community in Durban: descriptions of rituals, prayers, food and festivals, relationships, work, leisure, and aspirations. These early chapters concentrate on the social and familial; the strict adherence to 'traditional' values appears to build a cohesive identity.[22] Even the intercalated hierarchies of gender and age are respected rather than challenged: "They were a family, and all other considerations took second place" (57). But with the very next chapter (Chapter 7), with Chin's leaving the family after an altercation with his older brother Jack, the novel exchanges its generic affiliation with the family saga for that of an individualist novel of destiny. From this point on, the novel shifts from its preoccupation with the codes of collectively shared proprieties to the conventions of the picaresque and *Bildung*; that is, the novel now turns to the lone individual, Chin, and his adventures. It should be noted that Chin leaves home neither because of political activities nor because of the state's policies of eviction and forced removal, the two most common causes of involuntary mobility. Rather, he leaves home because certain cultural norms have proved intolerable. Strict rules of a patriarchal family demanded that Chin hand over his paycheck to the male head-of-household, his brother Jack. When Chin takes a small amount out of his wages to buy lunch, he is severely punished: "It was so swift, Chin didn't see it coming. The palm of the former South African

---

22   The construction of a corporate 'Indian' identity in this novel is quite different from Govender's much-admired play *The Lahnee's Pleasure* (1974), whose use of colloquial and working-class speech effectively renders a diverse group. It is as if the standardized English of the novel reflects the politics of respectability it espouses.

champion's smashed into his face" (58). This moment, "mixed with malevo-
lence and regret" (58), ruptures the familial bond and drives Chin out into the
unknown world beyond Durban.

The break with the family inaugurates, as I have said, a concomitant break
with the generic conventions of the family saga. The veering away from family
and community is a fundamental requisite of a picaresque novel; it is what
allows individual self-fashioning. Unmoored from the demands and expectations of a tightly knit Hindu family, Chin can now freely remake himself. He
leaves without "a penny in his pocket" and with only the clothes on his back
(69). Chin's self-fashioning is literalized when, with money in his pocket, he
can indulge himself by "wearing tailor-made suits [...and] silk shirts imported from England" (102). In this, the largest section of the novel, Chin moves
from location to location, from East London to Port Elizabeth, and finally to
the teeming, cosmopolitan Cape Town. His first stop, East London, is "a small
town [where] there were not many opportunities" (80); nonetheless, through
a stroke of uncommon luck, he becomes a "wine steward" and then a waiter
at the modest Tudor-style Royal Hotel (72). After an inauspicious beginning,
he "settled into a comfortable routine" (73)—though not for long. Chin moves
from location to location and from affair to affair; first with Mary, a Coloured
woman and the landlord's wife, a liaison which, when discovered, lands him
in a "hospital ward with a broken jaw and three broken ribs" (78); and then a
relationship with an older white woman, the sophisticated, worldly-wise, and
rich Greta Schmeling—whose relative affluence will underwrite Chin's own
success and financial security.

Removed from the reproach of his mother and older brothers, and therefore removed from the rigidities and constraints of customs and expectations,
Chin can parley his attractiveness, sexual and otherwise, from one lucrative
arrangement to another. "It seemed to Chin that [...] people in the Cape [...]
didn't seem as bothered about who you were and what your race was" (89). The
Durban chapters emphasized the dogged work ethic of an immigrant community: "Discipline, respect correct speech and behaviour, especially in front
of elders: this was the unwritten code, and you didn't dare break it" (15); Chin's
mercurial rise in Port Elizabeth exemplifies a new, dynamic, form of social
climbing. Hard work and aptitude may have their rewards here as well, and
Chin does indeed work hard; but his upward mobility is a direct outcome of his
charm, and, more pointedly, of his affair with Greta. While his father-surrogate
Mr. Reddy is proud of Chin's success, ascribing it to tenacity and industry—
"You must be the first Indian manager of a white hotel. It's a feather in the cap
of our people" (93)—the black doorman is a lot more knowing and "greeted
him heartily in the morning, but with a touch of irony. 'Mr. Chin, now you're
a big man—now I must call you baas!'" (93). Chin's entrepreneurial successes,

in which he is able to break free of the earlier rigidities of race and class, and from the dictates of tradition, are driven by associations that characterize modernity—that is, by accidental and arbitrary encounters. Breaking rules has its rewards, as it also has consequences, as Chin finds out when he is beaten up for his dalliance with the married Mary; yet, despite the scattered verbal and physical violence to which he is subjected, Chin rarely, if ever, pays a price. He routinely breaches boundaries, particularly racial, without any significant negative payback.

As the novel meanders along its way, both spatially and chronologically, through the decades, Chin goes from success to success. His setbacks are always temporary and in the end never impede his progress; the political changes, always referred to in casual conversation or asides, never quite affect the velocity of his upward mobility. After a long, eighteen-year absence, after he has acquired every symbol of success, money, property ("Govender's Modern Hotel") and "a practically brand-new" late-model, six-cylinder Hudson Terraplane car (185), Chin, the prodigal son, returns home to Durban and to his family, eager to bestow his "brotherly gesture of love and generosity" (200). His triumphant return is (mis)read as the "Karmic reward" (200) for the suffering his family has endured. It is important to remember that Chin's breach of the community's (and his family's) codes of decorum, and especially his sexual transgressions, take place far from Durban. This spatial distancing—segregation, in a sense—allows Chin to hide the inconvenient truths of his life. These concealments make it possible for him to return seamlessly to the family and for the novel to return to the generic affiliations of the sentimental domestic saga. But the return to form is possible only if Chin disavows his lovers, black and white, and denies his Coloured son. For only complete denial can allow the family—and the larger "imagined community" of Indian South Africans—to continue to define itself as ethnically marked as Tamil, Hindu, and descendants of indentured laborers.

If family sagas emphasize continuity, linear descent, and homogeneity, and its purpose is to show the connectedness of past to present; the demands of the bildungsroman are to illustrate the individual's ability to break free from family and from the past. While the generic codes of the domestic saga and *Bildung* seem irreconcilable (the novel has had to switch between the two conventions to accommodate Chin's story), what the two sections in *Black Chin, White Chin* have in common is a deep anxiety around politics. Whether as saga or as a picaresque novel, what is highlighted is the personal; and while history and politics exist, they do not occupy center stage. When politics finally breaches the boundary-wall between private and public, the conventions of both genres are thrown into crisis. It is to this crisis, and the novel's attempt to manage it, that we must now turn.

What Memory Resists

In Govender's fictionalized biography, Chin's life is "gleaned" from conversations—with Chin himself, but also with those who knew him well. 'To glean,' as any dictionary will tell us, is to discover (harvest) little by little. This slow reconstructive process of piecing Chin's life together from the many versions and fragments offered by others is a fine example of what J.R. Gillis calls "memory-work," which,

> like any other kind of physical and mental labour, [is] embedded in a complex class, gender and power relations that determine what is remembered (or forgotten), by whom and for what end.[23]

The work of remembering, as Gillis, among others, has shown, is always partial, discontinuous, and influenced by context and motive. Paradoxically, remembering requires that we also forget or repress. This combination—the effort to remember and the need to repress—makes memory-work in *Black Chin, White Chin* ideologically unstable.

In *Black Chin, White Chin*, 'memory work,' which celebrates the past and expresses disquiet with the present, is most obvious in its analeptic mode, which reorders the sequence of events—beginning in 1967, moving back to the 1930s, and slowly moving forward to the present—thereby producing the past *as though* it were the present. This strategic re-creation of the past-as-present is an act of preservation—of a community imagined as cohesive and homogeneous. The chronological reordering also postpones, though it cannot arrest, the moment of reckoning with the novel's present. The more the novel inches closer to the volatile anti-apartheid politics of the 1960s, the less is it able to maintain its strategies of containment. When Chin returns to Durban as a rich and successful entrepreneur, the novel attempts to 're-member'—that is, to reflect back on *and* to make the family whole—through scenes of conviviality and through the performance of rituals. The reunions are imbued, however, with nostalgia for a familial life that is now irrevocably lost.[24] The

---

23   John R. Gillis, "Introduction: Memory and Identity: The History of a Relationship," in *Commemorations: The Politics of National Identity*, ed. John R. Gillis (Princeton NJ: Princeton UP, 1994): 3.

24   One should note that the nostalgic recuperating of the family in its putative past of unity and harmony is itself a sign of its passing. More importantly, it is also a willed forgetting of the trauma (and violence) that has been present and which is brilliantly captured in the evasive paratactic phrasing that signal Chin's departure: "A family quarrel. Anger. A little violence" (59).

once extended Govender family, living under the same roof, which Chin had left behind him, has now been replaced by smaller, autonomous, nuclear entities, scattered in and around Durban. Amurtham, the formidable matriarch, no longer the centripetal force of the family, has retreated "more and more to prayer" (114). Politics, that explosive force that Chin has kept at arm's length, now threatens "the ordered life" that Chin had kept "so jealously private" (xiv). In the novel's present, when the domestic and the political intersect they do so with ferocity, leaving the apolitical Chin on the sidelines of his own narrative. Against the rapid and violent changes in South Africa over which he has no control—his hotel is confiscated by the apartheid state; he is evicted from his home; Guru is killed; his son Devs is arrested and imprisoned on Robben Island—Chin can only ruefully acknowledge his cowardice: "I was not brave when it counted" (277).

In the hurried, short chapters at the end of the novel, Chin's biography is superseded by that of the next generation: to Guru, his sister Chelamma's son, whom he adopts, and to Devs, who is his son with Grace Mbele. Their political involvement leads to their discovery that they are not only comrades, bound together by their politics; they are family, related to each other by blood and birth. This interlocking of kinship and comradeship—filiation with affiliation—finally connects family quite explicitly to history, segregation to commingling, apartheid to indenture. The overlapping of the familial and the political brings the novel to its ideological crisis. It also brings the forward momentum of Chin's biography to an abrupt halt. By novel's end, the worldly and cosmopolitan Chin, lover of women, successful hotelier, and property owner, turns back to ritual and prayer, surely as a solace, as an escape, perhaps even as a bulwark against the volatility of change. This move towards a religiously inspired spirituality is especially interesting when we recall that Chin had never been attracted to devotionalism: "Like his father and his brother Jack, Chin was not particularly religious" (55). Against the younger generation's fierce commitment to politics Chin posits the timelessness of devotion; against change, he can only offer quietude of detachment, askesis. "For the first time in his life, as he fought to hold back tears, Chin uttered that words that lay deep within his memory ... 'Aum naamasivaya'..." (278). The novel's last words are given over to a Hindu prayer—to the "song of the atman."[25]

---

25   As mentioned earlier, *Song of the Atman* was the original title of the novel. The new title, *Black Chin, White Chin*, points more to the irresolvable simultaneity of identities and histories. The space between black and white—the space occupied by Coloured and brown (to use apartheid's racial taxonomy)—is grammatically elided by the use of the comma. If anything, the burden of the narrative has been to show that Chin, though not black, can perhaps be considered as aspirationally white.

If, in the novel's past, politics had been relegated to the background in the novel's present, the explicit resistance to apartheid is not just disturbing—it threatens to undo the memory-work that had produced Chin's biography. Although references to punctual historical moments—indenture, the formation of the National Indian Congress, trade union and communist agitation—are scattered throughout the novel, they function more as chronological signposts. Faced with Guru's radical politics—he is a recruiter for the militant *Umkhonto wa Sizwe* and "ran secret workshops for young activists" (272)—Chin is at first resigned—"What can we do?" and then dismissive of "all this political nonsense" (266). Guru's unwavering allegiance not only poses a direct challenge to Chin's political reticence; he dares Chin to question his identification as an "Indian." To Chin's rhetorical question, "What can an Indian do about it?" Devs responds with a concrete, political suggestion: "Indians need to identify more with the struggle of African people, if they are to secure the future of their children" (229). In place of Chin's fealty to cultural identity, Guru and Devs, comrades and cousins, embrace a new, more complex conception, forged through anti-apartheid struggle; they are committed to a national, rather than any pre-given, communal identity. As Devs puts it, "I am not an Indian. I am a South African" (267). To reject what the novel designates, "the racial exclusivity of Indians" (89), as Guru does, would be to repudiate Chin's entire sense of self as well as the carefully presented collective identity. For Chin, the new definition of a national rather than ethnic identity is an untenable, unwelcome idea: "This shit about not being an Indian. This is ridiculous" (268). In a near-replay of the scene between a young Chin and his older brother Jack, who had smashed Chin's face with his boxer's fist for breaking the rules of the extended family, Chin confronts Guru for challenging his sense of identity. Unlike the scene thirty years before, this confrontation is not a physical but a deeply political one; one in which Guru has the last word: "I am South African—like your son Devs!" (168)

That the memorializing of indentured arrival provided the inspiration for novels such as *Black Chin, White Chin* is hardly a controversial claim; its connection to what Ndebele called "repression to expression" in TRC narratives may appear somewhat more tenuous. We would be right to ask what resonance the TRC's slogan 'Revealing is Healing' has for *Black Chin, White Chin*, as I claimed at the outset, and how it might complicate the memory-work of this narrative. After all, the novel's narrative time ends, in 1967, decades before the dismantling of apartheid and the commencement of the TRC hearings. Despite the chronological discrepancy, however, it is possible to argue that a novel published in 2006, whose dénouement motions towards forgiveness and reconciliation, cannot but be taken as a reference to the TRC,[26] even if the

---

26   The TRC's final report was handed to Nelson Mandela in 1998. However, the Amnesty
      Committee's findings remained incomplete at the time. The TRC also urged "free and

'truth' with which Chin needs to reconcile himself appears to be significantly different. Govender's fictionalized biography bears a close family resemblance to proliferating narratives of confession in the aftermath of apartheid, which were, as Michiel Heyns puts it, "structured towards self-revelation as a means of exoneration."[27] Indeed, *Black Chin, White Chin* begins with a confession and ends with Chin's attempt at reconciliation with a son he has failed, has refused to publicly acknowledge. We know that he has insisted to the world that Devs "was the son of a very good employee" and, as he admits, "Repetition had given it some plausibility" (xiv). Chin's confession (what Heyns refers to as "self-revelation") is strategically placed before the novel proper begins and structures the entire narrative. The "prologue" which follows, detailing Chin's journey to Robben Island, sets up our anticipation of the final scene of forgiveness, exoneration, and healing. The very end of the novel loops back to this moment, with Chin coming face-to-face with Devs, who is in his sixth year of incarceration: "Chin put his fingers through the grille to touch his son's hands. Devs looked into his moist, pleading eyes and gently touched his fingers" (277).

Within the diegesis of the novel, however, Chin neither acknowledges Devs as his son nor asks for his forgiveness. The sentimental reconciliation, of revealing in order to heal, is gestured at but never completed. Chin retreats, instead, into prayer.

While the novel ends without resolution, Govender tries to tie up the loose ends via an extra-diegetic paratext, the "Author's Note," This appendix, which has the *actual* last word in the printed text, radically modifies the entire preceding narrative. We learn that while "Most events in the book are true to the last detail," Govender has "used some licence in introducing fictional events" (279). In addition, he has introduced "imaginary characters"—among them "the Mbeles and sundry minor characters" (279). If the Mbeles are fictional characters, then logically so is Chin's son, Devs. This startling admission makes the frame—the journey to Robben Island and to a reconciliation—a fabrication, as it also alters our understanding of Chin. As readers, we have been privy to his darkest, most intimate and shameful secrets: we have known of Chin's transgressions; known of his many sexual indiscretions and infidelities; known

---

honest disclosure," which seems to be the narrative intent of *Black Chin, White Chin* as it is of a significant number of memoirs written in the post-apartheid moment. See Modhumita Roy, "'Is not the truth the truth?' Reconciling Truths in Gillian Slovo's *Every Secret Thing* and the Practice of Reconciliation in South Africa," in *Thinking and Practicing Reconciliation: Teaching and Learning through Literary Responses to Conflict*, ed. Leo Riegert, Jill Scott & Jack Shuler (Newcastle upon Tyne: Cambridge Scholars, 2013): 122–142.

27   Michiel Heyns, "The Whole Country's Truth: Confession and Narrative in Recent White South African Writing," *MFS: Modern Fiction Studies* 46.1 (Spring 2000): 45.

of his "African" son, Devs. From the moment we read the letter to Devs, we became, in effect, his secret sharer. But if Devs is a fabrication, then the sentimental ending, the touching reconciliation of father and son through prison bars, is also a convenient narrative construct. But for what purpose?

I want to end with a reminder of what this essay has been arguing. First, I want to reiterate that the form of the novel reveals its ideological unease: the novel's postponement of its inaugural moment, its generic shifts—now reading like a family saga, now resembling a lurid Zane Grey novel (which novels, interestingly enough, Chin voraciously reads till they "become predictable"), and now attempting to follow a coming-of-age realist novel in the form of a bildungsroman, *Great Expectations*, say—has something to do with a deep and fundamental discomfort with the political itself, and in particular with the politics of the novel's present. The novel cannot eschew politics; after all, the Indian South African community is a direct result of deliberate political and economic decisions of the late nineteenth century. The community is constituted and reconstituted in and through its imbrication in the larger political landscape of South Africa. Nor can the novel embody the political in the deep structures of its narrative syntax, having accepted culture—Hindu culture, in particular, presented in the novel as unchanging and eternal—as its mode of imagining community. By negating Dev's existence, not only does the narrative betray its readers. More consequently, it resists the politics embodied by Guru and Devs. *Black Chin, White Chin*'s memory work of reconstruction leaves us with the question: if Devs is a fabrication, then what are we now to make of the sentimental frame of confession and reconciliation? Perhaps more consequently still, what, in fact, in the novel's terms, is the riposte to Guru's radical vision of identity: "I am South African—like your son Devs!" (268).

Works Cited

Bhana, Surendra, & Joy Brain. *Setting Down Roots: Indian Migration in South Africa 1860–1911* (Johannesburg: Wits UP, 1990).

Brown, Duncan. "Narrative Memory and Mapping: Ronnie Govender's 'At the Edge' and Other Cato Manor Stories," *Current Writing: Text and Reception in South Africa* 17.1 (2005): 108–128.

Desai, Ashwin, & Goolam Vahed. *Indian Indenture: A South African Story 1860–1914* (Durban: Madiba, 2007).

Gallagher, Susan VanZanten. *Truth and Reconciliation: The Confessional Mode in South African Literature* (Portsmouth NH: Heinemann, 2002).

Galsworthy, John. *The Forsyte Saga* (1922; Oxford & New York: Oxford UP, 1995).

Gillis, John R. "Introduction: Memory and Identity: The History of a Relationship," in *Commemorations: The Politics of National Identity*, ed. John R. Gillis (Princeton NJ: Princeton UP, 1994): 3–26.

Govender, Ronnie. *Black Chin, White Chin* (New Delhi: HarperCollins, 2007).

Govender, Ronnie. *The Lahnee's Pleasure* (Johannesburg: Ravan, 1974).

Govinden, Devarakshanam Betty. "Healing the Wounds of History: South African Indian Writing," *Current Writing: Text and Reception in South Africa* 21.1 (2009): 287–302.

Govinden, Devarakshanam Betty. *A Time of Memory: Reflections on Recent South African Writing* (Pretoria: U of South Africa P, 2008).

Heyns, Michiel. "The Whole Country's Truth: Confession and Narrative in Recent White South African Writing," *MFS: Modern Fiction Studies* 46.1 (Spring 2000): 42–66.

Jameson, Fredric. "Third World Literature in the Era of Multinational Capitalism," *Social Text* 15 (Autumn 1986): 65–88.

Ndebele, Njabulo. "Memory, Metaphor, and the Triumph of Narrative," in *Negotiating the Past: The Making of Memory in South Africa*, ed. Sarah Nuttall & Carli Coetzee (Cape Town: Oxford UP, 1998): 19–28.

Popke, E. Jeffrey. "Violence and Memory in the Reconstruction of South Africa's Cato Manor," *Growth and Change* 30 (Spring 2000): 235–254.

Roy, Modhumita. "'Is not the truth the truth?' Reconciling Truths in Gillian Slovo's *Every Secret Thing* and the Practice of Reconciliation in South Africa," in *Thinking and Practicing Reconciliation: Teaching and Learning through Literary Responses to Conflict*, ed. Leo Riegert, Jill Scott & Jack Shuler (Newcastle upon Tyne: Cambridge Scholars, 2013): 122–142.

Rushdie, Salman. *Midnight's Children* (1981; New York: Penguin, 1991).

Stiebel, Lindy. "Crossing the *kala pani*: Cause for 'Celebration' or 'Commemoration' 150 Years On? Portrayals of Indenture in Recent South African Indian Writing," *Journal of Literary Studies* 27.2 (2011): 77–90.

CHAPTER 9

Imraan Coovadia's Representation of the Ambiguities of Indian Identity in Pre- and Post-Apartheid Durban

The Wedding (*2001*) *and* High Low In-between (*2009*)

M.J. Daymond

The fundamental ambiguity facing characters of Indian origin in Imraan Coovadia's first novel set in Durban, *The Wedding*, derives from the conditions imposed on immigrants by legislation that was passed in South Africa during colonial times and in the early years of the apartheid era. The general climate it created was profoundly contradictory: Indian immigrants were needed for labor but not wanted as persons; they could come to Natal but preferably not to stay; those who did choose to stay had little right to benefit from the fruits of their labors; they and those who came to trade could marry but their family lives would not be respected and, in many cases, their customs would not be recognized. Although 'race' was not always named in the legislation, the trajectory traceable in it is, as Ronit Frenkel has argued, one that imposed a supervening racial identity on people from the sub-continent of India.[1]

For his fiction, Coovadia has worked into the structural ambiguity created by this legislation another set of differences and ambiguities that stemmed from the Indian context of origin and manifests itself in the particular characters and actions he has devised in representing their immigration to Durban. The passenger Indians, who followed a decade after the indentured laborers (see the introduction to this volume), mostly in order to trade and to follow other opportunities, found "from the mid-1880s when [... they] started competing with white traders"[2] that their presence, and particularly all signs of their prosperity, were seen as threatening by the European settlers who ruled the colony. Bhana and Brain sum up the continuing measures taken in the period between the South African Wars of 1899–1901 and Union in 1910 (shortly before Coovadia's characters arrive in Durban):

---

1 Ronit Frenkel, *Reconsiderations: South African Indian Fiction and the Making of Race in Postcolonial Culture* (Pretoria: U of South Africa P, 2010).

2 Goolam Vahed & Surendra Bhana, *Crossing Space and Time in the Indian Ocean* (Pretoria: U of South Africa P, 2015): 63.

© KONINKLIJKE BRILL NV, LEIDEN, 2018 | DOI 10.1163/9789004365032_010

Whatever the differences between the Boer and the Briton in South Africa, they were in agreement about the Asians; they wanted them excluded from South Africa and the movement of those already in the country drastically curtailed.[3]

The Public Health Act and the Slums Act, both of 1934, "gave the Durban Town Council authority to clear areas considered to be slums."[4] Despite this and other relentless measures taken to forestall the penetration of Indian people into white areas, some Indian people who came as indentured laborers and some who came as passengers were gradually able to prosper through their own initiative and hard work. Those who did invested much of their wealth in the welfare of their community—in education, health, and sport, as well as religious and cultural activities—as is shown in many of the short biographies collected by Vahed and Bhana.[5]

In selecting and shaping these overarching conditions for a fictional representation that would convey "history's infinite specificities"[6] in *The Wedding*, Coovadia begins his story of immigration not from the oppressive circumstances in Natal but from attitudes in India which had shaped his immigrant characters' sensibilities. What he points to is that India was also a land of division, collision, and ambiguity, and much of the comedy in his narrative arises when this inherited conflict adds further levels of contradiction and irony to that produced by the structural ambiguities being created in the new land. But there was a great difference between the two places: divisions in India were ancient, arising from differences in religion, caste, class, and regional language, and were a matter of custom rather than law. Above all, they were not a product of legalized racist thinking as they were in South Africa. Although the immigrants were identified in Natal through collective, simplifying terms such as 'Indians,' 'Asiatics' or, even worse, 'Coolies,'[7] these people were in fact very heterogeneous and did not think of themselves in collective terms. Initially, at

---

3   Surendra Bhana and Joy Brain, *Setting Down Roots* (Johannesburg: Witwatersrand UP, 1990): 156.

4   Aziz Hassim, Sam Moodley, Len Rosenberg, Kogi Singh & Goolam Vahed, *The Making of Place: The Warwick Junction Precinct, 1870s–1980s* (Durban: Durban University of Technology, 2013): 28.

5   Goolam Vahed & Surendra Bhana, *Crossing Space and Time in the Indian Ocean*, 83–236.

6   Imraan Coovadia, *The Wedding* (New York: Picador, 2001): 221. Further page references are in the main text.

7   The word has its roots in Indian languages, where it is used disparagingly for lowly labourers (Tamil) or thieves (Gujarati). The indentured immigrants objected to this term. See Ashwin Desai & Goolam Vahed, *Inside Indenture* (Durban: Madiba, 2007): 83.

least, the nearest that the indentured peoples came to expressing commonality, or a shared sense of identity, was when they named themselves after their port of embarkation as 'Calcuttias' or 'Madrassis.'[8]

Coovadia opens *The Wedding* with the multiple divisions in India when his central male character, Ismet Nassin, a Memon-speaking[9] "Bombay registered clerk" (29), stares with deeply-ingrained dislike at the Sikh family who shares his railway carriage: "a slovenly turbaned race, he thought to himself" (4). They return his hostile suspicions which, in moments of high comedy, erupt into practiced verbal assault when he accidentally stumbles against one of their children as the train draws to a halt, and apologizes.

> "Sorry, ha! Sorry, ha!" said the man. "What does sorry do for us, eh? Sorry-sorry will pay the money to the bank, that is your feeling? Here you have come and made injuries to our person. And we have not yet laid a finger upon you. Even though you have been staring suspiciously. You hoped we would not notice this? You think we are stupid?" The man touched his forehead lightly with his open hand. "So because we are stupids, then it is all right from your point of view, you can go ahead to assault and accuse us?"
>
> *The Wedding*, 11

Verbal assault is probably the defining condition of the first five chapters of this novel, chapters in which Ismet Nassin first sees Khateja Haveri, "the most beautiful woman in the world" (3); pays a handsome dowry for her to a family much relieved to be rid of a difficult, headstrong daughter who has hitherto refused all thought of marriage because it is a loss of freedom; goes on a wearisome train journey to Hyderabad with his new bride; and discovers that although she has yielded to his purchase she will not allow any kind of physical intimacy with him. As in *The Taming of the Shrew*, her quick wit and sharp tongue are her only available form of defense. But the narrative also shows that, in a much divided population, verbal combat has become a habitual pastime for everyone, and is often one that they relish. Even the narrator, the grandson of this unlikely marriage, enjoys practicing for his own pleasure the acrobatics that the language customs of the sub-continent require, as when he describes

---

8   The spelling varies. This is used in Bhana and Brain, *Putting Down Roots*, 87. See also Frenkel, *Reconsiderations*, 11.

9   Memon speakers came originally from the north-west of the subcontinent, emerging from Sindhi-speaking Muslims, who were known as great traders. Memon did not become a written language. See also Vahed & Bhana, *Crossing Space and Time* (Pretoria: U of South Africa P, 2015): 32–33.

the trapped Ismet, who has fallen hopelessly in love with his bride, as "Webbed and spidered" (83) and represents Khateja as realizing that if she is to keep her balance in her new circumstances she must "wield a prudent foot [... and] turn on the discreet ankle" (74).

The process by which Ismet and Khateja unlearn these divisive habits of mind while finding themselves increasingly mired in a local set of race-based divisions which produce their own ambiguities begins as soon as they arrive in Durban and are ensconced in a flat in the Grey Street quarter. First they are earnestly advised by their landlord, Vikram Naidoo, that old divisions must fall away and "we must be together as Indians" (145). Ismet is reminded of the dubious basis of this appeal for solidarity when he finds himself "lumped directly into the Indian masses" by his prospective white employer, who tells him, "I like Indians" because they are "honest, hard workers" and preferable to "blacks."[10] Ismet is able to dismiss such thoughtless generalizing as "whites [... having] no conception of the subtleties in the world!" (151), but once he and Vikram enter an increasingly successful business partnership selling imported brooms, the more troubling ambiguities of Indian solidarity and success in the Durban context begin to present themselves. When and how do self-protection and self-interest escalate into damaging separatist thinking? The implications of separatism are more fully explored in *High Low In-between*, but in *The Wedding*, when Vikram, flushed with early successes, says he is expressing a fully understandable ambition to grasp current opportunities, he is matching present restrictions with the beginnings of a reciprocally separatist approach:

This is a new world for Indians, Ismet. We cannot imagine the opportunities. The next generation will be all professionals and whatnot. Doctors and solicitors! This country is literally made out of gold and diamonds. Tell me if it is a law of the universe that the Indians should not cash in also? My friend, is that a logical fact? You must decide. If we stick together as Indians, then the sky is the limit. That is the only proviso. We must be together as Indians. The blacks and whites do not have the time of day for us. Soon you will come to understand this.

The Wedding, 188

---

10   Ismet is employed to keep the books for the Birmingham Van Fruit Company, and when Coovadia has Campbell, the general manager, praise Ismet for speaking "the language" (151), meaning English, he provides a sly echo of the General Dealers' Licensing Act of 1897 which required all traders to keep their books in English. The Act was aimed at Indian traders but it also meant that 'white' businesses would have to employ book-keepers who could read and write English.

The narrator tells us that although Ismet remains silent, he disagrees with his friend on the grounds that such unity is unknown in India, which he thinks of as "a million squabbling fiefdoms and hostile tribes quarrelling over the land" (189), and because he wishes to dwell in peace in the new country. But Ismet's Indian response to Vikram's speech must be overlaid with a South African one which has been more fully shaped for the reader by the passage of time. In the first decades of the twentieth century, Ismet's time, there was still room for the would-be entrepreneurs to manoeuver, so for them it would have been a moot point whether Vikram's outlook would prove to be a means of resisting colonialism and apartheid's later policy of enforced separatism, or whether it would prove to be grounds for complicity with such policies. For him and Ismet, Durban was simultaneously a land of promise and an increasingly harsh withholding of that promise, but history has provided current readers with the certainty that the official policy of restrictions and limitations would triumph for the remainder of that century. We may also recall that, in a supreme irony, the apartheid government would, in the 1960s, claim Indian "cultural traditionalism, intactness, business acumen and motivation towards educational achievement and success" as a triumph that was "a result of enforced segregation."[11]

Ismet is also shown as reluctant to endorse Vikram's enthusiasm for aggressive solidarity, because he still does not see himself as a permanent settler in Durban. His coming to South Africa began with a set of muddled impulses. Among them were his hopes that life elsewhere might help to tame Khateja, hopes based on a story told to him by a family acquaintance who claims, with little concern for the truth, that "a few years in South Africa [... had made his wife] completely obedient [...]. Absolutely in love. Just seven years and it has done miracles on her" (117). Through what is a patent fabrication, Coovadia further alters the customary balance between mother country and colony (usually seen as a land of last resort for the needy and desperate) in stories of migration. Ismet was reasonably well-off when he decided to travel, and he did so in the hope that time in the colony might have a healing influence on his wife, a product of India's quarrelsome tendencies. As Frenkel puts it,

> This retelling of Indian migration to South Africa serves to dispel dominant misconceptions that Indians moved solely to alleviate poverty, and

---

11   Frenkel, *Reconsiderations*, 10. Frenkel is quoting Kogila Moodley, "Cultural Politics," in *The Indian South Africans*, ed. Antony J. Arkin, Karl P. Magyar & Gerald J. Pillay (Pinetown, s.a.: Owen Burgess, 1989): 101.

inserts heterogeneity into the narrative, widening the scope of history to reflect the diversity of migration narratives.[12]

In the telling of this family memoir (Coovadia is reflecting his own circumstances when he has his narrator asking his grandmother for more information about her migration to Durban), history is presented from the inside, the mood is optimistic, and the mode is mostly that of affectionate comedy. The questions about immigrant identity raised by the structural ambiguities that Ismet and Khateja find in Durban (being in Natal but not of it) cluster around the sense of belonging that they have. To whom or to what do they give their loyalty? To which place, to which ideas do they feel affinity? With whom do they identify; what gives them their sense of self? In Ismet's case, his newness in Durban (from the outset he is determined not to offend "customs and traditions" [149], although he has no clear idea what he means by this phrase) and his thwarted love for Khateja mean that questions of belonging do not extend beyond her into the socio-political realm. He is represented as a domestic creature by temperament who distrusts what he thinks of as "political fiddle-fiddling, intellectual log-rolling and stone-casting" (223), and so he prefers to ignore the restrictions which are increasingly pressing on Indian people. Preoccupation with his personal troubles dominates naturally over thought of the wider context, so that when, for example, he finds himself in a discussion about socialism and justice with two London-trained lawyers, he is at first silent and then,

> his voice half breaking [… he] asked the barristers, "How we all going to agree what is right for the world in one country when it is not even possible between one man and one woman?"
>
> *The Wedding*, 248

Khateja's situation makes her as powerfully introspective, but, unlike Ismet, this is shown to pull against her natural inclinations. She has come to Durban expecting to find endless fulfillment in tormenting her husband, but gradually their rows offer her less and less pleasure, and the small victories in her circumscribed world yield few rewards. In her village in India she had been "a child of nature"; now she feels like "a chicken in a coop. *His* chicken in his coop" (183; emphasis in the original). She has a small circle of friends but compared with having been "perfectly adapted to the culture and the tempo and the justifications of the land, its vicious assaults and feverish provocations" she

---

12   Frenkel, *Reconsiderations*, 67.

now feels herself an exiled outcast, a "misfit, a social joke" in Durban (211). She finds some solitary pleasure in reading novels, but still suffers because there is no one with whom she can discuss her reading. True to his comic outlook, Coovadia conveys this by imagining her meeting Gandhi in a carpet shop in Aliwal Street in Durban and trying to tell him about the concept of 'moral victory' in the face of material defeat which she has encountered with delight in the pages of Richardson's novel *Clarissa* (219).[13] Even when she has begun to return Ismet's love and her psyche expands in new-found happiness, her observation of events around her remains dominated by her experience of having once been trapped into marriage. Khateja's very personal focus is again evident at the end of the narrative when Coovadia imagines that she and Ismet meet Yusuf Dadoo (a well-known political figure who was campaigning for the communist party). When he came to their house, Khateja invited him into her kitchen and "quizzed him about the place of women in society" (263). Such was her energy that Dadoo advised his colleagues against inviting her to attend any further party meetings.

In the final chapter of *The Wedding*, the narrator tells us that as his grandparents slowly loosened their ties with India and became "mentally denationalised" (265), they settled, without much reflection, into permanence and prosperity on the fringes of the world of those who held power in South African life. When the Group Areas Act was invoked in order to appropriate their house in Wills Road, Greyville, and they were moved to a smaller and less conveniently located house in the segregated suburb of Reservoir Hills (264), they did not fight the decision, although they were impoverished by it.

Set some fifty years after *The Wedding*, in the decade after the first democratic elections in South Africa, the circumstances and attitudes of the Indian protagonists in *High Low In-between* have changed considerably. Their prosperity has continued, but a hardening of racial oppression in the intervening years has meant that they could not be represented as remaining oblivious to their wider sociopolitical circumstances, and, open-eyed in the post-liberation period, a fresh marginalization and a new kind of ambiguity are what they perceive. When democracy was inaugurated, hopes were high that the fringe-living

---

13   Mohandas Karamchand Gandhi first arrived in Durban in 1893; he moved his law practice to Johannesburg in 1903; a year later he launched *Indian Opinion* and started the Phoenix self-help settlement scheme outside Durban. Moral victory in the face of material defeat is the second of the principles which informed his thinking, which, Coovadia playfully suggests, were presented to Gandhi in Durban. The first was the "outrageous conviction that each disparate subcontinental belonged to the same nationality [...] in a sense Durban created the nation-state of India" (143).

of Indian people would become a thing of the past, especially as so many had stood side by side with their African comrades in the liberation movement.

Coovadia again draws on his family's history, this time from his parent's generation, in creating a family group that is "a scale model of humanity"[14] in these circumstances. Through it he dramatizes what it might mean for South African Indian people to have their eyes open to history, and to register the huge discrepancies between the newly elected government's official view of developments and reality on the ground. For some of the circumstances surrounding his central murder plot Coovadia draws on events that actually happened in Durban.

The ambiguities represented in this novel still arise from the old, legally created divisions in society, but where they differ from the earlier novel is that attention is now on the extent to which race, as a basis for division, resides within the characters' outlook and actions. During the passage of time from the first-represented fictional world to the next, the prevailing atmosphere of exclusion, distrust, and uncertainty has entered deep into the psyche of the characters we meet and a prevailing lack of faith has settled over the community. As Coovadia put it in an article published in 2009, the same year as *High Low In-between*,

> in the million minds of the Indian South African community, it is always five minutes to midnight.[15] It is always the beginning of the end [...]. Uncertainty is the major force in our lives: we don't know if our cars are going to be there the next morning, if our families are going to be there, if our country is going to be there. But every culture is nervous in its own way. Indians have a particular sense of insecurity because they have very few leaders who can tell them what is going to happen to them [...]. Durban may be an Indian metropolis but it is also the centre of Zulu urbanisation; there are times when Indians feel like an occupation force but without the weapons.[16]

There is one character who is an important exception to the dominant anomie, Arif, but he is murdered as the narrative begins. It is a death that can be read as the demise of principled action in the fictional world. Perhaps because of

---

14   Imraan Coovadia, *High Low In-between* (Cape Town: Umuzi, 2009): 46. Further page references are in the main text.

15   This is a reference to the Doomsday Clock.

16   Imraam Coovadia, "Midnight," in *Load Shedding*, ed. Liz McGregor & Sarah Nuttall (Johannesburg & Cape Town: Jonathan Ball, 2009): 46–47.

the impact of ambiguity on the psyche of Coovadia's characters, the questions raised in this novel also go beyond the social and political determinants of *The Wedding* and turn towards a more spiritual and philosophical realm.

In the novel's point-of-view narration, events are refracted in alternating chapters through the perceptions of Nafisa and Shakeer. This formal arrangement draws attention to one of several disturbing features of the novel: while the narrative mode offers a dialogue between the narrators that the reader may choose to follow, they themselves feel remarkably distanced from each other. There is a distinct absence of overt communication between mother and son although they think about, and second-guess, each other constantly:

> His mother, Shakeer thought, was as distant from him as those heads on Easter Island [which he had once photographed]. He couldn't imagine speaking to her directly. And she didn't want to be approached.
>
> *High Low In-between*, 42

A "defining fact of [… her] consciousness" is her keeping those about whom she cares in separate compartments in her mind and watching them "in her imagination" (28) rather than interacting directly with them. In this she is unlike her husband, Arif, "a rationalist who thought about people in their tens of thousands rather than one by one" (86). Shakeer, by contrast, feels that he will never understand any individual person, let alone his mother, but, having studied philosophy at one time, he is of a more speculative and spiritual cast of mind than his father.

Because the narrative opens on the day on which Arif, Nafisa's husband and Shakeer's father, is killed, the back-story of events leading up to his death has to be pieced together from the two narrators' remembered scraps and their moments of speculation. Arif (his surname is not given) had been one of the leading figures in the formation of the United Democratic Front, the internal wing of the African National Congress (59), in the 1980s, but despite the promises of a future democratic dispensation, he and other ex-leaders find themselves once again pushed to the margins after the first election. Arif is also a world leader in AIDS research, but as his findings are not compatible with the views of the country's denialist President, "he feels that his work isolating the [HIV/AIDS] virus has been completely squandered by the government" (18). The new cabinet is in the "intoxicating position" of thinking that it is "not important what others believed" (97) and that, against the evidence, they could simply assert their own Africanist view. This is what has given rise to what both Nafisa and Shakeer call, invoking Lewis Carroll's *Alice*, the prevailing "logic of the looking glass" (151). Indicative of the change of mood from *The Wedding*, the satire is mordant as Shakeer reflects that in the name of the "dignity of black Africans" life-saving drugs were rejected while

> the Health Minister [...] pass[ed] suitcases of illegal money to [the anti-scientist] Hansel Metzger at the Union Buildings [... and] ensured African dignity by drinking herself into a public stupor by lunchtime on a working day.
>
> *High Low In-between,* 151

Arif's being sidelined is accompanied by allegations of racism at the medical school where he taught, and several Indian doctors are under investigation. As a family friend observes, these men had all also been active in the UDF (153). In addition to knowing that thousands have died needlessly and that he has been politically eclipsed,[17] Arif has been forced to resign from the university, and the Minister of Health has filed a defamation suit against him (97).

Nafisa is a skin specialist who treats increasing numbers of AIDS patients. Her back-story works somewhat differently within the subject of the renewed exclusion of Indian people. Under apartheid, many Indian people, and others, had engaged in unlawful financial transactions which are now being used against them by the new government. Nafisa had opened an illegal bank account abroad in 1983. It was a time when the UDF was being set up, when Arif's arrest was possible at any moment, when police were raiding the houses of all suspects (65), when they might have had to flee the country in haste, and when, as she puts it: "Everyone did it who could afford it" (21). When a tax amnesty was declared in 1998 (229), however, she neglected to declare her assets. Besides the money in London, Nafisa has undeclared thousands in banknotes stashed in boxes in her cupboards at home. Now the Revenue Services are after her, threatening to repossess her house; when she thinks of their letter of inquiry lying at the bottom of her handbag, she reflects: "This new country they had helped to create was more treacherous than one might have anticipated" (25).

Her crime is one of the novel's many ambiguities. It began from a sense of necessity, even prudence, and she had sheltered in the belief that as long as she remained below the radar of the racist laws she could treat other illegalities as a technicality. We are invited to assume that she shared in a general contempt for legality felt by all (and this is one meaning of the title phrase, 'high low in-between') who had suffered under racist laws. Certainly it is only her husband,

---

17   Shakeer reflects: "mortality had increased by a thousand a day. The government of course objected to these terms. First of all, who was counting? Second of all, who were they to define a day? It was the logic of a looking glass" (151).

who believes in moral principles for their own sake, who is furious when he discovers the existence of the bank account. Although she continues to believe that she had acted sensibly and in their joint interests, after Arif's death Nafisa recognizes that she will have to pay dearly for her carelessness in not taking advantage of the tax amnesty.

The narrative opens with the murder of Arif on the day when the family is preparing a party to celebrate his retirement from the university. It ends with the death of his killer, Govin Mackey, in what might have been a road accident, or might have been suicide after Nafisa confronted him with his responsibility for her husband's death. The moral ambiguities and ironies in his case are weighty and comparable to those arising from Nafisa's own story: Govin had been Arif's star pupil and, preferring prosperity to research, has become a leading surgeon in the country, specializing in kidney transplants. He has recently saved Arif's life by operating on him, although it turns out that to obtain a compatible kidney he had resorted to the black market in trafficked organs. There is an inquiry under way into the conduct of Mackey and his partner Gerson, and this is why Mackey and Arif had quarreled violently on the day of Arif's death. Just as Arif had demanded that Nafisa bring back the money, he had, when he found out about the kidney, decided to write a letter to the Medical Council that would have brought Mackey's career to an end.

Confirming the attitudes behind the surgeon's actions, Shakeer is told by Mackey's partner that medical specialists consider themselves above the law:

> lay people are not the best judges of how professionals conduct themselves [... they] don't understand the pressures and responsibilities. If we have to break certain rules to prevent a death, so be it.
>
> *High Low In-between,* 261

This man makes the mistake of suggesting that Arif would have agreed with him. Shakeer, embarrassed but needing to correct him by asserting Arif's real views, suggests:

> for the basic questions which are also the deepest ones, you don't need specialised knowledge. You need the same soul we all have. You need to take care of that soul and make sure that it is working just like a kidney has to be working.
>
> *High Low In-between,* 261

Although Shakeer has ambivalent feelings about having to make such a point, at this moment he comes closer than any other character to escaping ambiguity.

As the murder weapon, his own gun, is found next to Arif's body, Nafisa thinks at first that he has committed suicide as a reproach to her, and Shakeer accepts his mother's view. But they soon recognize that Arif's personality made suicide impossible and that his political and professional marginalization would have made him more determined than ever to fight back. While the police seem indisposed to make progress with their inquiries and while mother and son brood on the classic question of who might have benefited from his death, they are not shown to follow a series of clues so much as to try, separately, to make sense of the changes in their material, sociopolitical, psychological, and spiritual worlds in order to identify what might have happened. Thus, Nafisa is shown back at work in her consulting rooms and in the hospital, which she thinks of as having become "a microcosm of the continent" (233). Her interactions with patients, nurses, and colleagues as well as her impatience with the demands of the tax man lead to her decision to resign from her job and to divest herself of all belongings in the hope of reentering her world as an equal with everyone else.

When she is told that her London bank account has been emptied, Nafisa is mystified but gradually realizes that there must be a connection between the money and the murder. She believes that if she can establish who among Arif's trusted friends was in London at the time (one who would have had authorized access to the account) she might be led to the culprit. In a move which salutes Edgar Allan Poe's "The Purloined Letter," Coovadia arranges his plot so that she finds the information she needs in the current copy of *The Lancet* which she had collected from the post and put on top of the fridge for Arif on the day of the murder. It records that Govin Mackey was in London at a conference during the week in question.

Shakeer, too, seeks terms for reentering the world he had left years before to become a professional photographer: he has been an onlooker, an itinerant who is at home nowhere and everywhere. First he tries to rekindle an old love, and, when that fails, he tries, at Govin Mackey's funeral, to imagine filling a ready-made but now empty social space by marrying the widow. It is as though the murder has enabled Nafisa and Shakeer to rethink the past and to imagine a future for themselves in what they think of as an unreal 'looking glass world.' In dealing with unreality, they have, as Nafisa puts it, to "turn it over" (188). Each concludes, for their own reasons, that they no longer want to participate in this world on the old terms. This revisiting and reassessment of their wonderland, their underworld, allows one to understand why Coovadia should have made Dante a recipient of one of his other literary salutes: the novel's epigraph is "you, a shadow, see a shadow."

In the flourishing of crime fiction over the past two decades in South Africa, two sub-genres have been most widely written: the crime thriller and the literary detective novel. The former is usually "formulaic, fast-paced, plot-driven, [has ...] more action than detection, is quite violent, and [...] ends with a climactic chase or physical show-down,"[18] while the latter has

> a detective figure who sets out to solve the puzzle; psychological analysis; philosophical insights; realism; a sophisticated use of stylistic devices; complex characterisation and an overall profundity.[19]

Coovadia's novel claims membership of the detective genre, but with one major difference: whereas the classic version has a "detective who embodies moral authority and eventually restores order when the puzzle is solved,"[20] *High Low In-between* departs radically from this model. It does not celebrate an authority figure who restores order, nor, incidentally, is there a psychopomp or guide to the underworld, such as Dante allowed himself in the figure of Virgil. Nafisa does indeed work out what happened, she does give the murderer a chance to make amends, and she does explain events and their connections to Shakeer; but no public resolution is announced and at the end of the novel it is difficult to say that their knowledge will in itself affect the future lives of Nafisa and Shakeer.

Shakeer's leaning to "the cosmic point of view" (259) is a source of some annoyance for his mother. Right at the end of the narrative, just after she has told him about Govin Mackey's part in Arif's death, mother and son bring their differences to a head. Nafisa tells Shakeer that she had once believed that he was destined to make his life with a childhood love called Leila, likening them to "two pieces of a jigsaw puzzle." He replies: "That assumes we're two pieces from the same puzzle" (259). Besides signaling the philosophical difference between mother and son, this reply also indicates the extent to which Coovadia wants his narrative to strain against the plot genre around which he has built it. In conventional detective fiction, all details would pertain to the crime being investigated, but in this narrative the parameters of the "puzzle" remain ambiguous, and so any final, satisfying coherence cannot be on offer. As the narrative mode has suggested, there is no single, coherent point of view to give definition to the puzzle. Ultimately, it is not just the position of Indian people in the new South Africa but life itself that is too ambiguous for mysteries to be resolved and order to be restored.

---

18   Sam Naidu, "Crime Fiction, South Africa," *Current Writing* 25.2 (2013): 127.
19   Naidu, "Crime Fiction, South Africa," 130.
20   "Crime Fiction South Africa," 132.

There have been several signals that this is the position towards which the novel is working, for in the world that Coovadia creates, ambiguity (difference and sameness) has philosophical as well as political origins. For example, Nafisa wonders if she is taking her bearings from people in her daily round whom she thinks of as "black swans," borrowing her term from the example of a person who, having seen one black swan, mistakenly "imagine[s] that the world contains nothing but black swans" (125). In South Africa, the categorization of people has a peculiarly fraught history; on the other hand, identifying membership of a set is likely, always and everywhere, to be a necessary sociolinguistic practice. As she reflects on her colleagues at work and her family at home, however, Nafisa realizes that the act of categorization need no longer lead to inequality between people (another nod to the title): "there was no clear and bright line between her, her family, and the rest of the continent. There were no exemptions. How much of her life had proceeded on the assumption that there were?" (133).

Each of the narrating centers of consciousness is allowed to hold to her or his different outlook to the end. When Shakeer continues their last, often silent argument by telling his mother that one's point of view shapes the meaning of events, she is irritated by his apparent nihilism:

> From far enough away everything is the same and, yes, it is useless. It is useless to get out of bed in the morning if you adopt the universe's point of view. But we don't live far away, Shakeer [...] We're right here and the cosmic point of view, your cosmic point of view is simply irrelevant.
> *High Low In-between,* 259

It seems that their differences cannot be resolved and so, keeping the balance between their approaches, the plot grants each one a fitting exit. Nafisa decides to give up all her possessions, to regain her health, to be like everyone else, and to try to live an untrammelled but productive life; Shakeer attends a religious ceremony, a ritual of consolation, at a Sufi mosque in Durban. Once it was "a festival of the vanishing minority of Shia in the city" (266) but now Sunnis, Jains, Hindus, and Parsees are all welcome to attend. Still grieving that the opacity of the lives of others causes him infinite sorrow, Shakeer loses himself in the procession, and finds, for the moment at least, a vision of the soul about which he had once attempted to speak. Nafisa's decisions concern herself in her moral-material world, while Shakeer glimpses spiritual possibilities. Each has moved beyond the sociopolitical determinants of the ambiguities facing Indian people; while their respective journeys do not suggest any certainty about questions for the psyche, it is something of a triumph that a novelist and his characters have reached such questions in South Africa at the end of the twenty-first century.

Works Cited

Bhana, Surendra, & Joy Brain. *Setting Down Roots: Indian Migrants in South Africa, 1860–1911* (Johannesburg: Witwatersrand UP, 1990).

Coovadia, Imraan. *High Low In-between* (Cape Town: Umuzi, 2009a).

Coovadia, Imraan. "Midnight," in *Load Shedding: Writing on and over the Edge of South Africa*, ed. Liz McGregor & Sarah Nuttall (Johannesburg & Cape Town: Jonathan Ball, 2009b): 44–52.

Coovadia, Imraan. *The Wedding* (New York: Picador, 2001).

Desai, Ashwin, & Goolam Vahed. *Inside Indenture: A South African Story, 1860–1914* (Durban: Madiba, 2007).

Frenkel, Ronit. *Reconsiderations: South African Indian Fiction and the Making of Race in Postcolonial Culture* (Pretoria: U of South Africa P, 2010).

Hassim, Aziz, Sam Moodley, Len Rosenberg, Kogi Singh & Goolam Vahed. *The Making of Place: The Warwick Junction Precinct, 1870s–1980s* (Durban: Durban University of Technology, 2013).

Moodley, Kogila. "Cultural Politics," in *The Indian South Africans*, ed. Antony J. Arkin, Karl P. Magyar & Gerald J. Pillay (Pinetown, S.A.: Owen Burgess, 1989): 93–102.

Naidu, Sam. "Crime Fiction, South Africa: A Critical Introduction." *Current Writing* 25.2 (2013): 124–135.

Vahed, Goolam, & Surendra Bhana. *Crossing Space and Time in the Indian Ocean: Early Traders in Natal, A Biographical Study* (Pretoria: U of South Africa P, 2015).

CHAPTER 10

The Limits of Unity in Ashwin Singh's *To House*

Food, South African Indian Ethnicity, and Drama from Durban

J. Coplen Rose

Although South Africa's post-apartheid constitution seeks to create a national psyche and legal system "committed to non-racialism," the material reality in the country is that racism and racial divisions continue to exist.[1] Even more problematic is the fact that the destruction of apartheid's system of racial categorization has caused specific ethnicities to experience further crises of identity and exclusion within the new democracy. For example, in her study of South African Indian fiction, Pallavi Rastogi records that many in this community during the 1990s felt excluded from a post-apartheid nationalism "that seemed to be still predicated along the black and white binary."[2] Rastogi's assessment highlights the extent to which apartheid-era ethnic and racial divisions still operate on a black–white binary, to the exclusion of other groups in the new democracy.[3] Responding to this challenge, Ashwin Singh's play *To House* foregrounds how systemic racism is preventing reconciliation among ethnically diverse communities, but also speaks to the unique crises of national inclusion and identity impacting the South African Indian community in areas like Durban.[4]

---

* This research was supported by the Social Sciences and Humanities Research Council of Canada. I also wish to thank Dr. Mariam Pirbhai, Dr. Maria DiCenzo, and Dr. Lynn Shakinovsky for their insightful and constructive feedback on this document.

1 Ashwin Desai & Goolam Vahed, "Identity and Belonging in Post-Apartheid South Africa: The Case of Indian South Africans," *Journal of Social Sciences* 25.1–3 (2010): 1.

2 Pallavi Rastogi, "From South Asia to South Africa: Locating Other Post-Colonial Diasporas," *MFS: Modern Fiction Studies* 51.3 (Fall 2005): 550.

3 Rastogi, "From South Asia to South Africa: Locating Other Post-Colonial Diasporas," 550.

4 While 'Indian' was the dominant apartheid racial designation for people of South Asian descent living in South Africa, 'South African Indian' is a term that has emerged in the post-apartheid moment to define this ethnicity. Ashwin Desai and Goolam Vahed use the term 'Indian South African' in their research; however, the present essay uses 'South African Indian' because a majority of the South Asian community in South Africa were born in Africa; they are principally South African, connected to India through ancestral ties rather than by citizenship or birthplace. See "From South Asia to South Africa: Locating Other Post-Colonial Diasporas," 539, for further information on this ethnicity's relationship with South African national identity.

For the purposes of this chapter, I define South African Indians as an ethnic group and not a racial identity because, as Frantz Fanon, Henry Louis Gates, Jr., Anton Krueger, and Brent Meersman have variously demonstrated,[5] race is a social construct and not a biological classification. As Meersman asserts,

> there is no such thing as race. The scientific/biological proof is incontrovertible; race exists only in the sense that it is a pigment of the imagination.[6]

Frank A. Salamone's definition is useful here. For Salamone, "ethnicity is (1) a combination of social identities, (2) a series of statuses, and, finally (3), a social persona."[7] This definition does not rely on a racial categorization based on skin color or physical features but, rather, on social structures that signify inclusion in an ethnic group within a social sphere. This definition is fluid and can help to identify characters in the play as representative of a broad ethnic community while also preventing us from reading each individual as solely defined by these communities in any fixed or homogenizing way. Salamone's definition of ethnicity also applies to black and white categories. In this regard, all ethnic groups must be understood as fluid, influenced by surrounding social and political conditions. As a "combination of social identities," ethnicity is open to constant change, a reality conveyed in *To House*.[8]

Even if one accepts that race does not exist on a biological level, as a social construct it still wields immense power in South African society. The undeniable influence of race over South African thinking is a result of apartheid's system of classifying citizens into four major racial groupings: African, Coloured, White, or Indian.[9] For whites, this system ensured privileges and wealth,

---

5   Frantz Fanon, *Black Skin, White Masks*, tr. Charles L. Markmann (*Peau noire, masques blancs*, 1956, tr. 1967; New York: Grove Weidenfeld, 1982): 111; Henry Louis Gates, Jr., "Writing 'Race' and the Difference It Makes," in *"Race," Writing, and Difference*, ed. Gates (Chicago: U of Chicago P, 1986): 5; Anton Krueger, *Experiments in Freedom: Explorations of Identity in New South African Drama* (Newcastle upon Tyne: Cambridge Scholars, 2010): 206; Brent Meersman, "The Problem is Not Black and White," *Mail & Guardian* (22 January 2012), Thought Leader, http://www.thoughtleader.co.za/brentmeersman/2012/01/22/the-problem-is-not-black-and-white/ (accessed 20 August 2012).

6   Meersman, "The Problem is Not Black and White."

7   Frank A. Salamone, "Persona, Identity, and Ethnicity," *Anthropos* 77.3–4 (1982): 481.

8   Salamone, "Persona, Identity, and Ethnicity," 481.

9   Sonja Altnöder, *Inhabiting the 'New' South Africa: Ethical Encounters at the Race-Gender Interface in Four Post-Apartheid Novels by Zoë Wicomb, Sindiwe Magona, Nadine Gordimer and Farida Karodia* (Trier: WVT, 2008): 1.

whereas for non-whites restrictive laws such as the Group Areas Act, the Immorality Act, and the Pass Laws Act curtailed property rights, sexual freedom, and movement. These categories, although wholly arbitrary and based on physical appearance, social status, and community opinion, continue to influence South Africans in the present day. As the cultural theorist Sonja Altnöder explains,

> South Africa has found, and still finds, itself in an ongoing phase of transition from racial oppression to majority rule. These post-apartheid processes of transformation span social, political and cultural reforms; yet, they are inevitably complicated by the deeply entrenched presence of apartheid's intricate mechanics of inclusion and exclusion, which cannot effortlessly be discarded in the sweeping movement of a new beginning. Rather, apartheid's four racial categories, White, African, Coloured and Indian, as well as their intrinsic hierarchies of power, continue to shape everyday life in a manifold of ways.[10]

Altnöder's discussion of "intrinsic hierarchies of power" is precisely where feelings of exclusion and isolation from the nation develop for ethnic minorities.[11] Their perceived difference, Otherness, and unique historical experiences marginalize them in post-apartheid national narratives. Although they are citizens of the nation, they are rarely viewed as full members, because cultural differences, unique classifications as 'racial' outsiders, or divergent histories mean they are located outside a nationalism that imagines the nation as being composed of black and white ethnic groups.

Apartheid entrenched the myth of the homogeneous Indian community, an ethnic identity which to this day still has both subtle yet complex indicators of difference and heterogeneity. While certain markers of difference have been largely eroded—for example, over ninety-five percent of South African Indians call English a first language—divisions still remain.[12] Frederic Landy, Brij Maharaj, and Helene Mainet-Valleix elucidate some of the major changes to the Indian diaspora after successive generations of settlement in South Africa:

> In South Africa, an ethnicity which may be called 'Indianness' was progressively built by combining many identity patterns, some of which have faded away, while others have been strengthened [...]. What is

---

10   Altnöder, *Inhabiting the 'New' South Africa*, 1.

11   *Inhabiting the 'New' South Africa*, 1.

12   Desai & Vahed, "Identity and Belonging in Post-Apartheid South Africa," 4.

remarkable, however, is that these identity markers are also mostly factors of heterogeneity inside the 'Indian' group. Those having gone are
caste and the original class structure. The factors that have remained are
region, language, religion and urban spatial segmentation.[13]

Although Landy, Maharaj, and Mainet-Valleix's assessment differs from Ashwin Desai and Goolam Vahed's argument that language has diminished as an
indicator of difference among this population, both camps agree that differences remain. It is possible that mutual feelings of marginalization form one
of the chief bonds between this ethnicity's members. As the editor Neilesh
Bose explains in the introduction to a collection of plays about the South Asian
diaspora, past marginalization informs present efforts towards unification for
South African Indians: "Today, the South African state celebrates its diversity,
but only after a long history of official attempts to repatriate and, at times, to
curtail the rights of Indians."[14] This ethnicity is heterogeneous, not homogeneous, a stance summarized by Rastogi's claim that "Indians are characterized
more by difference than by similarity."[15] And it is this type of cultural complexity that Singh portrays in *To House* through a range of characters with different,
and at times opposed, goals.

     Although this essay identifies Singh as a South African Indian playwright,
it does so to illustrate how his work breaks down fixed racial categories or
challenges stereotypes established during colonization. While the fixing of race
categories was central to apartheid's economic, geographic, and psychological
oppression of non-white populations, its legacy continues to taint the nation.
Racial categories remain institutionalized in state bureaucracy, appearing,
for instance, in the 2011 census.[16] Working from within a minority position,
Singh presents the South African Indian community as divergent from other
ethnicities in Durban, but also internally fragmented by class, gender, and
generational divisions. This contrasts with outside views of the community as
homogeneous. Furthermore, his play illustrates how fraught the problem of
racism is because ethnic groups not only experience racism but also racially
marginalize other groups, reaffirming divisions. In this sense, ethnic minorities do not fall into binary categories of black and white, but nor does racism.

---

13   Frederic Landy, Brij Maharaj & Helene Mainet-Valleix, "Are People of Indian Origin (PIO)
      'Indian'? A Case Study of South Africa," Geoforum 35 (20): 206.

14   Neilesh Bose, "Introduction" to *Beyond Bollywood and Broadway: Plays from the South
      Asian Diaspora*, ed. Bose (Bloomington: Indiana UP, 2009): 5.

15   Rastogi, "From South Asia to South Africa: Locating Other Post-Colonial Diasporas," 538.

16   Meersman, "The Problem is Not Black and White."

And yet, as ethnic minorities the South African Indians in this play have a unique history of being othered, a position that, drawing on Homi K. Bhabha's description of Otherness, is often "cited, quoted, [and] framed" by prevailing outsider views.[17]

Singh is an excellent example of a writer who is conscious of the challenges South African Indians face post-independence. Not only is he from Durban, an urban center where the Indian diaspora "make[s] up one quarter of the population," but reviews indicate that his play reflects real crises of integration facing the city.[18] According to the theater critic Gisele Turner, *To House* ambitiously "takes Durbanites right into the heart of one of the most pressing issues that we face as a community—how to live together!"[19] For others such as Illa Thompson, the play is unique because it "feature[s] a kaleidoscope of White, Black and Indian characters."[20] In another article, Thompson credits Singh with being "politically in-tune with the dynamics of living in a culturally complex city."[21] Focussing on the play's exploration of personal relationships, Caroline Smart argues that the play "defines the new cultural divide" in Durban by presenting competing views of familial bonds between two characters, Kajol and Sibusiso.[22] While Smart's review is positive, she is critical of the set's minimalism but attributes this to budget or time restraints. Chris Dunton also faults the dialogue with being "a bit stiff," but applauds the play's "neat devices such as the use of pieces of furniture in the multiple set [...] to highlight personal interactions and class differences."[23] Overall, most reviews praise *To House* for its focus on crosscultural exchanges after apartheid and discussion of social mobility.

So far, scholarly analysis of the play has been scarce. Charles J. Fourie's introduction to *New South African Plays* describes the work as "a clever vehicle to explore the lives of a diverse group of characters, who each come to terms with

17   Homi K. Bhabha, *The Location of Culture* (New York: Routledge, 1994): 31.

18   Landy, Maharaj & Mainet-Valleix, "Are People of Indian Origin (PIO) 'Indian'?" 204.

19   Gisele Turner, review of *To House*, by Ashwin Singh, Playhouse Company, Durban, *Artslink* (28 November 2006): online (accessed 28 November 2006).

20   Illa Thompson, "Premier of New Play at the Catalina," review of *To House*, by Ashwin Singh, *Artzone* (8 February 2005): online (accessed 28 February 2005).

21   Illa Thompson, "Art Matters: The Indian Voice Roars." *Artslink* (5 June 2010): online (accessed 5 June 2010).

22   Caroline Smart, review of *To House*, by Ashwin Singh, Catalina Theatre, Durban, *Artsmart* (3 March 2005): online (accessed 3 March 2009).

23   Chris Dunton, "New Writing for the Stage Projects Visceral Force and Visionary Intensity," *Sunday Independent* (28 May 2006): F8.

their own prejudices."[24] While characters make small efforts to unify, Fourie argues that continuing divisions persisting at the conclusion of the play indicate that "a long journey toward the integration of our cultural differences lies ahead."[25] Themi Venturas's foreword to *Durban Dialogues, Indian Voice* hails the play as an "intelligent work" that foregrounds tensions between old and new orders.[26] In doing so, the play "gives us insight into the emotional and intellectual complexity of having to deal with change."[27] Such drama configures the suburban space as a location testing national challenges on a micro-level. As Devarakshanam Betty Govinden's introduction in the same anthology explains, Singh's plays are "attentive to the struggle for survival in the city against the backdrop of the official story of the South African 'miracle.'"[28] Govinden also highlights Singh's general use of ethnic groups in his plays to create tension, depicting multiple cross-racial relationships to dispel stereotypes.[29] Lastly, Shantal Singh also provides a brief analysis of the play in *Durban Dialogues, Indian Voice*. For her, *To House* "exposes the underbelly of society's discomfort with dealing with crosscultural relations as it implodes into our living space."[30] In this regard, the play foregrounds people's reticence "to connect beyond superficial engagements," indicating that successful integration is improbable in the short-term.[31]

Prior to its debut, *To House* was a finalist at the 2003 Performing Arts Network of South Africa festival for playreading, "South Africa's foremost playwriting contest."[32] After gaining this award, it was first staged at the Catalina Theatre in Durban, on 2 March 2005.[33] The play was then published in Aurora Metro Press's 2006 anthology *New South African Plays*. Subsequently, the rights were bought by the Playhouse Company and it was re-staged in Durban,

---

24   Charles J. Fourie, "Introduction" to *New South African Plays*. ed. Fourie, foreword by Gcina Mhlophe (London: Aurora Metro, 2006): 8–9.

25   Fourie, "Introduction," 9.

26   Themi Venturas, "Foreword," in Ashwin Singh, *Durban Dialogues, Indian Voice: Five South African Plays* (Twickenham: Aurora Metro, 2014).

27   Venturas, "Foreword."

28   Devarakshanam Betty Govinden, "A Critical Overview," in Ashwin Singh, *Durban Dialogues, Indian Voice*, 14.

29   Govinden, "A Critical Overview," 14.

30   Shantal Singh, "Summary and Analysis," in Singh, *Durban Dialogues, Indian Voice*, 17.

31   Singh, "Summary and Analysis," 18.

32   Ashwin Singh, "To House," in *New South African Plays*, ed. Charles J. Fourie, foreword by Gcina Mhlophe (London: Aurora Metro, 2006): 88. Further page references are in the main text.

33   Smart, review of *To House* (3 March 2005).

5–17 September 2006.[34] Most recently, *To House* appears in *Durban Dialogues, Indian Voice*, a collection of five of Singh's plays published in 2014.[35]

To House assesses the limits of unity and integration in the new South Africa. Smart's review asserts that the title can have two meanings, either "'to accommodate' or 'to return home.'"[36] It is the earlier term that best connects with the play's themes, as *To House* portrays a racially diverse group of characters struggling to live together in a suburb called Oaklands. The plot develops when a mixed-race couple—Kajol and Sibusiso—move into the neighborhood. The couple's most powerful opponents are a white unemployed neighbor named Jason and a young South African Indian lecturer named Sanjay. Jason dislikes Sibusiso because he believes the new tenant is abusing his power on the executive board of Oaklands, gaining favor from white liberals because they wish to appear politically correct. In response, Jason coerces his niece, a student at the local university, to set up Sibusiso, a faculty member, for a sexual harassment charge. Like Jason, Sanjay believes that Sibusiso is being promoted faster in their law department because he is black. Sanjay blames the unfair distribution of resources after apartheid on affirmative-action policies and seeks to destroy Sibusiso's reputation by secretly funding Jason's malicious plan. At the same time, Sanjay is also considering an alternative career as a restaurant owner, because he assumes that his ethnicity decreases his chances of stable, long-term employment as a professor.

Sibusiso and Kajol's relationship is threatened not only by external forces but also by personal prejudices. The two struggle to adapt to each other's cultural differences and this, in turn, places significant strain on their relationship. Sibusiso dislikes Kajol's close ties with her extended family, and this pressure peaks when Kajol's mother needs to find a new place to live. Both parties disagree over how to handle the situation. The argument eventually draws Kajol's wealthy uncle Deena into the debate, a man who also dislikes Sibusiso and motivates Jason to tarnish the lecturer's reputation. By the end of *To House* Sibusiso has uncovered most of the plots against him; he counters the attacks by destroying Jason's job prospects and his relationship with his niece, by setting out to acquire Sanjay's job and by removing Kajol's family from his life by distancing himself from Kajol. The play's conclusion reveals that most characters harbor prejudices that prevent the formation of a unified community in Oaklands, especially Jason and Sibusiso, who resolutely hate each other. Sibusiso essentially wins by defeating all who oppose him and, although falling

---

34   Anon., "New Staging for 'To House,'" *Witness* (16 May 2006): 10.

35   Ashwin Singh, *Durban Dialogues, Indian Voice*.

36   Review of *To House* (3 March 2005).

out of favor with all characters, stands to be elected head of the body corporate, guaranteeing his influence over the larger community.[37]

Highlighting continuing divisions between ethnic groups, *To House* traces the complex road toward unification for all South Africans, especially those in urban centres such as Durban where competition for economic and geographic resources is high. Importantly, Singh locates the South African Indian community at the center of this discussion. In doing so, he uses food as a device to foreground social and cultural divisions affecting integration. Food operates as a key marker of inclusion and exclusion because it reflects shared or dissimilar tastes. As Anita Mannur contends, "writing about food is always contingent and conjectural: what food offers [...] is an alternative register through which to theorize gender, sexuality, class, and race."[38] In this regard, a study of food in Singh's *To House* can explore how it both delineates difference, reflecting unique class and cultural positions, and also attempts to break down boundaries between groups by functioning as a commodity of crosscultural or cross-class exchange. While food emerges in the play as a possible means to unify the neighborhood, it ultimately proves unsuccessful because racial prejudices are too deeply embedded. This leads to a conclusion indicating that unity in Oaklands will take years, if not generations, to achieve.

At the heart of the divisions in Singh's play are racial stereotypes that most characters openly, and readily, level against each other. These stereotypes fracture the meaningful efforts at unity that arise in the play. As Singh explains in the Playwright's Note, *To House* explores the conflicting narratives between "a false image" of successful national reconciliation depicted "in the media" and the general population's "true fears and prejudices" (88). This is the seam that runs throughout the play and divides people between what they envisage reconciliation to be and the reality of the divided community. He elucidates further:

> I believe there is much to be admired in our evolving democracy, but that true reconciliation between our different cultural denominations requires a deeper and more honest process than what has been forthcoming thus far.
>
> *To House*, 88

---

37 The community titles scheme in *To House* operates using a body corporate. Sanjay, Jason, and Sibusiso own parcels of land but pay fees to the body corporate to maintain and develop the public spaces within the suburb.

38 Anita Mannur, *Culinary Fictions: Food in South Asian Diasporic Culture* (Philadelphia PA: Temple UP, 2010): 19.

Attempting to present a more honest account of crosscultural exchange, *To House* shows audiences how supposedly liberated mindsets still fall back into prejudiced thinking when people feel they are losing power, wealth, or status. In this sense, all of the characters desire some level of cohesion within their community but largely fail to unify because of fear, greed, or racism; Sanjay dreams of opening a takeaway where people can gather (109), Sibusiso hopes to lead the board of the community titles scheme (134–35), and even Jason seeks an integrated community like his previous neighborhood, Redwood (118). However, each character's self-interest causes him to scheme against the others, rendering these dreams impossible. What fragments the suburb, then, is not a rejection of community but, rather, the selfish and prejudiced ways in which the residents interact with each other. Stereotypes based on ethnic, cultural, and economic differences divide Oaklands on both the public and the private level.

In *The Location of Culture*, Homi Bhabha explains the importance of stereotypes in establishing and maintaining power. For Bhabha, the stereotype "is a form of knowledge and identification that vacillates between what is always 'in place,' already known, and something that must be anxiously repeated."[39] That is to say, the power colonial discourse exercises over oppressed communities is established and maintained through its ability to label groups as different, and to construct those differences as unchangeable and everlasting. Bhabha's term for this is "fixity," and is established in terms of racial, historical, or cultural difference.[40] As Bhabha goes on to explain, stereotypes based on racial outsidership contain "a paradoxical mode of representation"; they establish a clear and concise order while also evoking a state of disorder.[41] The colonizer is always at the pinnacle of the cultural hierarchy while those being othered are at the bottom. This process works somewhat differently in *To House*, as independence has reversed who is empowered and who is vulnerable in the community. However, South African Indians must still contend with the stereotypes and othering established during colonization—such as fears that they oppose national unity by exploiting other racial groups. The Other is construed as different, socially contemptible, and outside the boundaries of regular society. Otherness is thus established on the assumption that one knows the Other's identity, history, and behaviors while at the same time reducing the Other's position to one of silence and negation. As Bhabha contends, "The Other loses its power to signify, to negate, to initiate its historic desire, to establish its own

---

39   Bhabha, *The Location of Culture*, 66.
40   *The Location of Culture*, 66.
41   *The Location of Culture*, 66.

institutional and oppositional discourse."[42] And it is in Bhabha's sense of cultural negation that characters in *To House*, especially Sanjay, are othered.

As one of the leading representatives of the South African Indian community in the play, Sanjay struggles to overcome numerous stereotypes and prejudices leveled against him by members of other ethnic groups, specifically Zulu and white. Although Sibusiso and Jason also level racial and cultural stereotypes against each other throughout the play, it is important to consider that *To House* is mindful of who was, and currently is, politically and economically advantaged in South Africa. While Sibusiso describes Jason as a failure because his inability to benefit financially from apartheid suggests that his "family must have been pathetic" (134), and Sibusiso is portrayed as empowered in the post-apartheid moment (134–35), Sanjay feels marginalized during both political periods. Sanjay's experiences suggest that he occupies a middle position, caught between the reversing power dynamics of black and white ethnicities. The play captures this by decorating Sibusiso and Jason's living rooms in similar fashion, differentiated only by the latter's coffee table (89). These lounges appear as one room, "with the coffee table being removed and replaced for the relevant scenes," as described in the stage directions (89). As furniture appears in Sibusiso's house, we deduce that his fortunes are on the rise, whereas disappearing furniture in Jason's living room reflects waning finances. In contrast, we never actually see Sanjay's house. The play revolves around Sibusiso's and Jason's abodes, meaning that South African Indians appear either as guests, in Sanjay's case, as temporary love interests (for Kajol), or as outside threats to the social order when Deena arrives. This suggests a particular mobility among South African Indians but also configures them as outsiders caught precariously between the reversing fortunes of black and white characters. In this case, the play's structure foregrounds the black and white racial binary Rastogi describes as continuing after apartheid's end, presenting the Indian diaspora as caught between the two polarities.[43]

Sanjay in particular feels trapped in this middle position. At one point he describes watching his cousins fight to defend cultural music and a sense of cohesive identity in the townships during apartheid (118), a sign of his own historical oppression, while on another occasion he complains that affirmative action policies have curtailed his economic and professional opportunities after independence (97). One of his greatest concerns as a junior lecturer is that he will not be able to publish an article without Sibusiso's support, because "few Indian academics are getting published in law journals these days" (97).

---

42   Bhabha, *The Location of Culture*, 31.
43   Rastogi, "From South Asia to South Africa," 550.

His sentiments reflect real doubts among the South African Indian community, who, owing to their minority status, heterogeneity, and diasporic history, feel marginalized in South Africa's colonial and postcolonial moments. This is not to say that this community is rendered solely as disadvantaged, as both Deena and Kajol are presented as successful. What the play underscores is that others presume this community to be driven by self-interest rather than shared goals, a view that hurts Sanjay most directly.

Characters tend to view Sanjay as an outsider motivated by self-interest, rather than by a desire to participate in South African nationalism. Examples of prejudices he encounters include Sibusiso's dismissive argument that if a career in academia does not work out a wealthy uncle will let him manage his shop (99), as well as Jason's use of the inappropriate term "coolie" when he is provoked to anger by an altercation by Sanjay with his domestic laborer Justus (120).[44] In both instances, stereotypes about Sanjay's diasporic history and identity are at the core of why he is perceived as different or suspect. Occasions such as Jason pointing out that Sanjay's "lotus music" does sound "quite funny sometimes" highlight how ethnicity separates him from the larger community (118). Responding to Sibusiso's remark that he can rely on a wealthy uncle to help him in a time of crisis, Sanjay broadens the impact of the insult by illustrating how it generally attacks the South African Indian community; his response to Sibusiso, that he "should share his views about Indian uncles with Kajol," foregrounds how Sibusiso's view of Sanjay's culture also applies to Sibusiso's partner (99). Ironically, as we later witness, Kajol explodes such beliefs by refusing to accept support from her wealthy uncle Deena after leaving Sibusiso (125).

The treatment of Sanjay as outsider or suspect reflects a long history of Indians as being viewed as secondary members of African nations. This sentiment intensified during decolonization. As Mariam Pirbhai explains, many South Asian communities who settled in Africa both prior to and during European colonization found themselves "caught uneasily between a racially divisive European ideology and an emergent pan-African consciousness" when African national movements gained momentum across the continent.[45] This tension

---

44   For a brief description of the term 'coolie' as a "denigration," see Alison Donnell & Sarah Lawson Welsh, "1966–1979 Introduction," in *The Routledge Reader in Caribbean Literature* (London: Routledge, 1996): 285. Jason uses the term in this way to insult Sanjay in Singh's play.

45   Mariam Pirbhai, *Mythologies of Migration, Vocabularies of Indenture: Novels of the South Asian Diaspora in Africa, the Caribbean, and Asia–Pacific* (Toronto: U of Toronto P, 2009): 67.

trapped South Asians as a "proverbial 'middleman' or 'Mr. Brown,'" an individual who was assumed to be complicit in colonization because of the financial or personal benefits it afforded them.[46] Such ethnic essentialism locates South Asians outside of African national movements, labeling them agents and beneficiaries of colonialism lingering in the postcolony.

Emblematic of the distrust many bear towards his ethnic group, Sanjay has few friends in his surrounding community. As Kajol points out, his inability to forge friendships leaves him feeling extremely lonely:

> I don't think Sanjay has many friends ... I'm not feeling sorry for him. I'm just saying that, besides his mother, I don't think he's close to anyone. I don't know. He just seems lonely.
>
> To House, 113

This loneliness is exacerbated by people's distrust, making it hard for Sanjay to form meaningful friendships. For example, his effort to reach out to and collaborate on a project with Sibusiso fails when the lecturer decides he would prefer to write the article with another colleague (97). While not stated at the time, Sibusiso's hidden belief that Sanjay secretly wishes to claim Kajol exclusively for his own probably has a bearing on his decision to reject Sanjay's proposal (110). Sibusiso's distrust of Sanjay is not misplaced, as Sanjay is indeed scheming against Sibusiso. But it is Sibusiso's rejection of Sanjay's project that ultimately leads Sanjay to enter into a pact with Jason, who has opposed Sibusiso from the beginning (102–103). In this sense, Sanjay's feelings of loneliness and isolation cause him to adopt the characteristics that form the basis of his exclusion from society. And while this leads him to form a bond with Jason, this connection dissolves when the hidden prejudices of both of them come to light.

In many ways. Sanjay's personal struggle for acceptance within the community directly reflects the broader crisis of integration in the post-apartheid nation. As Desai and Vahed assert, Indianness in South Africa occupies a contentious space in national narratives because of negative perceptions surrounding South African Indians; these include fears that they are uniting with white populations against black South Africans, that they are not patriotic members of the nation, by virtue of their diasporic history, and that they avariciously exploit workers, especially blacks.[47] Perhaps the most troubling

---

46   Pirbhai, *Mythologies of Migration, Vocabularies of Indenture*, 67.
47   See Desai & Vahed, "Identity and Belonging in Post-Apartheid South Africa," 3, 5, 10. In
       the play, Deena fulfills the stereotype that South African Indians exploit workers, whereas Sanjay also partially fulfills the fear that South African Indians will collaborate with

example of such sentiment is captured in a song by the playwright Mbongeni Ngema, who labels South African Indians "exploiters of Africans."[48] Desai and Vahed also cite Ngema's song as a prime example of the animosity aimed at this ethnic minority, a song which calls for a decisive physical response from strong Zulus.[49] The sentiment expressed in Ngema's song relates back to Pirbhai's discussion of the middleman stereotype, in which South Asians are viewed as financially self-interested shopkeepers. According to Pirbhai, stereotypes of "Gujarati merchants amassing commercial strongholds" were common during the influx of South Asian British subjects to the continent.[50] Such stereotypes still have currency in South Africa today, as examples such as Ngema's song and *To House* indicate.

Singh, renowned for his satire, uses the play to attack prejudices leveled at the ethnic minority community while also encouraging South African Indians to laugh at the stereotypes internalized through apartheid oppression and national exclusion. The humor produced is often self-deprecating, but hinges on laughing at what South African Indians are falsely believed to be. In Singh's play, the character who best encompasses this role is Deena, a personification of the colonial middleman stereotype. Deena's behavior replicates the fears and anxieties encapsulated in the middleman because he has no interest in national efforts to reconcile and unify citizens. Rather than supporting cohesive community ties and, by extension, national unification, Deena encourages Jason to hate Sibusiso by offering him a job if he can force Sibusiso out of the community (128). He also helps to end Kajol and Sibusiso's relationship by prematurely revealing Sibusiso's plan to request that the pair live apart for a period (124). In doing so, Deena exploits historical divisions for his own benefit, as do all of the male characters in the play. But Deena is perhaps most sinister, because he purposefully enters the community to create divisions, whereas the other men quarrel as a result of close proximity to one another and from the underlying fear that others will usurp their status or power.

Rather than interpreting Deena's appearance as unusual because he reflects negative stereotypes, Singh's decision to incorporate a contentious representation of South African Indians into his play should be interpreted as a sign

---

whites against the country's black population. In Sanjay's case, his position is complicated because he genuinely seems to want to create a sense of community, even though his prejudices prevent this dream from becoming a reality.

48   Landy, Maharaj & Mainet-Valleix, "Are People of Indian Origin (PIO) 'Indian'?" 213.
49   "Identity and Belonging in Post-Apartheid South Africa," 3.
50   *Mythologies of Migration, Vocabularies of Indenture*, 67.

of the community's health—it can laugh at itself. While the theater scholar Thomas Blom Hansen contends that self-mockery in South African Indian drama is "deeply ambivalent as it negotiates the slippery terrain of current Indian identity," he notes how one possible reading of "the ironic appropriation of the older 'coolie' stereotypes—funny accents, superstition, snobbery, and patriarchal control of women—seems to signify a celebration of the successful social mobility away from working-class life."[51] Such a claim is consistent with the role Deena occupies in *To House*, since his patriarchal views contrast sharply with Kajol's contemporary views on family structures and leadership, suggesting that Singh's play produces humor directed at historically-influenced stereotypes of South African Indians (125). At the same time, Deena provides a means of exploring generational conflict within the ethnic community.

He provides comic relief because his patriarchal mindset appears out of place alongside Kajol and Sanjay's more progressive and community-minded thinking. For instance, when Deena proclaims that he is "taking charge of the family again," expecting Kajol to listen to him as head of the family (122), she refuses his financial assistance and instead seeks Sanjay's help in caring for her mother (131). Reviews of the play describe Deena as an "interfering old man" who "brings movement and comedic relief whilst deepening the problems faced by the young Kajol."[52] Noting the humor in the performance of Deena, Turner cautions: "He is very watchable and entertaining—but look out for the cutting calculating edge that rescues him from becoming the buffoon."[53] The tension created by this character is significant because, were he to become a buffoon, his appearance would lose power. As Northrop Frye explains, the buffoon's function "is to increase the mood of festivity rather than to contribute to the plot."[54] Deena plays a more significant role than this because his Machiavellian thinking drives the play. For example, his furtive agreement with Jason to trap Sibusiso in a sexual harassment lawsuit (127–29) instigates much of the play's tension. It is Deena's malicious behavior and the way in which he undermines Kajol's efforts to support her mother (122), seeks to oust Sibusiso from the neighborhood (129), and manipulates Jason (128) that make him such a calculated and divisive character. He personifies the fear that South African Indians are exploitative for personal gain.

51   Thomas Blom Hansen, "Plays, Politics and Cultural Identity Among Indians in Durban," in *Journal of Southern African Studies* 26.2 (2000): 267–268.

52   Turner, review of *To House*.

53   Review of *To House*.

54   Northrop Frye, "Mythos of Spring: Comedy," in Frye, *Anatomy of Criticism: Four Essays* (Princeton NJ: Princeton UP, 1957): 175.

On a constructive note, Deena's appearance as an archetypal middleman may help to produce a sense of unity among South African Indian audiences while raising awareness for outsiders. The laughter directed at him suggests that he is not an accurate reflection of the community. More to the point, his appearance may help produce a more concrete sense of community by providing a target to laugh at. Hansen proposes that, thanks to the heterogeneity of the South African Indian community, self-deprecating humor can help in achieving a sense of unity by encouraging the community to view itself from an outside position:

> because the 'community' only seems to exist when it is talked about, or looked upon from the outside, the elusive sense of Indianness has to be tapped from negative stereotypes and from the long tradition of self-deprecation in community theatre.[55]

In this respect, characters such as Deena move South African Indian audiences outside because they do not accurately reflect most of the community, although some aspects may be relatable to it. For ethnic outsiders, Deena fails to reaffirm stereotypes because he appears alongside characters that reflect the community's diversity, undermining stereotypes of Indianness. In this sense, self-deprecating humor may help to open the community up to outsiders, while reaffirming its boundaries for insiders. Discussing the general fragmentation of South African society, the historian and cultural theorist Jared McDonald contends in a personal interview that, for unification to occur, "difference has to become non-threatening, and I think that's what comedy helps to achieve."[56] In this fashion, humor directed at the middleman stereotype can reduce outsider fears of exploitation, since Deena is denigrated by the community itself. Singh was adamant that the play premiere in Durban because of "its Durban setting and the multi-cultural theatre-going audience in the city," indicating that the humor in *To House* is intended to work with an ethnically diverse audience.[57]

Although certain aspects of the play are humorous, such as Deena's behavior and selfish attitude, the sense of isolation that many characters feel throughout is also quite troubling. For example, Sanjay is shown to have been historically marginalized by the apartheid government, but he also feels threatened by the post-apartheid black majority. His fears are reflective of a

---

55   Hansen, "Plays, Politics and Cultural Identity Among Indians in Durban," 267.
56   Jared McDonald, personal Interview (12 November 2013). Video.
57   Anon., "Confrontations and Surprises," *Witness* (15 February 2005): 8.

broader crisis—beyond his desire for acceptance—in which ethnic minorities believe they are being overlooked by affirmative action policies.[58] Reading
Sanjay's experiences as indicative of the broad challenge of integration facing
many South African Indians, his solution offers a resolution to the alienation
he experiences. Using food to forge community, Sanjay attempts to break down
racial and class divisions established by apartheid and to integrate his culture
into the mixed-race neighborhood.

Owing to Sanjay's fixation on all things culinary, food becomes one of the
important ways in which Singh maps inside and outside communities. Chris
Dunton captures the important role it occupies in his review of the *New South
African Drama* anthology. In it, he suggests that the play uses "food that's
passed around (good cook, bad cook) to highlight personal interactions and
class differences."[59] While his comments on the appearance of food are brief,
the point Dunton raises is salient to mapping the play's portrayal of a fragmented neighborhood. Food is central to understanding different characters'
views on culture, community, and national unification because, as the cultural
theorist Njeri Githire explains, "taste is intimately bound to mechanisms of inclusion and exclusion, of belonging and not belonging. Shared taste inevitably
connotes shared discrimination."[60] It is in this manner that food works as a
device to foreground differences and unified views among characters.

The individual most frequently associated with food in the play is Sanjay,
the presumed "good cook" in the "good cook, bad cook" binary Dunton establishes in his review. Sanjay employs food to forge connections on all levels of
his life. On the public level, it helps the junior lecturer form cohesive bonds
with colleagues and students at university (99). On a private level, food is a
vehicle for establishing bonds with Kajol and Jason. Responding to Kajol's
evaluation that Sanjay appears lonely, Sibusiso points out that Sanjay has few
friends at work. The one exception is Jenkins, who, Sibusiso argues, remains
loyal to Sanjay because he plies him with *samosas*. This moment leads Kajol
to respond with a pun: "you think he's trying to curry favour?" (113). Although
this dialogue is largely an aside in the broader context of the play, the moment
clearly indicates the differing functions of food in Sibusiso's and Sanjay's lives.

The pair's views on food are at odds. When Sibusiso and Sanjay disagree
over co-writing an article, Sibusiso seeks to hurt Sanjay by implying that his
fixation on food makes him unproductive:

---

58   Landy, Maharaj & Mainet-Valleix, "Are People of Indian Origin (PIO) 'Indian'?," 213.

59   Dunton, "New Writing for the Stage Projects Visceral Force and Visionary Intensity," F8.

60   Njeri Githire, "The Empire Bites Back: Food Politics and the Making of a Nation in Andrea
      Levy's Works," *Callaloo* 33.3 (Summer 2010): 857.

> You've worked hard! I [Sibusiso] work eighteen hours a day. While you sit
> in the canteen talking about your favourite food with students, I'm slog-
> ging in my office, or my study.
>   *To House*, 99

Sibusiso's rejection of the bond Sanjay forms through food is representative of
Sibusiso's general rejection of any sense of community kinship throughout the
play. We see from this how Sibusiso views food, eating, and dietary discourse as
a waste of time. More to the point, if we view food as a marker of community
because "taste is intimately bound to mechanisms of inclusion and exclusion,"
Sibusiso's rejection of the communal discussion of food in the cafeteria exemplifies how he sits outside the social community at the university.[61] In this
regard, both characters' views on food expose their feelings about community.
While Sanjay embraces his cafeteria talks as a way to forge friendships with
students (99), Sibusiso isolates himself from the communal space, preferring
to remain alone in his office; Sibusiso desires to lead the academic community
as a lecturer yet prefers to stay removed from social exchanges around him. He
exemplifies a similar sentiment when he campaigns to govern the body corporate (134–135) while simultaneously planning to ask Kajol to move out because
he wants his own space (124).

  In Sibusiso's mind, Sanjay's gifts of food are a kind of bribery that draws
people unwillingly in. In fact, hypocritically, he uses food in this way against
his own partner (96). Kajol's response to Sibusiso's criticism of Sanjay's food
exposes the ethnic basis of his animosity. Asking if Sibusiso means to imply
that Sanjay is "curry[ing] favour" with other faculty suggests that Kajol does
not agree with Sibusiso's view (113). In fact, her pun directly references Sanjay's
ethnic difference—curry representing the South African Indian community—
as a possible reason for Sibusiso's animosity. While food is the topic of conversation, the subtext is cultural misunderstanding and prejudice. Kajol's comment
is admittedly a subtle remark, but the message is a salient one. Although
Sibusiso and Kajol live together as a couple, the ethnic and cultural differences between them are captured in their divergent views on Sanjay's gifts of
food. Kajol's response to Sibusiso's comment highlights the fact that, in this
instance, Sibusiso is potentially misunderstanding—or misrepresenting—the
cultural significance of food in the South African Indian community.

  Sibusiso denounces Sanjay's cooking abilities, not only trying to pass Sanjay's food off as low-quality takeaway (110) but also making accusations that
Sanjay tries to pass his mother's *rotis* off as his own at faculty social events

---

61   Githire, "The Empire Bites Back: Food Politics and the Making of a Nation in Andrea
      Levy's Works," 857.

(110). As an outsider who does not share a taste for Sanjay's cooking, Sibusiso exists outside the food community Sanjay establishes. In contrast to Sibusiso's outsider position, Kajol indicates that she is an insider by having tastes similar to those of Sanjay. Able to detect the subtle distinctions between various types of curries, *rotis*, and *samosas*, Kajol comes to Sanjay's defense when Sibusiso accuses the cook of passing his mother's *rotis* off as his own: "No, he did [cook the *rotis* for the social event]. He's a very good cook [...]. He always gives me something nice after our yoga classes" (110). Also a member of the Indian diaspora, Kajol appreciates Sanjay's cooking, thereby exhibiting a more discerning sense of taste than Sibusiso. This is likely due to her cultural upbringing and the importance of food in defining her identity. The anthropologist Jon D. Holtzman affirms that "Ethnic identity forms a central arena in which food is tied to notions of memory," indicating that, for citizens of the diaspora, food plays an important role in sustaining links with other members of an ethnic group, but also the homeland.[62]

Although Sanjay and Kajol's shared appreciation and insider knowledge of South African Indian cuisine may suggest a closed community that does not accept outsiders, Jason's appreciation of Sanjay's cooking indicates that the community is, conversely, open and accepting: "You know, last week I felt for some samosas. So I went down to *Bobby's*. Hey. Very disappointing. Oily. And too crisp. Can't compare to yours" (108). Jason's comments emphasize that he, too, can clearly tell the difference between Bobby and Sanjay's cooking. In doing so, Jason and Kajol are both in agreement that Sanjay is the better cook. Initially, Jason's compliment and his ability to discern differences between *samosas* offers hope that food can succeed where national attempts at unity have failed.

The literary scholar Barbara Frey Waxman identifies the importance of food on the boundaries between cultures and how an appreciation of food can help to break down divisions between ethnic groups. In addition to operating as a link between the diaspora and its homeland, food can also form an important bridge between cultural groups:

> Food is clearly a link among generations of immigrants and exiles; those who cook and write about food are 'culture-tenders' and at the same time teach people outside the cultural community about that community's values, rituals, beliefs.[63]

62   Jon D. Holtzman, "Food and Memory," *Annual Review of Anthropology* 35 (2006): 366.
63   Barbara Frey Waxman, "Food Memoirs: What They Are, Why They Are Popular, and Why They Belong in the Literature Classroom," *College English* 70.4 (March 2008): 363.

As a character renowned for his transcultural sharing of *rotis*, *samosas*, and *kebabs*, Sanjay appears to be a type of "culture-tender" who shares the flavors and experiences of the Indian diaspora with people inside and outside his ethnic group.[64] In doing so, he attempts to subvert rigid conceptualizations of ethnicity. As characters such as Jason and, presumably, Jenkins begin to develop the heightened appreciation of taste that characters such as Sanjay and Kajol possess for *rotis*, *kebabs*, and *samosas*, the hope is that difference will gradually be undermined.

Because food often has specific cultural ties, crosscultural exchanges of food constitute important acts of cultural hybridity. As Githire explains,

> if diet is synonymous with culture and citizenship, one of those cultural traits psychologists claim humans learn first, we regularly venture beyond the borders of our accustomed tastes, and our cultural obsession with them.[65]

Githire's point is salient to Singh's play because most characters indulge in, and in some instances crave, food made by members of the Indian diaspora. This suggests that, for characters such as Jason, craving food with specific cultural ties indicates a willingness to embrace the codes and tastes of other ethnic communities. The importance of such a crosscultural exchange is powerful because it stands to change curries, *rotis*, and *kebabs* from being markers of Otherness to foods that cross historic ethnic and racial boundaries to form the basis of newly forged communities, or are normalized as a standard part of the South African diet.

Bhabha's metaphor of a staircase—used to explain hybridity—helps identify how foods from the Indian diaspora could be used to help establish an ethnically hybrid identity in Oaklands. The stairwell in Bhabha's text is described as connecting two separate floors, functioning as a "liminal space, in-between the designations of identity."[66] In Bhabha's example, the staircase that connects the two floors in Renee Green's *Sites of Genealogy*, an art exhibit upon which Bhabha builds his theory, also "prevents identities at either end of it from settling into primordial polarities."[67] The staircase prevents a definite polarity because it continues to maintain an open space for cultural exchange

---

64   Waxman, "Food Memoirs: What They Are, Why They Are Popular, and Why They Belong in the Literature Classroom," 363.

65   Githire, "The Empire Bites Back: Food Politics and the Making of a Nation in Andrea Levy's Works," 857.

66   Bhabha, *The Location of Culture*, 4.

67   *The Location of Culture*, 4.

between two different spaces of cultural identity. It is in this same instance that food occupies a middle space in Singh's text. While the staircase is a rigid structure that is part of an art installation, South African Indian food is a cultural product that circulates throughout the community, offering new tastes to other ethnic groups. In doing so, the food and culture of this minority community can be appreciated for its difference without "an assumed or imposed hierarchy" emerging.[68]

And yet, while *To House* explores the potential for food to open up new friendships within a divided community, it ultimately fails to overcome the embedded racism entertained by most characters in the play. Positive cultural exchanges such as Jason viewing Sanjay's cooking as equal in greatness to his prized Johnny Walker Black Label (100) in the end only reveal a craving for the food and not for those who produce it. In fact, while Sanjay views food as an indicator of friendship throughout the play—a view equally shared by Kajol— outsiders such as Jason and Sibusiso largely exploit Sanjay for his cooking. In Sibusiso's case, he accepts Sanjay's *rotis* only to claim them as his own when serving them to Kajol (109). In Jason's case, he accepts gifts of food without adequately repaying the friendship.

Jason demonstrates his failure to acknowledge the connection Sanjay makes between food and friendship when he offers to pay Sanjay to cook for him (117). Such an action would convert a marker of comradeship into a commodity, but also raises questions about Jason's commitment to Sanjay. A common enemy aligns the two, but otherwise Jason falls short of reciprocating Sanjay's kindness. This is most apparent when Sanjay proposes that the pair open an Indian takeaway restaurant. In Sanjay's mind, this is yet another aspect where food can help to bridge ethnic divides by drawing people in for nourishment and encourage crosscultural dialogue. He envisages the restaurant as a multicultural space "where people come to experience something different," a welcoming site where "people want to relax and chat" (109). Offering to partner with Jason to create "Oakhill's social meeting place," Sanjay's dream is the clearest example of how he hopes with his cooking to sustain the dream of the Rainbow Nation (109). Not only would this be a space for citizens of all ethnicities to congregate but it would also be a model for multi-ethnic business partnerships.

Jason's flat-out rejection of Sanjay's offer constitutes another way in which food holds out the promise of unity, only to fail in the face of prejudice. Afraid of rising costs related to his divorce, Jason sidesteps the offer (109). In doing so, he also expresses a lack of knowledge about Sanjay, claiming that "you have to be certain before you commit yourself to a partnership" and confessing that he is unfamiliar with Sanjay's "business acumen" (108). Much like Sibusiso's

---

68   Bhabha, *The Location of Culture*, 4.

earlier rejection, Jason's refusal to go into business with Sanjay is linked to ethnic stereotypes. Misunderstanding Sanjay's offer, Jason believes Sanjay's dream
is to become a shopkeeper (109), evoking the middleman stereotype of the
colonial-era entrepreneur. The stage directions note that Jason's misinterpreta-
tion irritates Sanjay, who must dispel the stereotype in the hope that Jason will
accept him as a "real businessman" and "Not a[n Indian] shopkeeper" (109). As
built-up as their friendship appears, based on Jason's love of Sanjay's food, this
bond breaks down very quickly when issues concerning money and ethnicity
arise.

Racism remains the primary division at the play's conclusion, as most of
the characters fall out with each other. Jason and Sanjay part ways because
the latter abuses Justus. Sanjay's affirmation that Justus was accosting a young
South African Indian couple turns racist when he claims that "Black men think
they can just get Indian women," a belief that likely influences his opinion of
Sibusiso, although never explicitly stated (119). In the ensuing argument, Jason
orders Sanjay to leave, and he departs with his *rotis* as a sign that their friendship has ended (120). Jason's effort to make amends by inviting Sanjay back
for food is unsuccessful; the two never appear together again (126). Similarly,
Kajol and Sibusiso's different histories lead to their separation. Sibusiso's desire to have his own space because he was historically prevented from doing
so destroys their relationship. Kajol's rejection of his excuse, "Oh please, don't
give me that" (125), indicates that her own failure to understand how Sibusiso's
upbringing living in close quarters due to apartheid restrictions causes him to
seek his own space. Kajol's belief that people who live together should never
try to rebuild a failed relationship means that, like Jason and Sanjay, the division here is irreconcilable (131).

The play's final scene contains the most sinister falling out as Sibusiso and
Jason square off for control of the body corporate. Neither felt friendship for
the other; however, until this point their animosity has remained veiled. This
sequence reveals the viciousness of both men as the plots they have orchestrated come to light. Jason's niece betrays him by sleeping with Sibusiso and
the latter uses this to provoke Jason, remarking tauntingly that instead of a
"Coloured boyfriend" she has "graduated to a Black man now" (132). In addition to uncovering, and defusing, Jason's plot, Sibusiso reveals that he has been
searching Jason's past employment records for blemishes. As he has discovered, Jason was fired for internal theft. Going public would violate his ethical code; so, as with Jason, Sibusiso's hatred remains secret. But he too reveals
prejudice by describing his fellow neighbors, people he believes will soon
elect him head of the body corporate, as "honkies" (132). This sequence illustrates that while racism and animosity are prevalent in Oaklands, they remain
hidden because social codes denounce bigotry. If either man were to come

forward as openly racist, he would automatically lose the election for the head of the body corporate. As a result, they hide their true views. Likewise, Sanjay's prejudices about blackness would further ostracize him from the community and his departmental colleagues. So it seems that these characters refrain from publicly voicing racist views in order to maintain status in their community, exclusively for personal gain. In this sense, the play suggests that the changing social and political landscape has driven racism underground, causing it to fragment communities in new, and at times unforeseen, ways.

In setting the final scene in Jason's house, Singh foregrounds the totality of Jason's fall. While Jason and Sibusiso do not appear in the same scenes throughout the play, damaging each other through schemes and comments made to other characters, the play ends with a direct confrontation. Jason lunges at Sibusiso, only to end up on the floor himself (134). Sibusiso assaults Jason in the struggle, aggravating an old leg injury that causes Jason to miss the election. The physical attack leaves Sibusiso to chair the meeting and ensures that he will be elected head of the body corporate. In addition to this political success, by the play's end Sibusiso is also the sole owner of a well-furnished living room. This is because Jason loses his recliner to his ex-wife in the divorce settlement. Symbolically, the ending represents the reversal of the pair's fortunes. At the conclusion, Sibusiso's future wealth and success seem guaranteed, while Jason stands to lose not only his house but also his job, because Deena will only hire him if he successfully drives Sibusiso out of Oaklands (129).

The only hope for unity at the end of the play is the relationship formed between Sanjay and Kajol. When Sanjay brings Kajol a snack, the two essentially carry on from where they left off at the beginning of the play, on a park bench discussing their lives. The major difference is that Kajol is now homeless, and needs to find a residence for her mother. Sanjay offers to help her but, as his wording indicates, he frames the offer as limited to their ethnic group: "We are Indians, hey. I mean, we must help" (131). So, although Sanjay comes across as the most community-oriented character in Oaklands—using both food and the dream of a takeaway to establish bonds—racism succeeds in destroying any hopes of inter-ethnic ties. The South African population's eagerness to indulge in the transnational flavors brought by the Indian diaspora seems to stop there, as racism, animosity, and fear isolate most characters. This perhaps contradicts the actual reception of curry in places like Durban, where playwrights such as Greig Coetzee claim that dishes like "bunny chow" have come to represent the region:

> The bunny chow originated in Durban and was a food of the working class but is now eaten across the line. It was also an apartheid meal,

created out of necessity when non-whites weren't allowed to sit down in restaurants.[69]

Coetzee's comments, reflecting on the appearance of bunny chow in his play *Happy Natives*, underscore the movement of South African Indian food from occupying a position outside regional discourses to a location that is clearly inside.

And perhaps, like Coetzee's view of bunny chow as representative of the Durban experience, South African Indian drama will continue to help embed this ethnicity in both the landscape and national identity. Neilesh Bose noted an increased interest in South African Indian drama in 2009:

> Figures like Ronnie Govender and Kriben Pillay are being noticed in non-Indian contexts, such as by the African practitioner Zakes Mda, the journalist Mark Gevisser, and by the many awards Govender has received from the South African theatre establishment.[70]

This interest suggests that many South African Indian playwrights are increasingly speaking both to their community and to other groups. In such an environment, plays like *To House* can positively influence regional discussions of unity by fostering dialogue among audiences composed of different ethnic, gender, and generational identities. Singh's continued success as a playwright and his recent publication *Durban Dialogues, Indian Voice* indicate that he is attuned to these trends, creating theater that reflects the everyday challenges faced by people in culturally diverse cities like Durban.

Works Cited

Altnöder, Sonja. *Inhabiting the 'New' South Africa: Ethical Encounters at the Race–Gender Interface in Four Post-Apartheid Novels by Zoë Wicomb, Sindiwe Magona, Nadine Gordimer and Farida Karodia* (Trier: WVT, 2008).
Anon. "Confrontations and Surprises," *Witness* (15 February 2005): 8.
Anon. "New Staging for 'To House'," *Witness* (16 May 2006): 10.

---

69   Quoted in Kuben Chetty, "Behind the Beer Ad," *Sunday Tribune* (7 September 2003): 3. Bunny chow is a Durban dish that typically consists of a mince curry served inside a hollowed-out loaf of bread. Currently it is largely served as a street food by vendors or in takeaway restaurants.

70   Bose, *Beyond Bollywood and Broadway*, 367.

Bhabha, Homi K. *The Location of Culture* (New York: Routledge, 1994).

Bose, Neilesh, ed. *Beyond Bollywood and Broadway: Plays from the South Asian Diaspora* (Bloomington: Indiana UP, 2009).

Chetty, Kuben. "Behind the Beer Ad.," *Sunday Tribune* (7 September 2003): 3.

Desai, Ashwin, & Vahed, Goolam. "Identity and Belonging in Post-Apartheid South Africa: The Case of Indian South Africans," *Journal of Social Sciences* 25.1–3 (2010): 1–12.

Donnell, Alison, & Welsh, Sarah Lawson. "1966–1979: Introduction," in *The Routledge Reader in Caribbean Literature* (London: Routledge, 1996): 282–297.

Dunton, Chris. "New Writing for the Stage Projects Visceral Force and Visionary Intensity," *Sunday Independent* (28 May 2006).

Fanon, Frantz. *Black Skin, White Masks*, tr. Markmann, Charles L. (*Peau noire, masques blancs*, 1956; tr. 1967; New York: Grove Weidenfeld, 1982).

Fourie, Charles J. "Introduction" to *New South African Plays*, ed. Fourie, foreword by Gcina Mhlophe (London: Aurora Metro, 2006): 6–9.

Frye, Northrop. "Mythos of Spring: Comedy," in Frye, *Anatomy of Criticism: Four Essays* (Princeton NJ: Princeton UP, 1957): 163–186.

Gates, Henry Louis Jr. "Writing 'Race' and the Difference It Makes," in *"Race," Writing, and Difference*. ed. Gates (Chicago: U of Chicago P, 1986): 1–20.

Githire, Njeri. "The Empire Bites Back: Food Politics and the Making of a Nation in Andrea Levy's Works," *Callaloo* 33.3 (Summer 2010): 857–873.

Govinden, Devarakshanam Betty. "A Critical Overview," in Ashwin Singh, *Durban Dialogues, Indian Voice: Five South African Plays* (Twickenham: Aurora Metro, 2014): 13–15.

Hansen, Thomas Blom. "Plays, Politics and Cultural Identity Among Indians in Durban," *Journal of Southern African Studies* 26.2 (2000): 255–269.

Holtzman, Jon D. "Food and Memory," *Annual Review of Anthropology* 35 (2006): 361–378.

Krueger, Anton. *Experiments in Freedom: Explorations of Identity in New South African Drama* (Newcastle upon Tyne: Cambridge Scholars, 2010).

Landy, Frederic, Maharaj, Brij & Mainet-Valleix, Helene. "Are People of Indian Origin (PIO) 'Indian'? A Case Study of South Africa," *Geoforum* 35 (2004): 203–215.

Mannur, Anita. *Culinary Fictions: Food in South Asian Diasporic Culture* (Philadelphia PA: Temple UP, 2010).

McDonald, Jared. Personal Interview. (12 November 2013). Video.

Meersman, Brent. "The Problem is Not Black and White," *Mail & Guardian* (22 January 2012), ThoughtLeader, http://www.thoughtleader.co.za/brentmeersman/2012/01/22/the-problem-is-not-black-and-white/ (accessed 20 August 2012).

Pirbhai, Mariam. *Mythologies of Migration, Vocabularies of Indenture: Novels of the South Asian Diaspora in Africa, the Caribbean, and Asia–Pacific* (Toronto: U of Toronto P, 2009).

Rastogi, Pallavi. "From South Asia to South Africa: Locating Other Post-Colonial Diasporas," *MFS: Modern Fiction Studies* 51.3 (Fall 2005): 536–560.

Salamone, Frank A. "Persona, Identity, and Ethnicity," *Anthropos* 77.3–4 (1982): 475–490.

Singh, Ashwin. *Durban Dialogues, Indian Voice: Five South African Plays* (Twickenham: Aurora Metro, 2014a).

Singh, Ashwin. "To House," in *New South African Plays*, ed. Charles J. Fourie, foreword by Gcina Mhlophe (London: Aurora Metro, 2006): 89–136.

Singh, Shantal. "Summary and Analysis," in Ashwin Singh, *Durban Dialogues, Indian Voice: Five South African Plays* (Twickenham: Aurora Metro, 2014b): 17–21.

Smart, Caroline. Review of *To House*, by Ashwin Singh, Catalina Theatre, Durban, *Artsmart* (3 March 2005): online (accessed 3 March 2009).

Thompson, Illa. "Art Matters: The Indian Voice Roars," *Artslink* (5 June 2010): online (accessed 5 June 2010).

Thompson, Illa. "Premier of New Play at the Catalina," review of *To House*, by Ashwin Singh, *Artzone* (8 February 2005): online (accessed 28 February 2005).

Turner, Gisele. Review of *To House*, by Ashwin Singh, Playhouse Company, Durban, *Artslink* (28 November 2006): online (accessed 28 November 2006).

Venturas, Themi. "Foreword," in Ashwin Singh, *Durban Dialogues, Indian Voice: Five South African Plays* (Twickenham: Aurora Metro, 2014).

Waxman, Barbara Frey. "Food Memoirs: What They Are, Why They Are Popular, and Why They Belong in the Literature Classroom," *College English* 70.4 (March 2008): 363–383.

CHAPTER 11

'Doing Time'

Temporal Disruptions in Dr. Goonam's and Fatima Meer's Prison Experiences

Farhad Khoyratty

In *Being and Time*, Martin Heidegger distinguishes between two types of temporality. The first refers to human (existential) temporality (*Zeitlichkeit des Dasein*) which enables human self-transcendence through ecstasy (as Being-outside-itself) and the second to the horizon within which the former takes place (as *ekstema*, general time), an ontological temporality (*Temporalität des Seins*). Conventional wisdom about time follows what Heidegger terms *Temporalität*—the convention of conceiving past, present, and future as distinct. Heidegger's later thinking (post-*Kehre*, post-change, dating from *The Fundamental Concepts of Metaphysics* in 1931) will lead him to conclude that in the end *Zeitlichkeit* is the only temporality.[1] Thus, the past does not exist as an independent reality that can be accessed, but only as the past-of-a-present. The past is, in other words, de facto, mediated by the present tense of phenomenon. And so is the future. Thus, when referring to either past or future, any research is discontinuous if it does not include an analysis of that past or future's present. Time is to be grasped in and of itself as the unity of the three dimensions—what Heidegger calls "ecstasies"—of future, past, and present.[2] *Zeitlichkeit* temporality also allows for an existential reading of various diasporic conditions instead, not in terms of causative strictures but in terms of atomic kernels of experience, each replete with a past-present-future continuum. This approach suggests that we go beyond common wisdom about causality and cultural essentialism.

* I am very much indebted to Dr. Felicity Hand (Autonomous University of Barcelona) for her usual generosity with her time for kindly providing me with material, sharing her views, and helping with editing the document. I am also very grateful to Associate Professor Meg Samuelson (University of Adelaide) and Dr. Abdool Cader Kalla for their timely help.

1 See Martin Heidegger, *An Introduction to Metaphysics*, Fourth Edition, tr. Ralph Manheim (wr. 1935, *Einführung in die Metaphysik*, 1953; New Haven CT & London: Yale UP, 1984), and Michael Inwood, *Heidegger* (New York: Oxford UP, 1997).

2 Martin Heidegger, *Being and Time*, tr. Joan Stambaugh (*Sein und Zeit*, 1927; Albany: State U of New York P, 1996).

An autobiography, an unusual literary device claiming to present the present and its presence, takes on its own life. Unlike existence itself, it takes an intentional form and gives shape to events in the form of such intentionality, seeking to produce an intended effect and a sense of ontological integrity to the person writing. Thus, Nelson Mandela's autobiography, *Long Walk to Freedom*, selectively downplays the role played by De Klerk and by Mandela's wife Winnie in the violence of 1980s and 1990s South Africa. Mandela was writing an autobiography for a future present, that of a statesman of the Rainbow Nation of reconciliation, not that of the freedom fighter. The retrospective nature of the autobiography allowed him even more to write for a strategic present. His writing—like that of Dr. Goonam and Fatima Meer—was to will a narrator's past and future for the authorial present. Similarly, Goonam's praise of President Mugabe of Zimbabwe in *Coolie Doctor*[3] argues for an approach that need not be absolutist, but only readable through the nexus of time.

In October 2015, a new biography of the Mahatma was published by two prominent South African academics of Indian origin, Ashwin Desai, Professor of Sociology at the University of Johannesburg, and Goolam Vahed, Associate Professor of History at the University of KwaZulu–Natal. *The South African Gandhi: Stretcher-Bearer of Empire* is a very studiously researched and well-written piece. Already, certain unsavory aspects of Gandhi's life were known, that he had been in certain ways a strong supporter of the caste system, of gender inequality, and of general conservativeness. Also—and this was shown with some candor in his autobiography, *An Autobiography, or the Story of my Experiments with Truth*, and in a number of other texts, including Meer's many accounts and testimonies—his personal life is shown to have been far from perfect, including paternalism at home, a certain Hindu nationalism, and questionable sexual experiments. *The South African Gandhi* show him as a proponent of Indian nationalism, but in terms of the superiority of Indian to native African identity during his time as a lawyer in South Africa between 1893 and 1914. Of his prison experience in 1908, for instance, he expresses indignation that he was being classed with the native Africans. It also describes a Gandhi who was not very clearly opposed to the British Empire. Reactions to the book have been varied, with most either truly disappointed, happy to be comforted in their suspicions, or scrambling to defend and justify Gandhi's 'honor,' arguing for instance,—somewhat disingenuously—that he was merely being a lawyer. Referring, inter alia, to Gandhi's autobiography, Desai and Vahed point out how Gandhi was being selective when representing his life:

---

3   Dr. Goonam, *Coolie Doctor: An Autobiography* (Durban: Madiba, 1991): 173.

As we examined Gandhi's actions and contemporary writings during his South African stay, and compared these with what he wrote in his autobiography and *Satyagraha in South Africa*, it was apparent that he indulged in some 'tidying up.' He was effectively rewriting his own history.[4]

In the midst of so many judgments, a phenomenological premise about being is commonly missing: time. Identity is generally imagined as continuous, as rational, as conscious, as self-conscious. Thus, whether the reaction is disappointment or confirmation, or anger, Gandhi is imagined to be a Mahatma beyond time. The unrealistic expectations originate in practices that remain shy of what Heidegger terms 'thrownness', the fact that beings are "thrown into" the world (*Geworfenheit*).[5] Whenever we become acutely conscious that we exist, we catch ourselves already in the world as it is. As it is, the world corresponds to social conventions, structures, and ties, such as those of family, nationality, and ethnicity. However, what we are thrown into can be overthrown, as is most obviously the case with activists, who even endure prison and threats to their lives as a result. Again, this is performed temporally, by first becoming aware of the 'thrownness' (past) and projecting (future), both actions actively taking place in the present—but the overthrow is never complete. Judgments, which are essential to understanding events, also need to be bracketed (*sous rature*) and not treated as final or definitive. Being is not truly accountable; any account of it is at best partial and needs to be contextualized as part of an intimate existentialism. Such bracketing[6] involves notable difficulties when connecting to public figures, especially icons of moral inspiration.

In this final chapter on South African 'Indian' writers, space must be made for two formidable activists whose prison experiences exemplify the determination and courage of so many anti-apartheid fighters from the 'Indian' community whose stories have not been sufficiently acknowledged. Kesaveloo Goonaruthnum Naidoo, better known as Dr. Goonam, published her autobiography, ironically entitled *Coolie Doctor*, in 1991. Fatima Meer, a sociologist and ardent anti-apartheid activist like Goonam, wrote *Prison Diary: One Hundred*

---

4   Ashwin Desai & Goolam Vahed, *The South African Gandhi: Stretcher-Bearer of Empire* (Stanford CA: Stanford UP, 2015): 25, italics in the original.

5   Martin Heidegger, *Being and Time*, 284.

6   Bracketing now refers to a Heideggerian (and Derridean) *sous-rature* or erasure. In Gayatri Spivak's words, in her defining Preface to Derrida's *Of Grammatology*: "Since the word is inaccurate, it is crossed out. Since the word is necessary, it remains legible"; Jacques Derrida, *Of Grammatology*, ed. Spivak (Baltimore MD: Johns Hopkins UP, 1997). In *sous-rature*, the (intended) lack of a neat taxonomy is here being replaced by a series of ghostly superimpositions.

and Thirteen Days 1976 in 2001. Both works, despite their limitations,[7] have added to the canon of South African women's autobiographies and have provided a gendered reading of prison narratives. As expected with autobiographies, the focus is here on relations of the self to itself. Arguably, the autobiography provides a locus like no other literary genre for exploring the inner life of a politics induced by apartheid, whose originary fractal organizes identities collectively, pits one ethnicity against another, but inevitably brings everything down to the issue of subjectivity, of the question of being (as *Seinsfrage*). Similarly, this fractal reveals itself most effectively through the condition of being imprisoned, a literal metaphor for living under apartheid. Prison autobiographies, according form to content, open a space of radical contestation, forcing an ambivalently elusive politics to face up to the only pertinent issue at hand: being (human).

Before the 1960s there were few, if any, published autobiographies by non-white South African women[8] and the growing number of women's memoirs in the years following the demise of apartheid demonstrates the therapeutic value of life writing.[9] The need for women to tell their stories and, in some cases, to cross the threshold between the private and the public has stimulated a great deal of autobiographical work. Life writing, which has mushroomed in the post-apartheid era, has, for Annie Gagiano, been "undertaken by some as a duty or a responsibility [and their] texts also testify (however modest in tone or intent) to pride taken by the author in his or her contribution to this society."[10] Gagiano goes on to say that the "autobiographer's burden to relate horrible memories can also point to a hope of eventually giving birth

---

7   As far as *Coolie Doctor* is concerned, Goonam took many years to conclude her work; had it not been for the intervention of Fatima Meer, it may never have seen the light of day. For reasons unknown, the text is very poorly edited, but this may not be attributable to Goonam herself.

8   Judith Lütge Coullie, "Introduction: Placing Selves in Question," in *The Closest of Strangers: South African Women's Life Writing*, ed. Coullie et al. (Johannesburg: Wits UP, 2004): 7.

9   According to Sarah Nuttall, "Reading and Recognition in Three South African Women's Autobiographies," *Current Writing: Text and Reception in Southern Africa* 8.2 (1996): 5, the first autobiography to be published in English by a black South African woman was Noni Jabavu's *The Ochre People: Scenes from a South African Life* (1963). See also Judith Lütge Coullie, "Auto/biographical Accounts in South Africa in Three Parts," in *Selves in Question: Interviews on Southern African Auto/biography*, ed. Judith Lütge Coullie et al. (Honolulu: Hawai'i UP, 2006): 24.

10   Annie Gagiano, "'… to remember is like starting to see': South African life stories today," *Current Writing: Text and Reception in Southern Africa* 21.1–2 (2009): 263.

to a better reality."[11] As regards the rationale of writing an autobiography of struggle in which incarceration features strongly, as is the case of Goonam's work, and Meer's daily account of the apartheid prison, both of which highlight "the brutal and inhumane prison conditions that denigrated and humiliated women,"[12] the question arises as to the purpose of composition. This is closely intertwined with the notion of empathy, as these accounts, which narrate police brutality and the horrors of detention in the apartheid era, cry out for social justice—or is the healing effect of writing the real objective?

Goonam's work, published just a year after the release of Nelson Mandela, illustrates what J.K. Gardiner has called "a privileged arena for moral action and creating psychological prerequisites to historical change".[13] The years during which the Convention for a Democratic South Africa (CODESA) was negotiating the transition toward a democratic state were fraught with indecision, doubts, and fears. Goonam's autobiography may have been intended in the present tense (*Zeitlichkeit*) to remind readers of the enormity of the challenges that the country faced. Several years later, Jay Naidoo, former secretary of the Congress of South African Trade Unions and minister in the Mandela administration, wrote in his autobiography *Fighting for Justice*: "We have not addressed the psychological damage we have all suffered [... there exist] deep underlying tensions and schisms in our society that we have papered over."[14] In this sense, *Coolie Doctor* seems to respond to what Naidoo would refer to almost two decades after the publication of her text. Fatima Meer was a tireless campaigner and author of some forty books on sociological issues, so *Prison Diary* responds to her personal experience of being deprived of liberty simply because of her ideas. In her conclusion, she states quite adamantly in the first-person plural (perhaps to signify a collective conscience) her purpose in penning this narrative:

> We were proud of our detention and even enjoyed a sense of the heroic. In retrospect, we would not have missed our time in prison for just about anything. It was a memory, an experience which was not just personal, it was historical, part of the people's memory. Thus this diary.[15]

---

11   Gagiano, "'... to remember is like starting to see': South African life stories today," 263.

12   Kalpana Hiralal, "Narratives and Testimonies of Women Detainees in the Anti-Apartheid Struggle," *Agenda* 29.4 (2015): 43.

13   J.K. Gardiner, *Rhys, Stead, Lessing, and the Politics of Empathy* (Bloomington: Indiana UP, 1989): 18.

14   Jay Naidoo, *Fighting for Justice: A Lifetime of Political and Social Activism* (Johannesburg: Picador Africa, 2010): 346.

15   Fatima Meer, *Prison Diary: One Hundred and Thirteen Days 1976* (Cape Town: Kwela, 2001): 210.

If 'black' women's autobiographies were relatively unusual before the abolition of apartheid, prison memoirs or resistance writing composed by women were extremely rare. In his survey of apartheid prison writing, Daniel Roux describes how the National Party used prisons "as a means to enforce a dictatorial form of social control."[16] Likewise, Paul Gready states that "the prison experience, particularly for the political prisoner, was essentially about violence"[17] and, as reflected in many prison narratives, about the relentless efforts by the warders to attempt to crush the prisoners' sense of humanity, to humiliate them, and ultimately to destroy their self-esteem. Clearly, a definition of prison writing is "that subgenre which responded precisely to the erosion of the rule of law and the concomitant emergence of the police state in apartheid South Africa."[18] As far as women prisoners were concerned,

> Prison authorities made women's political choices seem aberrant, inap-
> propriate [...] Implicitly, an ideal woman was one who was acquiescent
> to the state, a woman who remained in the confines of the domestic
> world.[19]

Apart from denying women their role as political agents, any collective identity was rarely understood as a personal sacrifice that women like Goonam were prepared to make for the common good, what Sam Raditlhalo has called "redemptive suffering [...] that form of suffering in which the autobiographical subject accepts such suffering in order to relieve the larger suffering experienced by those with whom he or she identifies."[20]

If South African prison writing tends to hover between a soul-searching confessional form of narrative and a clearly enunciated discourse of collective agency, both Goonam's and Meer's texts nestle themselves within the latter category as primarily autobiographies of struggle, which not only bear witness to the crimes against humanity committed by the apartheid regime but also vindicate the role of women—specifically Indian women—in the fight for a

---

16   Daniel Roux, "Writing the Prison," in *The Cambridge History of South African Literature*,
      ed. David Attwell & Derek Attridge (Cambridge: Cambridge UP, 2012): 546.

17   Paul Gready, "Autobiography and the 'Power of Writing': Political Prison Writing in the
      Apartheid Era," *Journal of Southern African Studies* 19.3 (September 1993): 495.

18   Judith Lütge Coullie, "Introduction" to *Selves in Question: Interviews on Southern African
      Auto/biography*, ed. Judith Lütge Coullie et al. (Honolulu: Hawai'i UP, 2006): 22.

19   Fiona C. Ross, *Bearing Witness: Women and the Truth and Reconciliation Commission in
      South Africa* (London: Pluto, 2003): 64–65.

20   Sam Raditlhalo, "Unzima lomthwalo—'this load is heavy': A Selection of South African
      Prison and Exile Life Writings," *Life Writing* 1.2 (2004): 31.

democratic state.[21] Against the will to make them invisible in prison, the autobiography provides an opening to the world, a public denunciation, and a personal antidote to its stealthy and hypocritical nature, the refusal of the drive
of State normativization. The prison autobiography is here intended to shame
the apartheid state by casting light onto its reality. Thus, the prison exposes
the truth about apartheid—that *it* is carceral. In the case of the autobiographies by Goonam and Meer, the public space provided by the autobiography
moves centrifugally from the private identity constructed in the home both
as women and as members of 'Indian' identities, which are also carceral. But
the mise-en-abyme of identity multiplies their bodies further into their diasporic condition, their specific religious background, regional Indian origin,
class, family history, psychic history. The fact of taxonomy itself becomes, in
essence, carceral.

Whereas Meer's *Prison Diary* covers mostly what its full title intimates,
113 days in jail, Goonam's autobiography spans most of her life, with the prison stories (one in particular) as kernels that qualify in many ways the rest of
the narrative. Yet, the other stories of Goonam's are far from incidental. They
provide details of the world she was 'thrown into.' However, the selection of
certain events rather than others gives Goonam's autobiography the more bildungsroman quality, a serendipitously deterministic approach to events that
creates an image of heroism rather than angst for the reader. This can help
maintain such illusions as that, since the fall of apartheid, the conditions of
the carceral ended—in South Africa or elsewhere.

The two accounts under scrutiny in this chapter were finally published after
the demise of apartheid, although Goonam's autobiography was started many
years before and the actual dating of the composition of Meer's work is unknown. This suggests that the two texts are subsumed under the category of
"retrospective prison memoirs."[22] Fran Buntman remarks, with reference to
Meer's text:

---

21   James Ocita comments on subversion in the adoption of the autobiography form by the
      non-white woman: "In choosing a form that has canonically been arrogated by bourgeois
      white males, whose claim to unique selfhood purportedly set them apart as the only indi-
      viduals capable of self-narrative, Goonam's autobiographical act opens up many fields of
      contestation as well as possibility."
         James Ocita, "Diasporic Imaginaries: Memory and Negotiation of Belonging in East
      African and South African Indian Narratives" (doctoral dissertation, Stellenbosch Uni-
      versity, 2013): 14.
22   Daniel Roux, "Writing the Prison," 553.

My best guess is that it was written in detention, in whole or in part. If that is the case, this makes it all the more valuable a contribution to resistance scholarship because most South African prison memoirs were written and reconstructed after, often long after, their authors were incarcerated. This gap in time reflects at least two of the practical facts of being in prison for anti-apartheid activities and sympathies: paper was often not available and it was usually not safe to record thoughts and feelings because these almost certainly would be found by authorities and used against inmates and others. But at least from historical and methodological perspectives, when and how the diary was written, and possibly edited, affects the understanding and reading of it, and it is frustrating not to be offered this basic information.[23]

Likewise, as Gready points out, "In order to penetratingly read prison accounts it is necessary to understand the circumstances in which, and reasons why, they were written."[24] Elizabeth Stanley, mostly comparing hers to Suttner's autobiography, argues, of Meer's diary:

> there is little political, social, economic or personal contextualisation of her imprisonment. Meer, a respected academic, has written a wealth of material to challenge apartheid practices, and also has close relationships with significant others in the movement. Yet, in this piece, there is little analysis of her condition. On one level, this is an unfair critique, as it is fundamentally a diary written under prison conditions, but its content raises many questions and, primarily, leaves them unanswered.[25]

Although such concerns are perfectly valid, they remain symptomatic of a metaphysics of presence (Derrida) signaling both presence (space) and present tense (time) as superior. Prison, especially as part of resistance, denotes the body's presence as exemplary. Such anxiety in the reader comes from her/his grappling with her/his own personal disorientation: for the struggle against the apartheid State has found resonance that stretches far and wide, but also in much of collective psychic history, as something Promethean. This feeds almost hagiographical expectations in readers of prison autobiographies,

---

23 Fran Buntman, "Imprisonment in Apartheid South Africa I: Personal Histories," *Journal of Southern African Studies* 31.3 (2005): 665.

24 Paul Gready, "Autobiography and the 'Power of Writing,'" 491.

25 Elizabeth Stanley, "Review: Meer, Fatima, Prison Diary: One Hundred and Thirteen Days, 1976," *Journal of Modern African Studies* 41.2 (June 2003): 333.

and therefore room for inevitable disappointment (as with Mahatma Gandhi above).

According to Dr. Goonam's daughter, Vanitha Chetty, "One of my mother's major complaints with the book was that chunks were left out and hence there was no flow."[26] This concern for narrative completeness is a literary reminder of how autobiographies are incomplete projects, but not because they need to be improved, but because they seem to promise more authenticity than they can deliver, since there is greater coincidence between the body writing and the body experiencing than in other literary forms, and since autobiographies (as ostensible fact) seem especially opposed to fiction. Above all, autobiographies can never record the present-as-present. Representation can never be complete, but autobiographies to most minds make an ontological claim: that being, full, non-chaotic, accountable, can be revealed and that the person writing has a privileged, self-conscious higher awareness of such a self. The defiant freedom fighter in the public political arena is expected to be a freedom fighter in the domestic sphere and in prison. In addition, expectations surrounding storytelling as retrospective means, for instance, that it is known that the story will end with the release of the prisoner and the end of apartheid, which impacts on our reading of the text in terms of the nature and trajectory of justice. These make of prison autobiographies a construction of heroism that fails to include the depth of despair that a true present tense of indefinite imprisonment and no notion of the end-time of apartheid implies. A sense of the temporal hiatus between the happening and the telling instead (the present's past) shows the real as never smooth or accountable, and is full of fissures of meaning, of breaks and interruptions, tied to the uncertainties of the ecstatic present, without the illusory comfort of a controlled past and future.

In a formal sense, the telling of *Coolie Doctor* is a quite distinct experience from that of *Prison Diary*. Meer's account—closer to classical definitions of the autobiography, as compared to Goonam's bildungsroman memoir[27] told in a narrative past—harbors some modernist overtones, favoring as it does a

---

26   Judith Lütge Coullie, "Mummy, the Coolie Doctor is at the Door," in *Selves in Question: Interviews on Southern African Auto/biography*, ed. Judith Lütge Coullie et al. (Honolulu: Hawai'i UP, 2006): 292.

27   Nicki Hitchcott defines the memoir as aiming to refer to "a context beyond itself, and to convey concrete objective information." Instead, autobiography "aims to express the addresser's emotional response to a particular situation, rather than a purely referential description of it"; Nicki Hitchcott, "African 'Herstory': The Feminist Reader and the African Autobiographical Voice," *Research in African Literatures* 28.2 (Summer 1997): 19, 20. My use of autobiography here is as a generic term. Memoir is only used strategically to differentiate from autobiography as a specific term—it only appears to make a point.

relative stream-of-consciousness immediacy, employing the present of narration. The illustrations to each book reflect the difference in writing. Goonam's autobiography contains black-and-white photographs, often family photographs with most of those photographed posing studio-style. Yet, the effect is not pompous, and is more along the lines of a good friend sharing photos from an old album. The overall impression is of an omniscient narrator. By contrast, the impression derived from Meer's book, with a title somewhat reminiscent of Gabriel García Márquez's novel *One Hundred Years of Solitude*, is more informal. The sketches that illustrate her book are by Meer herself and tend towards naïve art, with its candor and (studied) lack of formal perspective. Each in its own way, Goonam's and Meer's narratives show how incarceration exists in medias res, within the time of everyday living. In *Coolie Doctor*, the brutal intrusion into everydayness is represented more as content (through the closing of one prison and the sudden opening of the other), and in *Prison Diary*, this is experienced more through the form: since much of it describes experiential thought, the narrator's mind moves constantly from mundane everyday family concerns ('thrownness') to activist matters, and to preoccupation with her immediate bodily discomfort in prison. The descriptions and thoughts are mostly fragmented in terms of category and do not follow a set pattern—some of the discourse is recorded as sequential and quotidian, elsewhere as retrospective, sometimes experienced as profoundly intimate, at other times as familial, as communitarian, as national or as human. It follows the chaos of memory, itself further blurred by recollection through trauma. This memory (past) only exists as the past to a present. As was contended above with regard to the respective autobiographies of Nelson Mandela and Mahatma Gandhi, there are immediate pressures of the present that color representations of the past.

Goonam and Meer are first-generation *diasporic* 'Indians' born in South Africa. Given that no identity is ever a homogeneous category carrying recognizable cultural essentialism, diasporic conditions offer at least better potential for displacing 'thrownness': "The tradition, which is an ontic referential totality, is threatened when it encounters another tradition, which is inevitable in the case of the diasporic."[28] South Africa's time of first-generation migrants is already hybrid, already ontologically in contravention of apartheid laws.[29]

---

28   For a more detailed argument, see Farhad Khoyratty, "A Phenomenological Reading of Temporality and Natality in Relation to the Diasporic Indian Reception of the Bollywood Text with Reference to Mauritius," in *Diasporic Choices*, ed. Renata Seredyńska-Abou Eid (Oxford: Interdisciplinary Press, 2013): 21–34.

29   Most notably, this is in reference to the Immorality Act, 1927 (Act No. 5 of 1927), as qualified and further sustained by two Amendments in 1950 and 1957. One contemporary

In these laws was the refusal to recognize what was already happening (past progressive) in society. Thus, Goonam's autobiography affords a sense of how she is exposed to a number of cultural choices. Territorially, South Africa becomes not just ready-to-hand (*zuhanden*),[30] the territory into which she is thrown, but a choice over Scotland, India, and even Egypt. In *Coolie Doctor*, she tells how unaware of racism she was while she lived in her small world in Durban, only discovering racism when she encountered it retrospectively. For instance, only when she opened her medical practice and went on home visits did Goonam, who comes from a comparatively privileged background, state: "I discovered the depth of Indian poverty."[31] In South Africa she was Indian, and in India she became South African.[32] Like many others of Indian origin, Goonam in her autobiography reveals a sense of alienation in India while at the same time the freedom movement in India inspired their own struggle in South Africa. Goonam's mother, from Mauritius, is in a sense doubly diasporic, and opened up yet other cultural constructs, much as we learn that Fatima Meer's mother was white. Thus, even the term 'Indian' becomes present-at-hand (*vorhanden*): that is, noticeable.

One of the fundamental forms of violence in the apartheid regime was how it gave itself the privilege of naming others, subsuming every discourse under its own taxonomy. Choosing to call herself Dr. Goonam (and not Dr. Naidoo, admittedly a gesture that is common in South India) becomes a double act of resistance: she was trying also to overthrow the South Indian Hindu caste taxonomy which would have located her culturally within the Naidoo designation. Not only does she opt for her first name, she chooses a diminutive (Goonam for Goonaruthnum) but appends Dr., a personal, instead of an inherited, achievement, while demarcating herself from the average nomenclature for Indians: "coolie," the title of her book. Thus, in the construction of

---

example of its effects is mentioned centrally by the 'Coloured' South-African-born, world-renowned and celebrated comedian Trevor Noah, whose autobiography *Born a Crime* describes his birth, as the child of a black Xhosa mother and a white German-Swiss father, as a de facto crime under apartheid.

30   In *Being and Time*, Martin Heidegger refers to the world in terms of a "referential totality," a "totality of involvements," or a "context of assignments or references," of which a primary mode of relating to objects, the ready-to-hand (*zuhanden*), in which objects, such as a pair of scissors, do not exist with isolable properties but, rather, in terms of a referential totality in which scissors, paper, and a table relate to one another, and of the present-at-hand (*vorhanden*) where the objects become noticeable. Martin Heidegger, *Being and Time*, tr. Joan Stambaugh (Albany: State U of New York P, 1996): 76, 87.

31   Dr. Goonam, *Coolie Doctor*, 60.

32   This is a strength: "I had acquired a facility to move away, if uprooted" (*Coolie Doctor*, 151).

Indianness, South Africa becomes a space both of anxiety and of liberation for the younger Dr. Goonam, as with the younger Mohandas Gandhi. The diasporic condition temporalizes identity as never total, a becoming instead of a being that is mediated by a new Being-with-others, since we are individuals only in social relations with others. Thus, the taxonomic impositions can be said to have backfired. As James Ocita argues, comparing East Africa to South Africa:

> where Africanisation programmes in East Africa drive an insurmountable wedge between Africans and Indians, in South Africa, anti-apartheid struggle, under the umbrella of Black Consciousness, forges a non-racial alliance among the Indians, the Africans and the Coloureds.[33]

Within this communality with native Africans, however problematic, the pan-Indianness that the territory enabled was fostered by the possibilities of non-Indianness it offered as well as the possibility of categorization with native Africans by white hegemony, and pulled by the racist laws and institutions to 'revisit' it. Thus, contra what is often the case even in diasporic communities, Goonam and Meer do not seem to have a strong sense of religious difference (Hinduism, Islam) or regional Indian origin (Tamil, Gujarati), although these exist as context. Further, these women are not fighting against apartheid to be recognized as Indians or as women, but to achieve equality with any other human, endowed with individuality and choice (agency). In fact, apartheid did not encourage individuality within any body, being content to essentialize ethnic belonging. In Riason Naidoo's explorations of the representation of 'Indians' by predominantly non-white photographers of the 1950s, *Drum* magazine shows attempts at representing Indians as other than homogeneous under apartheid.[34] As well as the more stereotypical shopkeepers and agricultural workers, *Drum* had photographed 'Indians' who were sports celebrities, owners of jazz clubs, writers, gangsters, prostitutes, film stars, beauty queens (including Miss Durban 1960), women photographers, women stunt-riding, having a beer, posing on mopeds. In 1969, Meer's *Portrait of Indian South Africans* was the first solid attempt to engage with the varied ways of being Indian without falling into communitarianism.[35] The resistance and imprisonment of Goonam and Meer succeeded most effectively at subverting various stereotypes of the Indian in Africa as largely benefiting from, and implicitly or

---

33   James Ocita, "Diasporic Imaginaries," 23.

34   Riason Naidoo, "The Indian in *Drum* in the 1950s" (doctoral dissertation, Witwatersrand University, 2007): 18, 42.

35   Fatima Meer, *Portrait of Indian South Africans* (Durban: Avon House, 1969).

explicitly supportive of, colonialism, as well as the stereotype of the Indian woman as submissive and incapable of thriving outside of the domestic space.

While the diasporic condition enabled a ready-to-hand revisiting of all their layered identities, it also brought its own share of challenges. One of these, which seems to have troubled the younger Gandhi, is the connection between Indian identity and the native African. Starting with a mostly 'Indian' concern, the Natal and the Transvaal Indian Congresses gradually moved to embracing the plight of all who are oppressed. In this respect, Goonam and Meer's struggles rejoin the multiracial effort of Monty Naicker and Yusuf Dadoo by challenging at the same time the racist politics of the government and the conservativeness of South African 'Indians.' As well as the national pressures, there were major objections to Goonam's education by many in the 'Indian' community in Durban and only her Mauritian mother's determination helped at this early stage, even as she returned to Durban as a doctor and had to face criticism for being in-between: "There was objection to my western style of dressing, my outrageous habit of smoking in public, my carefree manner [...] politically and socially I was an outcast."[36]

The angst and panic expressed through public forms such as legislation and institutions play out on a personal level, much like other forms of more informal prejudice. Goonam recalls how her Afrikaner and English patients would ask if the 'Coolie doctor' was in.[37] The humor detected by proponents of the joke originates in taxonomy, a game of incongruity (ranging from gentle irony to laughter) that resides in the title of Goonam's book itself as a reappropriation of the signified 'Coolie doctor.' Evidently, and temporally, post-apartheid, the full sarcasm of the implied taxonomic oxymoron is fading. In "Jokes and Their Relation to the Unconscious" (1905), Freud famously describes laughter as a sublimation for aggression. It includes an exploration of how the joke involves an arrangement of people: a joke-teller, an audience/listener, and a victim of the joke, often involving two (the jokester and the listener) against one, who is often a scapegoat. If we stretch this logic, we can identify, in psychic terms, the maintaining of a community through in-jokes and the sacrifice of a scapegoat to found the new (virtual) city.[38] While he mostly focusses on their subversive nature, Freud fails to cover the more politically

---

36   Goonam, *Coolie Doctor*, 57.

37   *Coolie Doctor*, 92.

38   A general reference to another article by Freud where he discusses the scapegoat, though not in connection with jokes; Sigmund Freud, "Psychopathic Characters on the Stage," in *The Standard Edition of the Complete Psychological Works*, ed. & tr. James Strachey (London: Hogarth, 1953–74), vol. 7: 306.

conservative potential for jokes, of the order to the photographs by warders at the Abu Ghraib prison during the second Iraq war. Goonam's insistent attachment to the identity of a Scotland-educated medical doctor can be read as part of a bourgeois hierarchy both within the 'Indian' community and beyond, but above all, it is a hierarchy that she herself absorbed. Further (and we must remember the time of the narrative is anterior to the time of the narrating), such insistence is the result of original violence done to identity: already, during her first imprisonment, she was stripped of her sense of identity as a 'respectable member of society', a symbol of which is her insistence to have her glasses (116), in the face of the brutally demeaning questioning before she is locked up, where she is renamed a criminal, a prostitute, illiterate, and a witchdoctor (114, 115). Incidentally, we find out from Meer's autobiography that Goonam, by the time Meer was imprisoned, was well-known enough: "She was probably confusing me with Dr. Goonam, one of the Indian leaders during the 1946 Passive Resistance Campaign."[39]

Discussing Hugh Lewin's autobiography, *Bandiet*, Buntman argues:

> Lewin's astute descriptions of prison subcultures capture the near universal depravity of prison life. Central was 'a place of death and corruption' (p. 139), of forced sex, widespread informers, and the authorities' systematic toleration of forms of abusive behaviour.[40]

Prison autobiographies by both males and females in South Africa contain narratives of unspeakable physical indignities. Goonam was imprisoned eighteen times,[41] although in her autobiography she limits herself to describing her first stay in detail and her second experience only briefly. She bitterly recalls how isolated she felt because of the lack of information from outside—she is obliged to choose only one letter out of the dozen that had been sent to her—and the prohibition of even exchanging words with her fellow prisoners during her stay in Durban Prison. Paper was often not provided, and in any case letters or other written material would be censored by the prison authorities. Goonam was denied any subjectivity other than the category covered by the racial slurs 'coolie' (see above), 'swart' (black). She is faced with various forms of abjection, such as human excreta caked in her blanket. The first body search is physically

---

39   Meer, *Prison Diary*, 30.

40   Buntman, "Imprisonment in Apartheid South Africa," 663.

41   Devarakshanam Govinden, *'Sisters Outside': The Representation of Identity and Difference in Selected Writings by South African Indian Women* (Pretoria: U of South Africa P, 2008): 286.

brutal and morally demeaning. She is also forced to rinse her bed-pan and fill it with water for her ablutions. Her body is othered into the body of the sub-human: categorized as animal and/or criminal and/or sick. Meer served her 113-day sentence about thirty years after Goonam's narrated imprisonment, and her narrative probably reveals how prison conditions had improved since the 1940s. Meer, unlike Goonam, was allowed to write and draw. But the poignancy of Goonam's and Meer's experiences cannot be measured only in terms of the graphic violence they endured. Incarceration happens to you where you are and as you are, into the world that you are thrown into. Its first act of violence is to interrupt everydayness. The time inside is not a suspended time frame—it takes place in the midst of an intimate existence: after many days without it, Meer states: "I never realised tea tasted so good."[42] Meer's immediate concern when put in jail is to arrange for her mother to stay with the children.[43] One main concern throughout the ordeal is over food and relatives bringing food, at once a universal and a culturally specific concern. Food becomes not only good nourishment but also testimony to continuity with the quotidian out-side. The onset of diabetes becomes an existential prison within the prison. Fasting for Ramadan becomes part of a food-related desire to continue with normal everydayness unabated, except that, being in prison, she finds it hard to know when dusk falls so she can break her fast.[44] Goonam's attempt at such existential continuity is met with brutal awakening: "You think it a hotel?"[45]

The physical prison becomes a replication of the more general organiza-tion of space in society, as can be seen from Fatima Meer's account of find-ing a school/university for her daughter Shamim that does not ghettoize the Indian.[46] Far from bracketing it, prison in fact stages apartheid taxonomy, performing "apartheid time," a wishful temporal projection of racial segrega-tion, an extension of the society's effort to create 'docile bodies.' This becomes obvious from Meer's description of 'white' prison cells as beautiful and spa-cious.[47] Prisoners were segregated, too. In *Prison Diary* there is the essential-ized offer to Meer of a choice between 'European' and 'African' food. Outside status is maintained in prison—Meer herself admits that the body search ad-ministered to her is minimal, since she is well-known. Women are locked up

---

42   Meer, *Prison Diary*, 61.

43   *Prison Diary*, 50.

44   *Prison Diary*, 52.

45   Goonam, *Coolie Doctor*, 119.

46   Meer, *Prison Diary*, 46.

47   *Prison Diary*, 147, 163.

separately but also on different terms from men. Each is then treated differently in accordance with class. Meer writes:

> We were all women, but so classified and separated that we could not be women together: we were divided by the impregnable barriers of law and custom, in addition to race.[48]

If anything, prison tended to magnify social relations outside, concentrating apartheid in an isolable, controlled space, a hopeful blueprint on the inside for an often unmalleable present outside, and an inevitably miscegenated genetic past.

In *Prison Diary* there is a somewhat anticlimactic release from prison.[49] While this might not fit the reader's imagined promise of continued heroism, it reflects a grim reality that, like death, one of the existential salients of prison is that life goes on around it—and even within it. Goonam will find her privileges of education and travel reduced to a mere abstraction. Meer will find nothing much changed outside.[50] Goonam's and Meer's outspokenness in prison, even when faced with the worst humiliation, shows a heroic desire to maintain agency and autonomy, a refusal to be described and categorized, and a rejection of enforced carceral normalcy. Yet, none of these subversions can be maintained over time. The language used already predates the utterance and the two autobiographers are already thrown into their world, with its language, however disruptive their individual observations. Further, the retrospective nature of autobiography means that the true solitude of imprisonment remains uncharted, in fact unrepresentable. When implying solitude, literary representations of the inner life (much like other forms of art, such as the camera presence in mainstream cinema) in fact make of the reader a witness to events, which are subject to a certain degree of theatricalization. Rather than prompting questions of whether Goonam's or Meer's narrative is authentic, this demonstrates how autobiographical accounts fall short of conveying the real trauma of prison life. One example of this is just how disruptive of everyday relations (as Being-with-others) prison is, with none of the solace of a reader's presence.

Meer's autobiography makes the centrality of food (especially when connected with family) an arguably more acceptable concern associated with women in Third Wave, rather than Second Wave, feminism. While Second

---

48   Meer, *Prison Diary*, 209.
49   *Prison Diary*, 205.
50   *Prison Diary*, 207–208.

Wave readings might find in Meer a lack of commitment to the questioning of traditional gender roles, her very presence in prison reveals that she is transgressing spaces to which women (in many cases Indian women) were often restricted. But then, how feminist is the desire to preserve one's modesty when the male colonel visits the prison?[51] This is one among many questions that linger, though these are further offset by very frank accounts of love for, and the kissing of, her husband Ismail, more explicit than is conventionally acceptable in more conservative Indian and Islamic contexts. Goonam does not marry, and Fatima Meer's own marriage, to judge from her account, is one that in fact offers freedom. In many ways, Meer deals with prison as if she were running an extensive household with recalcitrant servants as a survival strategy, and while it exposes less savory aspects of the bourgeois world she is used to and finds comfort in, she is meting out a philosophical lesson to others—and to herself. There is no one way to be subversive, and it remains the case that the original pre-apartheid taxonomies were not perfect structures, no more so than post-apartheid taxonomies, as contrapuntally sanctified by the very real violence of apartheid. Pre-apartheid structures harbored their own forms of violence: colonialism, patriarchy, racism, class inequality. Many of these played out within given communities, such as Goonam's rejection by many within the Indian community itself. The language of apartheid is surreptitious to the point of providing the 'deep structure' grammar of psychic language. Thus, Meer's dreams in prison are colored by racial segregation, both of communities and of individual bodies:

> I found myself on the opposite side of the Durban docks where an Indian community was living and I was marooned with them, cut off from the city, which twinkled prettily in the distance [...]They were both dark in complexion, but they were living on the Esplanade, where only whites were allowed to live."[52]

While getting other inmates to sit in her cell is a poignant reminder of her continued activism even in jail, as transgression of the space allotted to them officially and a refusal to let themselves be defined entirely by State officialese, the chores for preparing food in Meer's autobiography still fall squarely on Irene, whose 'subaltern' position in terms of gender and class is left unquestioned by the author.

---

51   Meer, *Prison Diary*, 73.
52   *Prison Diary*, 69.

Relations and networks in prison do more than replicate the nature of the relations and networks of apartheid society at large. They reify the futural that is dreamed up and hoped for by the taxonomic structure existing in the present. The first act of apartheid violence is committed against time, and is existential. Once a medium like autobiography is used, the being that is uncovered is shown to be inevitably fissured. When set in an apartheid prison, a mirror of the carceral society outside, selfhood becomes further fragmented and attempts to put the pieces of Being back together can at best only reflect the temporal, something of the present tense—and the tense presence—of the reader.

Works Cited

Buntman, Fran. *Robben Island and Prison Resistance to Apartheid* (Cambridge: Cambridge UP, 2003).

Buntman, Fran. "Imprisonment in Apartheid South Africa I: Personal Histories," *Journal of Southern African Studies* 31.3 (2005): 663–679.

Coullie, Judith Lütge, ed. *The Closest of Strangers. South African Women's Life Writing* (Johannesburg: Wits UP, 2004).

Coullie, Judith Lütge. "Introduction: Placing Selves in Question," in *Selves in Question: Interviews on Southern African Auto/biography*, ed. Judith Lütge Coullie et al., 1–8.

Coullie, Judith Lütge. "Mummy, the Coolie Doctor is at the Door," in *Selves in Question: Interviews on Southern African Auto/biography*, ed. Judith Lütge Coullie, Stephan Meyer, Thengani H. Ngwenya & Thomas Olver (Honolulu: Hawai'i UP, 2006): 291–302.

Derrida, Jacques. *Of Grammatology*, tr. Spivak, Gayatri Chakravorty (*De la Grammatologie, 1967*; Baltimore MD: Johns Hopkins UP, 1997).

Desai, Ashwin, & Goolam Vahed. The South African Gandhi: Stretcher-Bearer of Empire (Stanford CA: Stanford UP, 2015).

Freud, Sigmund. *Jokes and their Relation to the Unconscious*, tr. & ed. James Strachey (*Der Witz und seine Beziehung zum Unbewussten, 1905*; Harmondsworth: Pelican, 1976).

Freud, Sigmund. "Psychopathic Characters on the Stage," in *The Standard Edition of the Complete Psychological Works*, ed. & tr. James Strachey (London: Hogarth, 1953–74), vol. 7: 303–310.

Gandhi, Mohandas Karamchand. *An Autobiography, or the Story of My Experiments with Truth*, tr. Desai, Mahadev (Ahmedabad: Navajivan, 1940).

Gardiner, J.K. *Rhys, Stead, Lessing, and the Politics of Empathy* (Bloomington: Indiana UP, 1989).

Goonam. (Kesaveloo Goonam). *Coolie Doctor: An Autobiography by Dr. Goonam* (Durban: Madiba, 1991).

Govinden, Devarakshanam Betty. "Healing the Wounds of History," in *SA Lit. Beyond 2000*, ed. Michael Chapman & Margaret Lenta (Scotsville: U of KwaZulu–Natal P, 2011): 287–289.

Govinden, Devarakshanam Betty. *'Sisters Outside': The Representation of Identity and Difference in Selected Writings by South African Indian Women* (Pretoria: U of South Africa P, 2008).

Gready, Paul. "Autobiography and the 'Power of Writing': Political Prison Writing in the Apartheid Era," *Journal of Southern African Studies* 19.3 (September 1993): 489–523.

Heidegger, Martin. *Being and Time*, tr. Stambaugh, Joan (*Sein und Zeit, 1927*; Albany: State U of New York P, 1996).

Heidegger, Martin. *The Fundamental Concepts of Metaphysics: World, Finitude, Solitude*, tr. William McNeill & Nicholas Walker (1929/30, Bloomington: Indiana UP, 1995).

Heidegger, Martin. *An Introduction to Metaphysics*, Fourth Edition, tr. Manheim, Ralph (wr. 1935, *Einführung in die Metaphysik*, 1953; New Haven CT & London: Yale UP, 1984).

Hitchcott, Nicki. "African 'Herstory': The Feminist Reader and the African Autobiographical Voice," *Research in African Literatures* 28.2 (Summer 1997): 16–33.

Hiralal, Kalpana. "Narratives and Testimonies of Women Detainees in the Anti-Apartheid Struggle," *Agenda* 29.4 (2015): 34–44.

Inwood, Michael. *Heidegger* (New York, Oxford UP, 1997).

Khoyratty, Farhad. "A Phenomenological Reading of Temporality and Natality in Relation to the Diasporic Indian Reception of the Bollywood Text with Reference to Mauritius," in *Diasporic Choices*, ed. Renata Seredyńska-Abou Eid (Oxford: Interdisciplinary Press, 2013): 21–34.

Kierkegaard, Søren. *Papers and Journals*, tr. Hannay, A. (London: Penguin, 1996).

Lewin, Hugh. *Bandiet: Out of Jail* (Johannesburg: Random House South Africa, 2002).

Mandela, Nelson. *Long Walk to Freedom: The Autobiography of Nelson Mandela* (Boston MA: Little, Brown, 1995).

Meer, Fatima. *Portrait of Indian South Africans* (Durban: Avon House, 1969).

Meer, Fatima. *Prison Diary: One Hundred and Thirteen Days 1976* (Cape Town: Kwela, 2001).

Naidoo, Riason. "The Indian in *Drum* in the 1950s" (doctoral dissertation, Witwatersrand University, 2007).

Naidoo, Jay. *Fighting for Justice: A Lifetime of Political and Social Activism* (Johannesburg: Picador Africa, 2010).

Noah, Trevor. *Born a Crime* (New York: Spiegel & Grau, 2009).

Nuttall, Sarah. "Reading and Recognition in Three South African Women's Autobiographies," *Current Writing: Text and Reception in Southern Africa* 8.1 (1996): 1–18.

Ocita, James. "Diasporic Imaginaries: Memory and Negotiation of Belonging in East African and South African Indian Narratives" (doctoral dissertation, Stellenbosch University, 2013).

Raditlhalo, Sam. "Unzima lomthwalo—'this load is heavy': A Selection of South African Prison and Exile Life Writings," *Life Writing* 1.2 (2004): 27–54.

Ross, Fiona C. *Bearing Witness: Women and the Truth and Reconciliation Commission in South Africa* (London: Pluto, 2003).

Roux, Daniel. "Writing the Prison," in *The Cambridge History of South African Literature*, ed. David Attwell & Derek Attridge (Cambridge: Cambridge UP, 2012): 545–563.

Stanley, Elizabeth. "Review: Fatima Meer, *Prison Diary: One Hundred and Thirteen Days, 1976*," *Journal of Modern African Studies* 41.2 (June 2003): 332–334.

Suttner, Raymond. *Inside Apartheid's Prison: Notes and Letters of Struggle* (Pietermaritzburg: U of Natal P & Melbourne: Ocean Press, 2001).

Index